Information for a New Age

Information for a New Age

Redefining the Librarian

A LIRT 15th Anniversary Publication

Compiled by

Fifteenth Anniversary Task Force
Library Instruction Round Table
American Library Association

LIBRARIES UNLIMITED, INC.
Englewood, Colorado
1995

Copyright © 1995 American Library Association,
'on Round Table
Reserved
d States of America

nay be reproduced, stored in
iitted, in any form or by any
al, photocopying, recording,
ior written permission of the
publisher.

LIBRARIES UNLIMITED, INC.
P.O. Box 6633
Englewood, CO 80155-6633

1-800-237-6124

Project Editor:	Stephen Haenel
Copy Editor:	Jason Cook
Proofreader:	Lori Kranz
Indexer:	Nancy Fulton
Design and Layout:	Kay Minnis

Library of Congress Cataloging-in-Publication Data

Information for a new age : redefining the librarian / compiled by
  Fifteenth Anniversary Task Force, Library Instruction
  Round Table, American Library Association.
    xiii, 192 p. 17x25 cm.
    "A LIRT 15th anniversary publication."
    Includes bibliographical references and index.
    ISBN 1-56308-278-0
    1. Library science--United States. 2. Library science.
  3. Library orientation--United States. 4. Library orientation.
  I. Library Instruction Round Table (American Library Association).
  Fifteenth Anniversary Publications Task Force.
  Z665.2.U6I54   1995
  020'.973--dc20
                                                    94-41934
                                                        CIP

Contents

ESSAYS

Membership of the 15th Anniversary Task Force

CO-CHAIRS

Lois M. Pausch, University of Illinois at Urbana-Champaign
Mary Pagliero Popp, Indiana University, Bloomington

PROGRAM SUBCOMMITTEE

Madeline Copp, co-chair, University of Washington
Bonnie Gratch, co-chair, Syracuse University
Tobeylynn Birch, California School of Professional Psychology
Eugene Engeldinger, Carthage College
Esther Grassian, University of California-Los Angeles
Sheila Laidlaw, formerly University of New Brunswick
Mary Jane Petrowski, University of Illinois at Urbana-Champaign
Beverly Sandifer, Chicago Public Library
Milton Wolf, University of Nevada-Reno

PROMOTIONS SUBCOMMITTEE

Marilyn Barr, chair, Free Library of Philadelphia
Michele Gendron, Free Library of Philadelphia
Kathy Key, University of West Virginia
Carol Penka, University of Illinois at Urbana-Champaign
Lynn Randall, Caldwell College

PUBLICATIONS SUBCOMMITTEE

J. Randolph Call, chair, Detroit Public Library
Linda Dougherty, Chicago Public Library—Clearing Branch
Gary Hyslop, Indiana University, Bloomington
Carolyn Leopold Michaels, University of South Carolina
Emily Okada, Indiana University, Bloomington
Trish Ridgeway, The Handley Library and Catholic University
Thelma Tate, Douglass College—Rutgers University

PUBLIC RELATIONS SUBCOMMITTEE

Elizabeth Margutti, chair, University of Virginia
Mary Noel Gouke, Ohio State University
Kelly Janousek, University of California-Long Beach
Charles Dintrone, San Diego State University

EX OFFICIO–CHAIR OF THE LIRT 1992 PROGRAM COMMITTEE

Cindy Cunningham, University of Washington

Introduction

A recent article stated, "Information is to our age what coal and iron were to the Industrial Revolution" (Miericke 327). What information did you need today—to do your job? to make a purchase? to plan for the future? Where did you get that information? Did you ask a friend or relative? Did you read a book? Did you watch TV? Everyone needs and uses information. And everyone agrees that there is too much information. The statistics about publishing output and the emergence of new information are well documented.

Computers have made finding information both easier and more difficult. Just to begin to find information, one must choose from an extraordinary array of information resources, and often what Oberman (1991, 190) calls the "cereal syndrome" occurs. Too many possible choices lead to anxiety and avoidance. Once some information is found, one must evaluate the materials and determine what is useful. This evaluation process is actually two steps, evaluating citations or actual resources to determine if they are relevant and assessing the content of each source (Kissane and Mollner 1993, 486). Further, information users need to know "how their questions can build upon one another" and to see the interconnectedness of information (487).

Technostress further complicates the information picture. Many people, particularly those who are older, lack experience with computers and find them daunting. Miericke (1991) comments that "without the confidence which comes from successful experience, many people are understandably hesitant to approach an automated system, including those increasingly found in modern libraries. Librarians, then, must approach potential end-users; they must proactively interact with them in their own environments and on their own terms" (333).

Exponential growth in the amount of available information, of sources for that information, and of the technology to access those sources has made the ability to cope with information an acute need. To succeed in the Information Society, one needs to be information literate, which is defined as follows:

> To be information literate, a person must be able to recognize when information is needed and have the ability to locate, evaluate, and use effectively the needed information. . . . Information literate people are those who have learned how to learn. They know how to learn because they know how knowledge is organized, how to find information, and how to use information in such a way that others can learn from them (American Library Association, Presidential Committee on Information Literacy 1989, 1).

To assist library users in the development of the skills they need to support democracy, to make a living, to keep businesses competitive, and to live more fulfilling personal lives, librarians offer programs and services, including those aimed at enabling patrons to become more information literate. Bibliographic instruction (BI), in focusing on the need to help library patrons become more proficient in locating and using information, is a major contributor to that learning skill. The authors of the papers in this volume describe their approaches to proactive interaction with library users, ranging from the Ohio State University Gateway system, which combines an expert system and computer-assisted instruction, to development of coalitions and information consulting programs, and to changes in school curricula. All of these are done with one goal: an information literate society.

The centrality of information literacy to the library mission has been acknowledged by the American Library Association and other library groups. These organizations provide opportunities for the discussion of activities, programs, and problems of instruction in the use of information in all types of libraries. Each association contributes to the education and training of librarians for library instruction; promotes instruction in the use of libraries as an essential library service; and serves as a channel of communication between its members and other library/professional groups.

In recognition of the vital role of bibliographic instruction in library service, the American Library Association has supported the work of two units, the Library Instruction Round Table (LIRT) and the Bibliographic Instruction Section (BIS) of the Association of College and Research Libraries. In 1992, these two groups celebrated 15 years of growth and service with a day-long program entitled "Information for a New Age: Reinventing the Librarian." Included was a keynote address by Robert Silverberg, well-known science fiction author, who provided unique perspectives on the information society, on literacy, and on technology. The annual programs of both organizations followed.

The Library Instruction Round Table also sponsored a competition for papers presenting innovative ideas in the development of information literacy skills. The award-winning papers are included in this special anniversary publication, along with invited articles by acknowledged experts in the field, the Silverberg address, and the papers presented at the LIRT program. In preparing this publication, LIRT works to fulfill its mission, which focuses on the dissemination of ideas, suggestions, recommendations, and research into information literacy and on the provision of practical assistance to librarians in school, public, college/university, and special libraries.

In his article, Evan Farber issues a challenge to all of us to improve on what we do. This book includes many good ideas for such improvement.

LOIS M. PAUSCH
MARY PAGLIERO POPP
Co-chairs, 15th Anniversary Task Force

REFERENCES

American Library Association. Presidential Committee on Information Literacy. 1989. *Final Report*. Chicago: American Library Association.

Kissane, Emily C., and Daniel J. Mollner. 1993. "Critical Thinking at the Reference Desk: Teaching Students to Manage Technology, in "Library Literacy," ed. Mary Reichel. *RQ* 32: 485-89.

Miericke, Susan. 1991. "Creating Hospitable Environments for Technologically Naive Users: Y'all Come Back Now, Hear!" *Library Trends* 39: 327-34.

Oberman, Cerise. 1991. "Avoiding the Cereal Syndrome, or Critical Thinking in the Electronic Environment." *Library Trends* 39: 189-202.

Information for a New Age: Fantastic Technology or Institutionalized Alienation?

Robert Silverberg
Keynote Speaker

In the course of slouching toward the ballroom, I picked up a copy of the LIRT program evaluation—a fascinating document. And I see that one of the things you're supposed to express your opinion on is: "The keynote speaker had enough time. Strongly agree, strongly disagree." And you're given a spectrum of five numbers there. Well, that's interesting. I think I should tell you the real problem is whether the keynote speaker will have enough voice. If I suddenly go mute after about forty-two minutes, Milton will finish my speech for me. Five days ago I had no voice at all. I've done a lot of traveling this spring and have picked up various exotic microorganisms as I went and they all got to me last week. But I think I can make it through.

I'm also fascinated by the raft of initials that Dianne Langlois called off. It's been about six months since I knew I was appearing here, and I have not managed in all of that time, because I've been partly very busy and occasionally sick, to master the meaning of L.I.R.T., let alone all of the other ones that I see on the various badges. I've been thinking about it. I came up a little while ago with "Librarians In Retrograde Transit" and "Library International Rehabilitation Therapy." I imagine that the *L* is "Library," the *I* is "Information"—but the *R* and the *T*?—"Rapid Transit"? "Retrieval Techniques"? I don't know. But anyway, I'm glad to be here, whoever you may be.

And, finally, I see by this document that what we're doing is discussing "Information for a New Age: Fantastic Technology or Institutionalized Alienation?" I'm not sure we have a dichotomy here, but these are the themes of today. I'd like to begin by reading a few things to you to demonstrate the nature of information as it is sometimes shown in fiction.

I'd like to read to you from a book called *Shadrach in the Furnace*, by Robert Silverberg. This takes place not too far in the future, but a very bedraggled future in which most of the planet is struck down by a plague. I wrote this book in 1975. And the protagonist is the physician, Shadrach Mordecai, who is the physician to the dictator of the world, Genghis Mao. And Shadrach, in his morning routine, is passing through the outer offices of Genghis Mao's headquarters on his way to the great man.

The room just on the far side of Interface Three is a cavernous sphere known as Surveillance Vector One. It is, in a literal sense, Genghis Mao's window on the world. Here a dazzling array of screens, each five square meters in area, rises in overwhelming tiers from floor to ceiling, offering a constantly shifting panorama of televised images relayed from thousands of spy-eyes everywhere on the planet. No great public building is without its secret eyes; scanners look down on all major streets; a corps of government engineers is constantly employed in shifting the cameras from place to place and in installing new ones in previously unspied-upon places. Nor are all the eyes in fixed positions. So many spy-satellites streak through the nearer reaches of space that if their orbits were turned to silk they would swathe the earth in a dense cocoon. At the center of Surveillance Vector One is a grand control panel by means of which the Khan, sitting for hours at a time in an elegant thronelike seat, is able to control the flow of data from all these eyes, calling in signals with quick flutters of his fingertips so that he may look at will into the doings of Tokyo and Bangkok, New York and Moscow, Buenos Aires and Cairo. So sharp is the resolution of the Khan's myriad lenses that they can show Genghis Mao the color of a man's eyes at a distance of five kilometers.

When the Chairman is not making use of Surveillance Vector One, the hundreds of screens continue to function without interruption as the master mechanism sucks in data randomly from the innumerable pickup points. Images come and go, sometimes flitting across the screen in a second or two, sometimes lingering to provide consecutive sequences many minutes in length. Shadrach Mordecai, since he must pass through this room every morning on his way to his master, has formed the habit of pausing for a few minutes to watch the gaudy, dizzying stream of pictures. Privately he refers to this daily interlude as "checking the Trauma Ward," the Trauma Ward being Mordecai's secret name for the world in general, for that great vale of sorrow and bodily corruption.

He stands in mid-room now, while observing the world's griefs.

The flow is jerkier than usual today; whatever giant computer operates this system is in a twitchy mood, it seems, its commands moving restlessly from eye to eye, and pictures wink off and on in a frenzied way. Still, there are isolated flashes of clarity. A limping woebegone dog moves slowly down a dirt choked street. A big eyed, big bellied Negroid child stands naked in a dust-swept ravine, gnawing her thumb and crying. A sag-shouldered old woman, carrying carefully wrapped bundles through the cobbled plaza of some mellow European city, gasps and clutches at her chest, letting her packages tumble as she falls. A parched Oriental-faced man with wispy white beard and tiny green skullcap emerges from a shop, coughs, and spits blood. A crowd—Mexicans? Japanese?—gathers around two boys dueling with carving knifes; their arms and chest are bright with red cuts. Three children huddle on the roof of a torn-away house rushing swiftly downstream on the white-flecked gray breast of a flooding river. A hawk-faced beggar stretches forth an accusing clawlike hand. A young, dark-haired woman kneels at a curb, bowed double in pain, head touching the pavement, while two small boys look on. A speeding automobile veers crazily from a highway and vanishes in a bushy gulley. Surveillance Vector One is like some vast tapestry of hundreds of compartments, each with a story to tell, a fragmentary story, tantalizing, defying comprehension.

All of that is data flooding in on this enormous room-size screen from all over the world. How is the data handled? What is the experience of the handler of the data? I dealt with that in a book called *The Time-Hoppers,* ten years earlier, with a somewhat similar setup and a somewhat similar world dictator, who is Kloofman. And I have a little scene from his point of view as the data comes flooding in, with some sense of his emotions.

Kloofman rested. After a while, he had himself withdrawn from his nutrient bath and taken to his office. He had not been to the surface in sixteen years. The upper world had become slightly unreal to him; but he saw no harm in that, since he was well aware that to most of the inhabitants of the upper world *he* was slightly unreal, or more than slightly. Reciprocity, he thought. The secret of effective government. Kloofman lived in a complex of interlocking tunnels spreading out for hundreds of miles. At any given time, machines with glittering claws were energetically at work extending his domain. He hoped to have the world girdled with a continuous network of High Government access routes in another ten years or so. His personal Midgard Serpent of transportation. Strictly speaking, there was no need for it; he could govern just as effectively from a single room as from any point along a world-rimming tunnel. But he had his whims. What was the use of being the supreme leader of the entire world, Kloofman wondered, if he could not occasionally indulge a small whim.

He moved on purring rollers to the master control room and allowed his attendants to attach him to contact leads. It bored him to depend on words for his knowledge of external events. One of the many surgical reconstructs that had been performed on him over the years allowed a direct neural cut-in; Kloofman could and did enter directly into the data stream, becoming a relay facet of the computer web itself. Then, only then, did a kind of ecstasy overwhelm him.

He nodded, and the flow of data began.

Facts. Births and deaths, disease statistics, transportation correlations, power levels, crime rates. Synapse after synapse clenched tight as Kloofman absorbed it all. Far above him, billions of people went through their daily routines, and he entered in some way into the life of each of them, and they entered into his. His perceptions were limited, of course. He could not detect individual fluctuations in the data except as momentary surges. Yet he could extrapolate them. At this very instant, he knew, a hopper was departing for the past. A life was subtracted from the present. What about mass? Was it conserved? The data on planetary mass failed to take into account the possibility of the sudden and total subtraction. Two hundred pounds abruptly removed from now and thrust into yesterday—how could it be possible, Kloofman wondered? It was done, though. The records showed it. Thousands of hoppers thrust out of his time and into the time of his predecessors. How? How?

Kloofman brushed the thought from his throbbing mind. It was an irrelevancy. What was relevant was the sudden, unthinkable possibility that the past might be altered, that all of this might be taken away from him in a random fluctuation against which no defense existed. That struck horror into him. He filled his brain with data to drown out the possibility of total loss. He felt the onset of his delight.

Caesar, did you ever have the whole world running through your brain at once?

Napoleon, could you so much as imagine what it might be like to be plugged right into the master computers?

Sardanapalus, were there joys like this in Nineveh?

Kloofman's bulky body quivered. The mesh of fine capillary wires just beneath his skin glowed. He ceased to be Peter Kloofman, world leader, lone human member of Class One, benevolent despot, sublime planner, the accidental inheritor of the ages. Now he was everyone who existed. A flux of cosmic power surged in him. This was the true Nirvana! This was the ultimate Oneness! This was the moment of full rapture!

There we have the future of data processing, the ecstasy of knowing it all at once. But before we get from here to there, we have certain problems that must be dealt with.

The following is an article. It's in a science fiction magazine but it's nonfiction, by my dear friend Isaac Asimov, who I trust at this moment is working on his eight-hundredth book. And before Isaac began writing most of those books, or during the time, he was in fact a professor of biochemistry in Boston and did research in biochemistry. And this is an article talking about the difficulties in keeping up with the flow of knowledge in biochemistry, and especially in preparing new editions of the textbook that he and a collaborator had written on the subject.

In preparing future editions of the text, the one great problem is bringing it up-to-date. And for that, *Chemical Abstracts* is absolutely necessary. With the second edition done and the third edition a gleam in our eyes, my own method is to grab Dr. Walker's issue of *Chemical Abstracts* as soon as it comes in, and preferably before Dr. Walker gets his hooks on them.

Fortunately, *Chemical Abstracts* segregates its paper listings into over twenty subdivisions of chemistry, and I can ignore sections dealing with industrial chemicals, paper and papermaking chemicals, electro-chemistry, photography and so on. Unfortunately, the listings under bio-chemistry, which itself is subdivided into ten sub-subdivisions, is the longest in the periodical. I cuddle up with 100-150 large pages, containing 1,000-1,500 articles twice a month in other words, and read dizzily through the titles.

Sometimes a title is short, like "Iron Metabolism," which usually indicates a review. All reviews are automatically noted down by me provided they are in a journal I can obtain. In one place or another in Boston I can obtain almost all the unimportant journals and all the important ones. I can obtain almost all the important ones by going to my school library two floors below my lab.

Sometimes the title is long, like, for instance, "Use of Ion Exchangers for the Separation of Some Amino Acids Formed During Enzymatic Degradation of Cysteinesulfinic Acid. Application to the Isolation of Hypotaurine [acid 1-aminoethanesulfinic acid]," which is the real title to a real paper. Long titles like this are fashionable not because scientists are queer but because a good title is one which will give you a complete idea of the contents of the paper without your having to read anything further. That's not laziness on our part, friend, that's one of our barriers against insanity.

If a title of a paper is interesting, I read the abstract itself. If the abstract looks interesting, I note the volume of *Chemical Abstracts*, the number of its column and its position in that column in a special volume of our second edition of our text book which has a blank page between every two printed pages, and make the entry oppose the place in the book where I think it belongs.

The results? Well, they can be harrowing. Take the case of the function of the metal molybdenum in the human body. In the first edition of our book, it wasn't even worth mentioning; and we didn't mention it. By the time we wrote the second edition, some workers had showed it to be a constituent of an important enzyme known as *zanthendehydrogenoas*. We stuck in molybdenum therefore and gave it seven lines. In the not quite a year since we finished reading proof on the second edition, I've come across ten papers which seem to me worth reading in connection with this seven line passage. Comes time for the third edition, there'll probably be thirty papers which will have to be read or at the very least glanced through if we are to increase the space devoted to molybdenum from seven lines to say two paragraphs and do it intelligently. And this despite pruning the number ruthlessly by first picking only those with interesting titles, and of those only the ones with interesting sounding abstracts.

And this isn't really enough, you know. Even *Chemical Abstracts* isn't up-to-date. They're anywhere from six months to a year behind the journals. And I'm off therefore to glance at the titles of the most important journals as they come out but then the journals aren't up-to-date either. A paper which is accepted for publication by the *Journal of Biological Chemistry* may have to wait six months to a year before seeing the light. The *Journal* has that great a backlog of accepted papers. Besides that, a paper deals with work that is completed. There's other, newer work in progress. And so there are all sorts of conventions.

The American Chemical Society holds annual conventions in various parts of the country. The Federation of American Societies for Experimental Biology, which includes six subsidiary societies, holds annual conventions. So does the American Association for the Advancement of Science. So do innumerable smaller groups. At each one of these, papers are presented. Hundreds of papers are presented at the largest gatherings, where several subgroups are usually giving a series of papers simultaneously in different rooms of the hotel. Sometimes in different hotels, and sometimes even in different cities. It is impossible for one man to hear more than a fraction of these, and he must choose his spots with care and hope for the best.

Of the three of us, Dr. Boyd is the most indefatigable attender of conventions. In recent months he has been to New York, Philadelphia, French Lick, Indiana and Paris, France, in order to get together with others, give papers, listen to papers and most important of all get together over a glass of beer and find out what's doing in the other guy's lab right at that moment. And so it goes.

There is now a whole branch of human effort devoted to attempts to coordinate the cumulating data of the physical sciences at a rate roughly equivalent to that at which it is accumulating. This includes the formulation of special types of indices and codes, the use of screening programs, the preparation of special punched cards, microcard files, and so on.

In connection with this I would like to quote a passage from a letter written by Carl F. Hyman, Director of the Chemical Biological Coordination Center of the National Research Council, to Mr. Ken Devaney, Jr. of Millington, New Jersey; a carbon copy was forwarded to me. The passage reads: "Mr. Devaney. In answer to your question recently about data handling, I would like to give you a short bibliography but it is not possible. There has been a great increase in the work in this field which has resulted in the scattering of documentation references among various abstracting services. . . ."

In other words, the literature relating to efforts to handle the literature is too great to be handled easily. There's no way and each year it's getting worse. And so, if you are ever up Boston way and enter the Boston University School of Medicine and pass my lab and hear the sound of panting, you may think it is the result of my chasing some female around and around some desk, but you'd be wrong. It's just I. Asimov trying to keep up with the literature; a task which is much more futile and far less likely to reach a satisfactory conclusion.

As you listen to this, you may have picked up certain clues as to the age of this document, the reference to punch cards, for example. And, in fact, this is the June 1955 issue of the magazine that was then called *Astounding Science Fiction.* Thirty-seven years have gone by. We have new and advanced technology, not dreamed of in the days when Isaac Asimov wrote this piece.

Is the situation any better? Do we have greater access to information than we had in 1955? Yes, we do. Are we closer to the kind of instant plug-in ecstasy of total data input that my world dictator, Kloofman, was able to get? No, I don't think so. In fact, I think Isaac's point is still valid, that we fall farther and farther behind as we march onward into the future, despite the new technologies. You all know this. You all also know, of course, that discussions of this kind will largely rehearse information that you have felt in your bones all along; that's what you come here for, to be confirmed in your deepest beliefs.

It's impossible to keep up. Is this inherent in the situation? Yes. I think it is; you think it is. Is it deplorable? Yes, it is. And then you go on from there.

I see that some of you have managed to frighten yourselves, if I'm correct in understanding the theme of this program—"Information for a New Age: Fantastic Technology or Institutionalized Alienation?" And I said at the opening that I don't see any dichotomy there. The "Fantastic Technology" will indeed result in "Institutionalized Alienation," if it's allowed to. It will also provide you with a way of scanning through an entire bibliography in a tenth of a second looking for the references to whatever molecule it was that Dr. Asimov was talking about.

The power to mess ourselves up is always in our hands. And it's easy indeed to make dire predictions of what is going to be. You all are aware that we are probably the last print-medium generation. And this has caused a lot of hand-wringing concern and, I'm sure, many panel discussions like this one.

Actually, I don't think that this is true. I think that the book is still a very useful way of carrying information up to the podium. I suppose I could have clicked a cube into a transmission unit and a screen behind me, and all of what I have read to you would have appeared, which would have been much easier on my voice, but it would not be fundamentally different from what I just did. It would still require information packets known as *words.* The medium by which they travel is irrelevant. I'm sure there was great hand wringing in Mesopotamia when clay tablets were replaced by inscribed scrolls. But, nevertheless, they managed to transmit their information, and we still have it, as a matter of fact.

The most positive thing I have seen about the information revolution that is galloping toward us has to do with the articles that say 60 percent of all American households did not buy a single book in all of 1991. You know what the people you have to deal with every day in your libraries are like. Yes, fewer and fewer people are reading books, yet, mysteriously, my friends in the publishing industry tell me they have never sold more books. Who are they selling them to? What is happening? Are they on a conveyor belt going round and round? At any rate, despite the fact that nobody is reading anymore, more books are being sold. An interesting paradox, and one that I rather like, because I earn my living by selling books.

Here is a hopeful sign, found in the *Wall Street Journal* in a column called "Information Age":

> In the midst of the general apocalypse of literacy, computer use by illiterates grows at work. The information world is supposed to have no place for illiterates. For some time now doomsayers have predicted that illiterate and uneducated workers won't be able to handle tasks that require them to measure, record and analyze everything by computer. But that may not be the way it plays out. [And do remember that sentence, "But that may not be the way it plays out," because the science fiction writer who deals professionally with the future does a little humility exercise every day before he goes to work, for the way he writes it may not be the way the future plays itself out.] Instead of forcing workers to become smarter, computers may make it easier for some illiterates. They may also help some foreign-born workers who cannot read English. In some warehouses, forklift drivers who can't read the labels on a soda machine get directions from talking computers on their belts. Instead of writing up work reports, construction workers can touch pictures on a portable pen-based computer screen to store work records.
>
> From a short term, bottom line point of view, perhaps that's sensible. It's cheaper to invent new technology to cope with illiteracy than it is to eliminate illiteracy itself and it keeps workers on the job, even if they don't have computer skills. But the longer term penalty may be having fewer workers who can think. And an illiterate worker who is dependent on the technology that one company has fine tuned will have trouble finding another job if the employer flounders.

So we have the trend being decried by the spokeswoman for Laubach Literacy Action, a Syracuse, New York, group that organizes literacy training efforts of a thousand local groups, at the same time we have a Raytheon spokesman talking about how wonderful it is that people who can't read can still process information and so on.

This is the future happening right around us here in the late twentieth century. New technologies have advanced into our lives. We all talk learnedly of MS-DOS and things that we knew nothing about ten years ago. And in two years we won't even talk of MS-DOS; we'll talk about Windows, and so on.

The future will not be held back. Unfortunately, we are proceeding into it one second after another, unstoppably. And since I began talking, we have gobbled up a half-hour of the present and moved that much farther into the future.

The future brings for you people, I suppose, the problem of information literacy. It's a phrase I don't like at all. How many of you think *information literacy* is a nice term? You can put your hands up. And how many of you think it's a repellent neologism? Good. I don't like it, either. I don't like the "jargonative" use of *literacy* to mean "ability to function" or "ability to know" or "ability to use tools." There are other terms for that. Literacy to me is the ability to use words. And when you start extending it into *information* literacy, I see another good word beginning to get very blurry around the edges. And we'll go on—quickly, I suppose—into *baseball* literacy, and then ultimately into *literacy* literacy. And I hope I'm not here to see that day.

But I'm puzzled by the ostensible topic that we're here to discuss, because it seems to me, despite the glitzy new term that has been introduced to me in the last few hours, the concept behind information literacy is the very thing that you as librarians have been doing all along, and which, in fact, librarians have been doing since the days of the Alexandrian Library, probably even earlier—controlling the flow of data in such a way that that data is useful to the people who need or want to use it.

Do we need a new term for library science, which I take *information literacy* to be? I don't know. I worry about these things. I see Abigail Loomis received an award for the paper—probably an excellent, crisp paper—called "Building Coalitions for Information Literacy." With all due respect for Ms. Loomis's paper, which I have not read but hope to someday when I can access the data, when I read about building coalitions, I reach for my revolver. And *information*? I don't know. I find the word as well as the phrase *information literacy* disturbing; and I hope to have it explained to me better as I sit here how and what the problem is.

I have here before me "Information for a New Age: Redefining the Librarian." Do you want to be redefined? Yes. Do you need to be redefined? Apparently. Are you afraid of something? Yes. I would like to hear, as this morning unfolds, what it is you are afraid of. And I, who spend most of my time, professionally, in the future, even since I was a small boy, will try to soothe you with examples, if I can find them, of how the frightening and inchoate future always turns out, when you get there, to be the present. And you know about the present, you've lived your entire lives in it. It's a matter of catching the hot rivets in the bucket as they are tossed to you and putting them in the right place.

As Isaac indicated, we live in a very complex society that grows more complex all the time. And if we don't learn ways of processing the data that comes in, we will be inundated and swept away. As I tried to indicate in the two passages from the two books I read, technology will not only provide new inundations but will provide ways of coping with those inundations. And librarians today, as always, are what we now call the "interface" between the inundation and the dike. You are the finger in the dike, plugging it with your ability to guide the users of data in the ways it can be used.

I have here a manifesto, or at least a proclamation, from the Library Instruction Round Table Fifteenth Anniversary Task Force, and I suspect I have fragments of that Task Force all around me here ready to hurl me from the podium. It says: "It is vital to clarify the instructional role of libraries and librarians in the 1990s and beyond." How will it change? What aspects will stay the same? What I want to propose to you now is that it will change; it will stay the same. This may sound like Zen koans to you. But, in fact, you will be facing the age-old problems of how to deal with this mess: Where do I file this? and Where do I find it again? How do I tell them, when they can barely ask the questions, what their answers are? These are not new problems. They just have new glitter on them, new gleam. The fundamental problem of all of us who deal with data—those who create it, those who process it, those who organize it, those who retrieve it—is this: these are all pieces of the same continuous spectrum. The fundamental problem is *thinking*. Thinking is not only the fundamental problem but the essential function that we perform. All the rest, requiring the coalitions, the initialed groups, all the rest is simply a matter of polishing the hardware.

The hardware you will have to learn how to polish and massage, and then be terrified of some revolution—a *double revolution* of illiteracy, in the old sense of the word: ignorance and increasing data. Now the paradox we've struck here is that people are consuming less and less information all the time, but more and more information is flooding in upon the libraries. How can this be? As this paradox complicates your lives, you will discover that technology yet again simplifies them. Those of you whose hands touched a computer keyboard before 1981 please raise those hands now. Wow! Before 1971. I'm surprised it's even that many. I would say that's about 5 percent of you. Those of you whose hands have never touched a computer keyboard to this day, if you dare raise your hands now. There you have it. Either some are afraid to admit it, or, more likely, you are all computer literate.

Nobody, including Dr. Asimov with his punch cards, could have foreseen that in 1955. The problems that he was facing then, which caused him to write the essay "The Sound of Panting," now seem laughable. *Chemical Abstracts,* I'm sure, is on CD-ROM, though, if it isn't, it will be next year. And it will then be possible to put the lovely little disk into the machine and type in "thiotimoline"—ah, there are some knowing snickers from the people who are Asimov experts—and get back not only all the available information on thiotimoline but neat printouts, stapled and bound, if necessary. None of this was imaginable in the days of the Alexandrian Library. Somehow, we got from here to there; somehow we, and you particularly, will get from here to the terrifying twenty-first century.

2

Librarians or Technicians?
Which Shall We Be?

Deanna B. Marcum

Technology is neither inherently good nor bad. It has become a fact of life for most of us, even if we find in our literature as many articles against it as we find for it. Unfortunately, I frequently hear librarians referring to technology as something with a life of its own. We talk about what computers can and cannot do. We have added technology in our libraries in order to make resources available, but we have not considered the consequences, necessarily.

Why should we be so concerned about technology? We convince ourselves that computers are just like cars—you simply *drive* the car; you don't have to understand how it works. It gets you to the place you are going. So it is with computers. We use them for our work, but they do not have any influence on what we do. Or do they? The truth is, many librarians spend far more time these days learning about how the computer works and what it can do than nearly anything else. That, in and of itself, is not a bad thing, but it does have enormous implications for our profession.

Recent changes in our profession can be best summarized in the words of one of my history faculty colleagues who recently lamented, "Librarians used to be our colleagues and allies. They talked with us about the latest historical literature, and when the library budget was under consideration, they could always count on us to support their need for additional money. Now, librarians speak a new language. They tell us about the latest computer based on-line catalog, how fast the transaction speed is, all the bells and whistles. They speak in a language totally unfamiliar to us. When library budget time rolls around, they want support for more terminals, more work stations, cables and wires. We want to help the library, but we are reluctant to talk about these things we do not understand. The need to upgrade seems never ending, and we begin to wonder if we will ever see history books again." Historians do not speak for everyone, certainly, but we need to be concerned about how we are perceived by others. I am reminded of the adage from the 1960s: "You are what you do, not what you say."

I would like to use my brief response time to outline what I believe to be the most important changes that have resulted from a new emphasis on technology.

1. Library education has become increasingly technical. As needs for technical training increase, historical and philosophical subjects are more often ignored by students as they choose electives. Even worse, such subjects are often eliminated from the curriculum altogether. Consequently, students know more about how to do certain tasks using a computer, but less about how the profession developed and what its ethical and philosophical bases are.

2. Technical skills, not subject knowledge, more frequently form the basis for professional positions. Librarians are hired for their expertise in online searching or microcomputer applications in libraries. In many ways, the emphasis on technical skills in library school grows directly from the employment situation.

3. Staff training has become more technical. In the 1970s and 1980s, staff development received great emphasis. Courses and workshops in many aspects of organizational development, management, and interpersonal skills were made available to library staffs. Librarians were beginning to work in groups to solve problems and share knowledge. Work today, much of it computer-based, is more likely to be solitary.

4. Library instruction has changed its focus as well. In earlier years, librarians concentrated on teaching research skills to library users. Today, the emphasis for both groups is on technical skills. Librarians and users alike must learn how to use machines in order to find the information they need. Little time and few resources are left for the broader utilization of information types of courses.

Though I believe technology has resulted in a new emphasis, I do not mean to suggest that technology is an altogether new force. Libraries have been as aggressive as any other institution in adopting technology for the purpose of improving services and reducing costs. Starting with Melvil Dewey's campaign for the first School of Library Economy in 1884, technology has been singled out as the way to improve library services.

If we find ourselves now wondering if technology is overemphasized, perhaps it is because we have been so ambiguous about what the library is supposed to be and what role it is to play. We seem to be caught in the transition from the late-nineteenth-century progressive institution to the postmodern world of individualism. When the modern American public library was created in the late nineteenth century, its development coincided with the emergence of professions. Librarians, just as other educated groups, sought recognition for their special contributions. They emphasized the missionary nature of librarianship, for they truly believed that books could improve people's lives. They thought reading good books would influence individuals from all sectors of society to be better humans. I think that is the reason we still hear so many personal testimonies to the transforming power of the library. When the topic of libraries comes up in general conversation, it usually leads to a story about how someone's life was totally changed because that person discovered books and reading at a local public library. As highly sophisticated "information professionals," we cringe when hearing such stories, for we know that libraries are much more than repositories of books. These inspirational stories about the library leave out a very important ingredient—librarians. We want everyone to know that information is available in many different formats and that we are ready to serve it up to anyone who needs it, even if the person does not know that he or she needs it.

We like to say that the library is a *service*, not a place. With a vast arsenal of technology to assist, we can introduce our clients (no longer "patrons") to the world of information that is waiting to be tapped. We are eager to tell people about what is available through *this* online search service or *that* bibliographic network. We want our clients to realize that we have the professional knowledge to cut through the complicated start-up procedures for these technologically mediated services and get to the heart of the information needed.

The reader, who in the past gained a great deal unconsciously as he or she roamed through the stacks, opening books from time to time, looking for the right information, is now handed a list of citations or texts that resulted from matching words in a database. Specificity of language becomes more important than anything else: Did your word capture the exact nature of the topic? Does it match the thesaurus terms in this particular database? It seems to me that when technology is the mediating force in retrieving information, the purpose is to limit as much as possible. Creativity and expansiveness seem to be discouraged, because they result in lack of specificity.

The remarkable quality of books is that knowledge comes in a synthesized form. The raw material of the topic has been questioned, explored, and summarized in a form that gives us complete thoughts, not just information. Even if a book is not particularly well written, we have a certain level of assurance that the author of the book spent a good bit of time thinking about the issues before thoughts were committed to paper. When we retrieve information from online sources, we also find some material that is highly structured and synthesized, but it usually coexists with informal remarks, works in progress, and electronic messages from uninformed individuals.

The point of all this is that librarians are more than processors of information. If we continue to focus on how to make machines work in our libraries, we fundamentally change the nature of what we do, but we also become members of a different community. No longer are we allies of scholars; no longer are we active researchers ourselves into the substance of an academic discipline; no longer are we the experts on our collections. Instead of seeing us in the stacks, our users will find us bent over a CD-ROM player trying to repair it or connecting it to the printer so students can find the information they want and leave quickly. Students begin to think of us as the technicians who will change the paper, not the experts who will help them think through the substance of important questions.

We should be concerned about technology because it *allows*—not forces—us to become a quite different type of professional. We may actively seek that result, but I am fearful that we have given too little thought to the historical and even the present contributions of the librarian. It is not fashionable to speak in the missionary-like language of the late nineteenth century when librarians first began to define their roles. Yet, I am convinced that books and reading play important, sometimes transforming, roles in people's lives. We deny our users a precious commodity if we begin to think that all information has equal value and that our job is that of the information retrieval specialist.

We should not blame technology if our students seem more interested in grabbing quick citations on the run. We have created that world for them. In this new world, students are confronted with more information than they can possibly assimilate. If we do not teach them how to assess the quality of what they retrieve, what is the point of teaching expert retrieval? In emphasizing the role of technology, we cannot ignore the role librarians have played, and must continue to play, in transforming information into knowledge.

3

The Death of the Librarian in the (Post) Modern Electronic Information Age[1]

Robert H. Kieft

Even to those who do not follow the vicissitudes of post-structuralist thought, the bibliothecal version of its postmodernist assault on the humanist self as the unifying, transcendent term of individuality will be familiar.[2] The story is told in almost every journal and at every conference, and its very simple plot reads as follows: The death of the librarian will result from a fusion reaction between computers and wide-band communication networks as both are involved in a physics of capital, geographical dispersion, personal convenience, sheer hurry, and technological progress peculiar to the post-everything "information society" we live in. The librarian and the library, in the old world of print and paper the essence and the end, the cohering terms, of the universe of information,[3] will fragment and deliquesce as the infinitude of decentering possibilities released in this reaction blazes into every info-dark nook and cranny of the planet. This death will occur just as certainly as God met its demise under the Nietzschean bludgeon and the author was buried at the behest of Roland Barthes.

At the decentered center of the postmodernist self, then, is a struggle with the humanist subject and with the corollary questions of identity and agency, and I want to take as my text in these pages the striking image with which Michel Foucault begins his inaugural discourse at the College de France.[4] That image is the oxymoronic tableau of his standing before his audience to outline a personal research program from a lectern that honors the highly individuated, aggressively central voices of France's most original thinkers and, at the same time, to wish he were absent, to wish that he himself could be present in effect merely as a figure in a timeless rhetoric, as an oratorical node in the infinite unfolding of a discursive network that precedes any individuation or beginning.

Foucault's self-subversive image comes to mind when I enter a library lobby and see platoons of cathode-ray tubes guarding a distant, or nonexistent, librarian, or when I read the eschatological prognostications of those who threaten, welcome, or simply speculate about the death of the library and the librarian at

15

the hands or, better, chips and Internetted electrons, of the very technologies those librarians have bespoken to speak for them. Librarians have eagerly embraced various electronic technologies for a good many reasons,[5] and, although some of those same librarians suspect that this embrace may well leave them in the position of the small-town gas station after the new interstate highway has been built, many in the business emerge from it sufficiently invigorated that they urge us all to buy up the neighboring farmland for information truckstops and 24-hour information minimarts. A part of me, however, wonders, in the context of the postmodernist question of agency, whether that electronic embrace doesn't miss at least part of the point and, at that, miss it in some ways that are dysfunctional with respect to many educational goals. Academic librarians are, after all, in the education business, not the information business, and I wonder whether assigning the importance that they do to these technologies doesn't take too facile a way out of the admittedly difficult tasks of the educator, only one of which and, in the four-year undergraduate program, not the most important of which, presumably, is the task of purveying information or making resources available.[6]

Before I develop what I mean by this last statement in the postmodern, agentless world of electrotechnology, I want to offer some rules or assumptions for librarianship.

First, students do not want to learn how to use a library. With varying degrees of ambition, they want to get their work done, but almost none of them wants to learn "library." Although electronic technologies offer value that the average card catalog, printed index, National Union Catalog, or even photocopy machine never thought of, these same statements apply in the incipient electronic library as well.

Second, librarians are not in the business of teaching students how to use a library. Rather, they are in the business of teaching students how to think research problems and papers, how to perform a variety of intellectual tasks. Learning to think library and learning about things in the library are aspects of this endeavor, but they are not the goal of the endeavor.

Third, students are concrete and circumstantial. They have difficulty abstracting from experience with one course or one research project to others, and very little in their educational experience, with the possible exception of brute repetition, encourages the development of the ability to do so.

Fourth, students tend to cast all their relationships in the mode of social relationships. What adults think of as working relationships, relationships with multiple dimensions of authority, responsibility, accountability, and friendship, are largely foreign to them. Furthermore, a great many social and developmental facts of both adolescent and adult life inhibit the successful interaction of students and librarians. Students' lack of experience with or their anxieties about institutional settings work together with the way they modalize their relationships to make their feeling comfortable or effective in libraries and with librarians difficult.

Fifth, with all due respect for the hard work undertaken by teachers throughout the country, students do not receive enough, let alone systematic, instruction in how to go about the work assigned to them. Students have been trained to look at their grade as the main, even sole, indicator of their success, and neither professors nor TAs are trained or encouraged by their publish-or-perish circumstances or by their own training to give students and student work the kind of attention that would be required to correct this situation. Indeed, very little in the system of higher education trains students in the ways of researching, reading, thinking, and writing that characterize effective work. Perhaps, more destructively, very little in U.S. culture does much, in spite of protests from the "real" world of business that people cannot write a decent sentence, to encourage that they seek such training.[7]

Sixth, although modern librarianship came into being simultaneously with the laying of the groundwork for what we have come to think of as the information explosion, academic librarians are not now nor have they ever been "major players" in the information game. The view that they are or have been is, to a large extent, an exercise in self-justification, an epiphenomenon of their workplace, that is, of the part they have played in the gathering, organizing, and caring for print collections and the large buildings and bureaucratic institutions that have grown up around them. All the good work librarians have done in this regard has obscured the reality that most people find what they want or what they are willing to settle for without the direct intervention of most of the people who work in libraries. If, then, librarians are operating with a misplaced or even exaggerated notion of their profession's role in the pre-electronic information world, the advent of the electronic revolution and its potential for displacing that profession suggest that librarians look to functions other than those of gathering, storing, or delivering information as their true functions.[8]

With these rules in mind, I revert to my statement that librarians are in the education business, not the information business, and take the position that, important though it is for librarians to make the raw materials for research, reading, thinking, and writing available to students, they are finally, as educators, responsible for achieving other goals. That is to say that librarians must finally be more interested in and more responsible to the whole work of enhancing human capacity than of providing students with information and the instruments for obtaining it. To emphasize technology, as the profession tends to do these days, and here I run the risk of false oppositions, is to value means over end, information over knowledge, tool over product, turnover over completeness, delivery over destination, detail over perspective, and so on. To say that what students need is information is like saying that what we need to do to correct the social ills of the country is to give everyone a job—it's simply too limited a view.[9]

I want, then, to advocate for librarians what, for want of a better locution, I will call an erotics of teaching. One can, of course, sublimate the eros of human pedagogical interaction into an eros of machine interaction, part of the human project being to produce things in humanity's own image. In that an erotics depends, however, on a balance of similitude and difference, on a complex of qualities and characteristics that together establish an attraction, other human beings are likely for the foreseeable future to function better, for most of us, as sources and objects of attention than are machines. In this view, education is much more than information or training, it is a life. As human life, it exists necessarily as a whole governed, in specific contexts, by negotiation, judgment, and a complex layering of relationships and experiences. Thus, librarians' business as educators is, in its largest sense, the growth of souls and the finishing of spirits, which means that librarians, like all teachers, must engage in nurturing students to create themselves as knowledgeable human beings by passing along to them the authority not only of their knowledge but of their experience of themselves as knowledgeable beings.

Informed by my six rules, this pedagogical role I advocate would make the following prescriptions for librarians' work:

First, because students tend not to reveal themselves or state their needs unless encouraged to do so, and because they tend to be most tolerant of and most receptive to people they can simply fall in with, librarians must get out of the office, the conference room, and the convention hall, out to the reference desk and into the classroom, out to participate in institutional programs and events that would make them a part of the students' community. Librarians must manifest personal interest in the questions and projects the students work on. They must engage students in conversation about that work, and, by their intellectual fluency, ambition, and engagement, they must demonstrate that education matters in real life, matters as more than a credential giving access to certain futures, as something that one lives rather than simply hurdles. I hesitate to say they must be "role models," because overuse has tended to drain that locution of its power, but that is indeed what education is, in large part, about.

Among other pressures, not the least of which are the cultural and social forces that make education problematic for students, the pressures of organizational and professional life for librarians militate against such behavior. In consequence, some of the very ways in which librarians define their professionalism create a subversive turn away from contact with college students. Librarians must, therefore, change the reward system of their work to encourage interaction with students and must ally themselves with those forces in the academic world currently calling for a new emphasis on teaching.

Second, beyond being personable and personally involved, librarians' help must be repeated and concrete, highly individualized and attentive. It should look like the sort of consulting advice that many would call spoon-feeding or taking by the hand. Students need to be *shown* how it's done, not pointed to how it's done.

Third, librarians must be widely educated, that is, they must be well-read in and want to talk about what the students and faculty work on. A librarian gains credence among students with interest in and knowledge of the subject matter of their papers, and of materials related specifically to them, not with knowledge of "the library." The most instruction most students receive from most professors with respect to assignments is "go to the library and look up some articles"; when they arrive, not only are the mechanics of looking for such things unknown to them, but they do not have a good idea of what use to make of the material once they have found it. Thus, librarians must not only work with professors to design meaningful assignments, assignments that teach thinking and judgment and not simply "using the library," but they must be able to pick up both the procedural and substantive slack with which so many assignments leave students.

Education programs for librarians must insist, therefore, not only on a broad background of learning but should include advanced education in the humanities, social sciences, or sciences in much the same way that some teacher education programs conflate a subject master's and a teaching credential. Education for librarianship should offer courses in the history, research methods, and literature of the disciplines, taking account especially of the scholarly debates that shape ongoing work. Librarians should finish their graduate programs knowing the major monographs and serials in the liberal disciplines and should be acquainted with the history of higher education and its curriculum.

Fourth, librarians must want to work with and know the people at their institution. The reward structure for the profession must be changed to value institutional contributions and institutional loyalty over professional activity and professional loyalty.

Fifth, librarians must simplify organizations so that they don't need so many people as "managers" and can, therefore, devote more staff to working with students.

Sixth, librarians must reexamine whether and in what ways the current technological keeping-up-with-the-Joneses in which so many of us are engaged fits enough of the needs of students. They must ask more searching questions than are being asked today about the value of putting such vast quantities of institutional resources into information access.

Having entertained these prescriptions, readers will proceed to adduce a host of reasons why they are all very well and good but even in the short run unworkable, all very bad philosophically as well as practically, or all simply out of touch with reality. All that such readers say may well be true, and doubtless much else besides. That concession made, however, and although I will not go so far as to subscribe to the opinion that the "ideal college" would consist of Mark Hopkins, the influential president of Williams College in the mid-nineteenth century, "on one end of a log and a student on the other,"[10] I will insist that senior human beings are preemptively important in the formation of their juniors, that no substitute exists for the careful, humanly enfranchising attention that only the adult can give to youth. If the librarian is an educator, then the librarian's task is to cultivate students, not simply provide them with information, and librarians, together with the institutions in which they work, must find ways to enable librarians not simply to make information more accessible but to engage the minds and lives using it.

This view of the librarian as educator returns me, in conclusion, to Foucault, for in the conclusion of his lecture he recognizes an important sound in the discourse he had wanted to find himself immersed in, an important presence in the Beckettian absence he had wanted himself to be at the lectern. That sound, a speech that is speaking through him, he recognizes, is the voice of a teacher, Jean Hippolyte. He thus locates himself finally not as a vacant space filled by an agentless irruption of language out of silence and nothingness or as the voiceless voicing of an unindividuated discourse, but as an echo, a resumption of and tribute to, the voice of his teacher. He realizes his own voice in the cadences of that other and finds his proper discourse, his origin, in the teacher's presence to his memory and work. The voice of the teacher is, thus, a preeminently human voice, the voice of the individuated intellect, the voice of the powerful agent, saturated with a plenitude of influences. The voice is not a mechanical one, not the discourse of unarticulated information or sheer discursiveness, but that of the master speaker. Electronic technologies cannot yet themselves speak in this complex way, much though they facilitate the work of speaking. In the end, one skillfully *uses* a technology, but one *knows* a teacher, and in knowing a teacher, one comes to be oneself.

NOTES

1.   Early on in the telephone conversation during which Cindy Cunningham (University of Washington) suggested that I might participate in the 1992 LIRT program at which I presented a version of the present essay, she made it clear that what she wanted on the panel was a point of view that would fall on a technology continuum running, say, from village idiot to quixotic recusant. Inclined to fit on that continuum, I developed the position you read here. As the emphasis on *emphasis* in the essay suggests, however, the position I take does not so much try to claim that electronic technologies are pernicious or distracting, wholly wrongheaded or ultimately trivial, as it tries to stake a claim for the continuing, even increased, importance among those technologies of human beings. Because I wanted this essay to retain the flavor of the original presentation, whose purpose was to stake out a certain territory on a panel, it tends to assert a position rather than argue it; however, in that the essay has some more room in which to maneuver than did the original presentation, I have added some qualifications to the text and have resorted to notes when, if not to argue a point, I wanted at least to recognize its arguability. I concern myself with the class of library users called "students," and by this I mean late-adolescent college students, who, rather than faculty or graduate students, are not only the most numerous but arguably the most important clients of our academic libraries. By "librarians," I mean primarily those responsible for reference and instruction.

2.   What constitutes humanism and what constitutes the poststructuralist deconstruction of humanism are matters for debate, and I cannot enter that debate here. Furthermore, so as not to muddy waters that my failure to engage in this debate already makes murky enough, I have been scrupulous in avoiding mention of humanism's conceptually even slipperier cousin, "liberal education," a character ever willing to participate in and confuse discussion of the purposes, goals, and methods of higher learning. I also avoid completely in these pages the theoretical questions of whether a postmodern humanism is possible and of the relationship between technology and the postmodernist sensibility.

3.   The question of whether or to what extent such a statement was ever true of librarians remains open, even though the number of people who are anxious about the electronic displacement of librarians from the center of the information arena to the remote tundras of its periphery suggests that a great many in the profession would give an affirmative answer. See note 8.

4.   Delivered December 2, 1970, published as "L'ordre du discours" (Paris: Gallimard, 1971), and translated into English by Rupert Sawyer as "The Discourse on Language," the translation being done originally for the journal *Social*

Science Information (April 1971: 7-30) and appearing later as an appendix to the English-language edition of Foucault's *The Archaeology of Knowledge* (New York: Pantheon, 1972).

5. Not the least of these good reasons is that electronic information technologies allow librarians faster, more flexibly, more completely, and on a larger scale to do their traditional work of gathering, storing, organizing, retrieving, and disseminating the recorded products of intellectual labor. The problem before the profession, however, is the extent to which a(n overwhelming) concern for the means of doing that traditional work not only complicates the reasons for doing it at all but obscures them. In effect, that concern not only potentially moves that work out of libraries and librarianship but threatens those very reasons themselves.

6. One is reminded of the old saw about the demise of the railroads. Many would argue that once libraries and librarians recognize that they are in the information business rather than the library business, they will prosper. At least for academic libraries, my position takes exception to this view. Students certainly need the raw materials for doing their work, and they should learn contemporary methods for gathering those materials; but they need a great deal more than that from libraries and librarians, a great deal more than the current tendency to equate the work of librarianship with the delivery of information would give them.

7. That said, a dimension missing from the arguments of most of those who criticize the research orientation of colleges and universities is a recognition of the frustration that working with students can induce. In such critiques, students are generally portrayed as hungry for the very fruits of knowledge that a cynical, lazy, self-absorbed, and professionalized professorate deny them. Anyone who teaches is abundantly aware, however, of the difficulties, as well as the pleasures, of working day after day with adolescent young adults. Those same people do not wonder for long why research and writing are so attractive to so many college professors when so many students take no interest whatsoever in what interests them, are poorly prepared to do the kinds of work they require, and live in a culture that is deeply ambivalent about intellectual work and workers, that affords those workers no clear mandate for what their job is or what skills and knowledge they want students to have, and that subscribes in any case to a cynical myth of success, a myth that has little to do with what students do in school and is largely concerned with the accumulation of money and power.

8. From this point of view, the current discussions of access and ownership, the grimly visionary job descriptions for the librarian in the electronic age, and the speeches and articles that begin with and proceed quickly to wallow in such conditional statements as "If librarians are to remain major players, then, . . ." are the emperor's new clothes of that old librarianly battle with the knowledge that people will find things without us, a knowledge substantiated in new and even more powerful ways by computers and their networks. The current anxiety among librarians is easy to understand; after all, people tend to feel the validity

of their work reduced if history changes things so as to make that work no longer necessary. Do we have any reason, though, to think that the library profession should continue to exist as we have come to think of it in the last 100 years? If in the age of electronic technology those things that libraries stored and librarians cared for are indeed going to bypass libraries and the librarians in them to go directly to office and home computers, librarians must look elsewhere in the educational establishment for their niche. That some of the goals of education and research may well be achievable without the profession of librarianship as we know it and that those goals may be achievable even without the kind of human interaction that has been one of the librarian's main stocks in trade does, of course, make the educational role of librarians more problematic; at the same time, however, these circumstances argue for paying renewed attention to what education is about, namely, the lives and minds and characters of students.

9. My point of view here dovetails with the tradition represented by Neil Postman's critique of the culture of technology in *Technopoly: The Surrender of Culture to Technology* (New York: Knopf, 1992).

10. James A. Garfield quoted by Frederick Rudolph in *The American College and University: A History* (New York: Knopf, 1962, p. 243).

4

Bibliographic Instruction, Briefly

Evan Ira Farber

Earlham College
Richmond, Indiana

The idea that teaching use of the library is important has been around for over a century. This brief introductory essay will try to convey something of its history, a bit about its methods, and offer some speculations about its future. The viewpoint is necessarily a personal one. To be sure, it is based on long experience, wide reading, and many conversations with others in the field, but it still represents one person's views.

Throughout the years, there have been various terms for teaching use of the library: library orientation, bibliographic instruction, training in use of the library, library instruction, library user education, library use instruction, information literacy, and perhaps even others. The term most widely used for it now (in higher education, certainly) is *bibliographic instruction*. That term is hardly one that comes trippingly off the tongue, so among librarians it's generally referred to as BI. For reasons of convenience, as well as space, we'll use that acronym here.

The rationale for BI is straightforward and is based on the fact that most individuals do not use libraries efficiently or effectively: if they find the information they're seeking at all, they spend much more time than necessary; just as often, or even more often, they don't find the information they're seeking, or, rather, they don't find the information that, if they had found it, would much better meet their needs. Asking a reference librarian would help obviate this problem, of course, but reference librarians are not always available and, even if they were, many persons are reluctant to ask them for help. Another part of BI's rationale is that the very bibliographic apparatus that helps organize the chaotic world of publications is complicated, and most users either don't appreciate that fact or don't take the time to sort through the complications. Moreover, as the world of information has become more complicated, the number of pieces in that apparatus—indexes, abstracting services, online and CD-ROM databases, bibliographies, handbooks, and so on—has increased. More essential, only with some sort of instruction will library patrons use these resources or even know about them.

Such instruction is important for all library users, and not just because of the immediate or short-term impact. In the short run, it will help students do better work, get to materials they otherwise could not have, and go beyond the textbook, even beyond the instruction; in other words, it will help students become more independent learners. Just as important is the change in attitude on the part of those who receive instruction: their "library-anxiety" level will be reduced and so they will make better use of the library and especially of reference librarians. The long-term argument for BI is based on the fact that, in many ways, our society is rapidly becoming—if, indeed, it has not already become—information-based, and in such a society, success or failure will increasingly be measured in terms of one's ability to find, organize, and use information. Learning how to use a library effectively may not automatically bestow that ability, but it can provide an impulse that will help one attain it.

The opening sentence of this essay mentions teaching use of the library, and the following paragraphs are also related to libraries. Today, however, with the new information technology, technology that is so "user friendly," it is becoming increasingly easy for individuals to find practically unlimited amounts of information from their offices and homes. Information overload rather than information deprivation will be more and more recognized as the problem. BI librarians, therefore, are becoming increasingly concerned with teaching ways of sorting through the information, and are giving increasing attention to instruction that is more conceptual, instruction that attempts to give users an understanding of how information is organized, so that they can know better how to select and evaluate information.

EARLY HISTORY

While the contemporary BI movement is really only about twenty-five years old, efforts to provide instruction in use of the library began over a century ago. In the latter part of the nineteenth century, academic librarians began to write about their role as educators. In an 1880 government publication entitled "College Librarians as Aids to Instruction," Justin Winsor, the Harvard University Librarian, wrote that the college librarian should become "a teacher, not that mock substitute who is recited to; a teacher, not with a text book, but with a world of books."[1]

That was not an unusual sentiment, and, in many institutions, including Cornell, Colorado, Oberlin, and Bowdoin, librarians offered courses or lectures on the use of libraries. A survey conducted by the U.S. Bureau of Education in 1914 found that about 20 percent of the 446 colleges and universities and 56 percent of 166 normal schools provided instruction to their students in the use of the library.[2] In 1922, the H. W. Wilson Company, recognizing the growing interest, published the first of many editions of *Guide to the Use of Libraries: A Manual for College and University Students*, by Margaret Hutchins and others.

Primary and secondary schools were also active—surprisingly so (at least to this writer). Various articles on the history of BI had given this writer the impression that in those early years little was going on below the college level. However, a look through the *Bibliography of Library Economy*, the periodical index covering professional literature from 1876 to 1920, quickly changed that impression: it lists dozens of articles on the need for both library instruction and individual programs in elementary and high schools, with a few of these items even appearing in the 1890s. Nor was this a temporary spurt of interest; *Library Literature, 1921-1932* shows a good bit of continuing attention to the subject, with one additional aspect: a number of manuals were published, both those meant for persons teaching use of the library and workbooks to be used by students. Again, the interest of the H. W. Wilson Company indicates a recognition of the substantial involvement by librarians with instruction. In 1928, Wilson came out with the first edition of Zaidee Mabel Brown's *The Library Key*, a manual used over the years by generations of students (a later edition was used by this writer in the 1950s). A superb summation of all this early activity appeared in 1960 when George S. Bonn came out with his *Training Laymen in Use of the Library*, in which he reviewed "some of the significant contributions" from the over 1,100 articles, books, and theses on BI that had been published between 1876 and 1958.[3] The items he reviewed involved the spectrum of libraries—elementary and high school, public, special, college and university, even graduate and professional school libraries—and he noted the wide variety of methods and materials used by these libraries. What strikes today's reader of Bonn's work, aside from the impressive interest in instruction shown by the number and variety of programs and studies, and by the many guidebooks and manuals, is the individualism (one might even say the *anarchy*) exhibited in all of this activity. Nowhere is there any indication of a concerted effort to get beyond individual programs or publications, either through conferences, cooperative projects, or organizations devoted to instruction.

In higher education, the instruction movement seemed to have reached a plateau in the 1920s and 1930s. One possible reason, paradoxically enough, was the development of reference work as a standard aspect of academic librarianship, with a concomitant focus on answering questions and finding materials rather than on instruction. The academic and social environment of the two decades undoubtedly also contributed to the lack of progress in bibliographic instruction. That is, educational reformers were trying new methods—honors courses, independent study, reserve readings, for example—methods to which the library had to adjust in terms of procedures or even organization but that did not demand the librarian's involvement in the teaching process. Also, of course, the economic crisis of the 1930s meant, in many cases, staff reductions or at least static budgets, so librarians were reluctant to take on additional responsibilities.

Another possible factor was that, with the rapid growth of university libraries after 1900, and especially in the 1920s, professional concerns among academic librarians were increasingly tilted toward university libraries. That meant emphasis on those activities that supported graduate and faculty research—acquisitions, special collections, administrative theory and structure, and so on—rather than on those activities relevant to the education of undergraduates; thus the attention of reference librarians increasingly moved toward reference services for scholars rather than for students. That emphasis also affected the training of new librarians, so that, even if they worked in under-graduate institutions, their interests reflected those of university librarians and their constituents.

But if the BI movement in higher education seemed to have reached and remained on a plateau these years, a few statements and studies, primarily on the college level, came out that would have a significant, though delayed, impact on its practical and conceptual development. In the 1930s, B. Lamar Johnson, Librarian and Dean of Instruction at Stephens College, broke new ground in integrating instruction in use of the library into the curriculum. He reported this in a speech at the ALA conference in 1933, and then wrote about it more formally in his book *Vitalizing a College Library* (Chicago: American Library Associa-tion), published in 1939. Only a year later, Harvie Branscomb's *Teaching with Books: A Study of College Libraries* reported the results of his visits to more than sixty college libraries. What he found, of course, was that the libraries were not used very much. "They do not use the library's books because in a great deal of their work they do not have to; they can do quite acceptable work, in some cases possibly better work, without doing so."[4] To correct the situation, he made a number of suggestions about administering the library differently, but his major emphasis was on the need to teach students how to use the library. As one reads Branscomb today, one is struck by his insights and can't help but wonder, especially because his book not only was sponsored by both the Carnegie Corporation and the Association of American Colleges but also was widely and favorably reviewed, what its impact might have been if it had appeared at any other time but on the eve of America's involvement in World War II.

Another individual of some peripheral interest for the history of BI was Louis Shores, perhaps best known as the head of the library school at George Peabody College for Teachers from 1933 to 1942; he was also the head of the library school at Florida State University from 1949 to 1967. His idea was the "library-college," in which he envisaged the roles of librarians and teachers merging, and all instruction being given in one building, the library. It was an idealistic notion, but so vague conceptually and so utterly impractical politically that it had little impact on the mainstream development of BI. However, its emphasis on librarians as teachers did get a number of librarians to think about that role, and it provided a forum for those who became interested in pursuing the issue in more practical ways.

The writer with unquestionably the greatest impact on the practice and theory of bibliographic instruction was Patricia B. Knapp. She was responsible for a number of significant publications, most of which were on the experiment she carried out at Monteith College in 1960-1961. That experiment was based on the approach that competence in using the library entails a complex of knowledge, skills, and attitudes that can only be developed over a period of time through repeated experiences and that such experiences should be built into regular course assignments, assignments that should be "an integrated part of content courses . . . throughout the four years of [a student's] college education. . . . And they should provide sequence through increasing breadth and depth of the knowledge, skills and attitudes required."[5] She went on to describe types of assignments, emphasizing that the librarian had to take responsibility for the program's initiation and much of its implementation.

The Monteith experiment was the most significant attempt up to that time, and perhaps even to date, to totally integrate BI into the educational curriculum. It was bold and creative in its conception, yet sensible and precise in its method. Even though it did not continue, its thrust and conceptual framework were looked to by instruction librarians as a paradigm, one that perhaps could not be repeated on another campus but could be looked to for guidance, even inspiration.

Responding to a 1965 survey, 126 college librarians indicated that some library instruction was given but no one approach seemed to generate real enthusiasm. If those 126 programs had anything in common, it was the feeling that instruction was very much needed but that not nearly enough of it was being done.[6] Why, then, did the BI movement take off in the next few years? It is interesting to speculate on the relationship between that surge of interest in BI and the Zeitgeist of the times. Perhaps it was a product of the experimentation and innovation taking place in higher education during that period; perhaps it was due to a new generation of reference librarians. In any case, there were a number of events in the late 1960s and early 1970s that seemed unrelated at the time, but in retrospect were obviously part of a movement.

In 1964, Earlham College had begun a program of bibliographic instruction that was built on cooperation between librarians and teaching faculty and extended to many disciplines, including the sciences, and entailed some sequential instruction. These features made the program particularly interesting to other academic librarians, and in 1969, at a meeting of the College Library Section of the Association of College and Research Libraries, the program's purpose and methods were described. The response was impressive:

> [We] expected the usual two- or three-hundred attenders. . . . This was the first time, as far as we knew, that there was a public presentation on bibliographic instruction. . . . To our surprise and delight, the room was overflowing, and there were, we estimated, at least eight hundred in the audience. Moreover . . . [t]he obvious enthusiasm, the questions we got there, and the follow-up letters and inquiries all indicated that there was an enormous reservoir of interest in the subject.[7]

Shortly thereafter, responding to that interest, the Ad Hoc Committee on Bibliographic Instruction was formed within the Association of College and Research Libraries. It began activities with enthusiasm, and it was soon obvious that permanent status was desirable. In 1977, the Bibliographic Instruction Section of ACRL was formed, a group that became one of the most active in professional circles and central to national efforts in BI.

Another important factor was the Council on Library Resources, which initiated two programs in 1969 that involved user education in academic libraries: a fellowship program for midcareer librarians, and a College Library Program, jointly sponsored with the National Endowment for the Humanities. The College Library Program was based on Patricia Knapp's work, and "provided thirty-six institutions with grants to explore innovative ways of enhancing the library's participation in the educational process." The programs ranged widely but they seemed to show enough progress to start yet another program in 1975, the Library Service Enhancement Program.[8] Again, the results ranged widely, and while the proportion of long-term successes was not great, the Council's support contributed to institutionalizing a few programs, providing them and others with national exposure, and permitting an even larger number of individuals to get involved, many of whom became important to later developments. Perhaps one of the most important results was the prestige, the "official" recognition, so to speak, given to BI.

One important long-term result was LOEX (Library Orientation Exchange). In 1971, as a result of its CLR-NEH grant, Eastern Michigan University held the first Annual Conference on Library Orientation for Academic Libraries. The enthusiastic response not only guaranteed succeeding conferences but demonstrated the need for an informational center. LOEX was established the following year to serve as a clearinghouse for sample instructional materials. While its initial interest and membership were focused on college and university libraries, it has gradually extended its services to include a number of public, school, and even special libraries, though its original focus is still paramount. Its importance as a factor in the development of BI cannot be exaggerated: its annual conferences (the twentieth was in 1992) have permitted BI librarians to share experiences and ideas; its quarterly newsletter carries all kinds of news about BI; it has permitted libraries of all types to borrow BI materials developed by other libraries—handouts, workbooks, publicity, videotapes, audiotapes, and so on; and, finally, its success has encouraged the establishment of a number of other BI clearinghouses operating on a state or regional level.

Meanwhile, a good bit of activity relating to instruction had been going on in the American Library Association, and, in 1966, an Ad Hoc Committee on Instruction in the Use of Libraries was set up, with a standing committee established the following year. It had a wide set of purposes, aimed primarily at gathering and disseminating information about instruction vertically as well as horizontally throughout the profession. The Committee was able to provide a forum for discussion during the annual conference so that additional interested parties could participate.[9] Then, in 1972, the Committee sponsored an exhibit of instructional materials at the ALA annual conference in Chicago. The exhibit included audiovisual as well as printed materials and represented all types of libraries. With the interest shown in that exhibit, it became very obvious that an organization was needed that would permit librarians from all types of libraries to meet and work together on matters relating to instruction. The many developments on the college and university level, as productive as they were, could not meet the needs of school and public librarians, and the Committee, as active as it was, could not provide a large enough arena. A committee was formed to work toward such an organization, and, in 1977, the ALA Council approved the establishment of the Library Instruction Round Table (LIRT). Since then, through its many programs, conferences, and publications, LIRT has been another active player and important factor in the BI movement.

The growing interest in BI was also reflected by the amount of publication. Whereas the annual number of articles on the subject averaged thirty-five between 1958 and 1971, in 1974 *Library Literature* listed more than seventy. In that same year, John Lubans Jr.'s *Educating the Library User*, containing thirty-nine original essays on many aspects of instruction at all levels, was published.[10] His book was a milestone in BI history, not only because of the prominence of many of the contributors and the quality of their contributions, but because of its breadth. It treated various aspects of instruction—its rationale, its applications and implications, even the design of buildings as a factor—and it was the first book on instruction that covered the entire library spectrum, from elementary school through the university, even extending to public libraries. One could almost consider it a reference work on BI as of the early 1970s, and as such, it gave BI librarians a common point of reference.

From that time on, BI has continued to develop and is one of the most active areas of librarianship today. Its role in the educational process has become established, not for all educators by any means, and not even for all librarians, but for *enough* to have made an impact. Though a few librarians are still skeptical of BI's importance, even of its usefulness, most librarians understand its contributions to the various levels of education, to lifelong learning, and to more effective use of libraries in general.

BI METHODS

Until the 1970s, BI was provided by one or a combination of several methods. All of them have been written about innumerable times, but a brief survey of them seems appropriate.

Probably the oldest method was the *separate course*, sometimes optional, but more often either required or carrying credit; these were given at a number of colleges and universities even in the nineteenth century. Such courses, varying greatly in content, in format, and in educational thrust, are tempting to offer because the instructors—almost always members of the library staff—can have complete control over content and method. A course, then, can be consistent and effective in itself. Its main disadvantages are two: first, most students are not really interested in learning how to use a library for itself; second, it's expensive, requiring a good bit of staff time for the benefit of relatively few students. For advanced students, however, and especially graduate students, whose motivation is strong, and whose research skills are critical, its high cost can be justified.

Library tours, or *library orientation sessions*, are sometimes included among the methods of BI. For this writer, however, they are practically useless for teaching use of the library, although in larger, more complicated buildings, they may be useful in acquainting students with the location of various library services and types of materials. They may even be counterproductive in some situations: most students are only interested in learning about a library when they need it, and tours simply reinforce students' negative attitudes about libraries and librarians (libraries are boring and librarians are simply custodians). Electronic enhancements—interactive video tours, for example—can make such "instruction" much more palatable, but still do very little in the way of real teaching.

Seminars and *term paper clinics* are just two of the common types of small-group, "on demand" instruction. They have the advantage of being easy and inexpensive to organize, and they obviously meet particular learning needs.

Unfortunately, they reach a relatively small number of students, primarily the highly motivated. Again, they work best at an advanced level.

The *library workbook*, or *library manual*, providing descriptions of library materials and procedures along with a series of questions relating to their applications, has long been used at the school level. Manuals designed for individual college and university libraries go back at least to the 1920s; workbooks used on a large scale came into their own in 1969 when UCLA developed one to teach library skills to minority students. It worked so well that UCLA quickly adopted it for all first-year students and since then a substantial number of college and university libraries have used modified versions of it.

Course-related instruction is the method most commonly used in college and university circles. In this approach, the instruction relates to particular courses in order to help students find information for the assignments in those courses. Usually, the assignment is a research paper of some kind, but it can be any kind of assignment—a book review, an annotated bibliography, material for a speech, whatever—for which information is needed. The instruction, then, takes advantage of what students are really interested in—saving time and getting better grades. *Course-integrated instruction* carries the method one step further: the instruction as well as the assignment is built into, is integrated into, the course itself.

In the 1970s, with the computer beginning to occupy such an important and ubiquitous role in library operations, it was only natural for librarians to look to it for help in BI. Yet a decade later there was then not much evidence of its practicality, and a consequent waning interest in *computer-assisted instruction* (CAI) certainly compared with the flurry of interest in the early 1970s. The decline in interest was due to several factors: the high cost of equipment and its rapid obsolescence; the time and expertise necessary for programming; the focus of attention on other uses of computers in libraries, especially for administration and processing; the burst of activity in more traditional approaches to bibliographic instruction. Recently, however, with the usefulness and presence of computers in libraries taken for granted, with more librarians entering the field who feel comfortable using computers, and with computer hardware accessible to most students and in an increasing number of homes, there has been a renewed interest in CAI. Many librarians feel that basic BI will be taken over by machines. Terminals, or, rather, workstations, are increasingly accessible and not just in libraries, but in homes, classrooms, and dormitory rooms. It will be much easier for users to learn how to find information, or to learn how to use even the most complex library tools. All that will be built in. The Gateway Project of the Ohio State University Library, as sophisticated as it is, is only a beginning, but it points to the logical direction for CAI.[11] In not very many years, even the most unsophisticated users will be able to get infinitely better results from their online public access catalogs (OPACS) than most veteran library users got yesterday from both card catalogs and reference collections. As more libraries have moved to automated catalogs, and as individual uses for online databases continue to grow, instruction for users of these systems will increasingly be built into their operation.

Will it do a good job? Probably. An adequate job? Undoubtedly. Artificial intelligence and expert systems will permit computers to do an even better job—certainly if the number reached is part of the equation—than we do today. Remember, the computer has infinite patience, doesn't take coffee breaks or need to go to the restroom, can be infinitely versatile in its responses, and will be able to adapt to individual needs and requests—requests not just typed out, but spoken (speech, after all, can be transposed into binary units). The next generation of computers will not only be more powerful, but may well have the capacity to reason so that users will be able to interact with them in ordinary conversational language, even to the point of replicating a model reference interview. Just as a good reference librarian does, the new generation of computers might not require users to be very exact about their needs, because they will have some reasoning ability, and could be able to tease out from the user, through questions and suggestions, just exactly what it is the user wants to do or know. Moreover, the "gee-whiz" factor—users marveling at what the computer can do and giving credence to whatever it does (Theodore Roszak, in his book, *The Cult of Information* [New York: Pantheon, 1986], aptly terms the phenomenon "technological idolatry")—gives CAI an appeal that most instruction librarians cannot compete with.

What instruction will be left for the librarian? Though there will still be many individual reference works that will be in print form and will need explaining—indexes, handbooks, encyclopedias, and so on, as well as locally produced materials—this will be a minor part of service, and, eventually, computer programs will be designed locally by individual libraries to provide that service. But the major job for librarians will be to provide individualized reference assistance, much as reference librarians do now, but on a more specialized level, because the basic instructional needs will be taken care of by computers. The role of reference librarian will be even more important than it is today. The OPAC, which is rapidly becoming as standard an item in every library as the card catalog used to be, can provide through the Internet and other information channels we don't even know about yet not only an unlimited number of sources of information but sometimes even the material itself. That will become common. Students in many secondary schools, and even in elementary schools, are doing online searching now through DIALOG and other information systems. As more of these systems provide full text, information will be so easy to get that users will be overwhelmed by the sheer amount and the incredible variety. Not only will the information be easy to get, but there is again that "gee-whiz" factor, the mystique of the computer, its apparent infallibility, which will cause users to be even more unquestioning than they are now about the information they get—and the less sophisticated the user, the more overwhelmed and unquestioning he or she will be. Librarians will have to act more as teachers, as "information counselors," or, as one of my colleagues put it, as "guides in the wilderness of information."

What are the implications for the role of BI librarian? Gail Lawrence, of Ohio State University, in an essay on the computer as a device for bibliographic instruction, concluded more than a decade ago that "the challenge of automation is a total redefinition of the role and function of library user education."[12] Up to this time, BI has focused on specific tools—the card catalog, individual indexes and other reference works, and more recently, online databases. The winter 1991 issue of *Library Trends*, titled "Toward

Information Literacy—Innovative Perspectives for the 1990s," calls for a different thrust, one that entails much more conceptual approaches to instruction. It is a bit early to know whether this is the direction BI will go (and this writer has some pragmatic doubts about it), but there's not much question that BI will have to change.

That raises a different but rather immediate and very practical question: If BI is going to be very different, why spend time now putting all our energies into an outdated approach? Why spend time fixing up a jalopy? Why not just wait for the new model?

To be sure, the main occupation of today's BI librarians—teaching users how to find information—will be taken over by technology. The other function— helping users shape their searches, showing them how to evaluate information, serving as "information counselors"—will increasingly become the librarian's role. Expert systems, after all, have real limitations. Computers, according to an article by a foremost authority on artificial intelligence, have been able to emulate human intelligence in areas "in which the domain of dialog is restricted to a certain topic (such as *wine* or *psychological problems*). . . . [Where] there are no restrictions on the scope of the dialog [human-level intelligence] has not yet been achieved by a machine." [13] Some reference work involves problems that are relatively narrow and limited in their ramifications, but much of it doesn't. But, one might respond, sooner or later technology will even take care of much of that kind of reference work. "We will begin to see reports that a computer has passed Turing's Test [used to determine if a machine has achieved human-level intelligence] early in the next century, but these reports will be premature until at least the year 2000." [14]

There are, it seems, three responses to why we should keep trying to improve on doing what we do.

The first response is the very obvious one: It will be a while before the computer replaces much of what we do, and there's a lot of work to be done until then. Not only do we have library users today who need to be educated, but we also have a continuing flow of new means of storing and accessing information, means that are available to these users; the content and methods of our instruction, then, need almost continual updating. We only used to have to worry about incorporating new reference materials into our instruction; now we have to keep in mind that users can get information in ways very different from what they used to.

The second response is perhaps just as obvious: As professionals, we're obligated to improve what we're doing. If we don't, we're letting down those who prepared the way for us and those who follow us, to say nothing of the rest of our professional colleagues. Continually working to improve what we've been doing and what we believe in is part of our professional nature.

The third response is more speculative, perhaps, but also more practical: The application of artificial intelligence concepts to expert systems is the most important key to all of CAI. But the basis of expert systems is, of course, expert advice. That is, the way in which an expert responds to a query or solves a problem, or performs an operation is translated into a program for a computer. So an expert system is no better than the advice of the experts it is based upon. If, then, we want those machines to do really expert jobs, we need to keep improving our methods, systematizing them, so that they can be translated into steps a computer can follow.

Are we, then, preparing the way for ourselves to be replaced? To a large extent, yes, as machines can do better much of the kind of instruction we do now. But when it comes to talking with a child about the kinds of subjects he or she is interested in, or helping a beginning student shape an embryonic, vague notion into a manageable topic, or reacting to a more advanced student's conjecture about some evidence for an idea, or all the other kinds of assistance most of us have given at one time or another to those eager but naive and unsure users, it's hard to imagine being displaced. But it's not just our knowledge that will continue to be important, because even as knowledgeable and efficient as computers are likely to get, it's unlikely they'll ever provide the eye contact, the reassurance, the friendly words that some users will always need.

NOTES

1. *Circulars of Information of the Bureau of Education*, no. 1-880 (Washington, D.C.: U.S. Government Printing Office, 1880), 7.

2. Henry R. Evans, comp., "Library Instruction in Universities, Colleges, and Normal Schools," *U.S. Bureau of Education Bulletin*, no. 34 (1914): 3.

3. George S. Bonn, *Training Laymen in Use of the Library*, vol. 2, pt. 1, *The State of the Library Art* (New Brunswick: Graduate School of Library Service, Rutgers, State University of New Jersey, 1960).

4. Harvie Branscomb, *Teaching with Books: A Study of College Libraries* (Chicago: American Library Association and Association of American Colleges, 1940), 52.

5. Patricia B. Knapp, "A Suggested Program of College Instruction in the Use of the Library," *Library Quarterly* 26 (July 1956): 224-31.

6. Barbara H. Phipps, "Library Instruction for the Undergraduate," *College & Research Libraries* 29 (September 1968): 411-23.

7. Letter from Evan Farber to Larry Hardesty, April 8, 1981, quoted in *User Instruction in Academic Libraries: A Century of Selected Readings*, comp. Larry Hardesty, John P. Schmitt, and John Mark Tucker (Metuchen, N.J., and London: Scarecrow Press, 1986), 231.

8. Nancy E. Gwinn, "Academic Libraries and Undergraduate Education: The CLR Experience," *College & Research Libraries* 41 (January 1980): 5-16.

9. Helen M. Brown, "ALA Activities to Promote Better Instruction in the Use of Academic Libraries," *Drexel Library Quarterly* 7 (July & October 1971): 323-26.

10.   John R. Lubans Jr., *Educating the Library User* (New York and London: R. R. Bowker, 1974).

11.   Philip J. Smith and Virginia M. Tiefel, "The Information Gateway: Designing a Front-End Interface to Enhance Library Instruction," *Reference Services Review* 20, no. 4 (winter 1992): 37-48; and Virginia Tiefel, "The Gateway to Information: The Future of Information Access . . . Today," *Library Hi Tech* 1, no. 4 (1993): 57-66.

12.   Gail Herndon Lawrence, "The Computer as an Instructional Device: New Directions for Library User Education," *Library Trends* 29, no. 1 (July 1980): 150.

13.   Raymond Kurzweil, "The Paradigms and Paradoxes of Intelligence, Pt. 2: The Church-Turing Thesis," *Library Journal* 117, no. 13 (August 1992): 73.

14.   Ibid.

5

Information Literacy and Public Libraries: A Community-Based Approach

Susan Jackson

Reference Librarian
Monroe County Public Library
Bloomington, Indiana

Within the last two or three decades, library instruction has developed into a substantial professional movement, but it has never become a major programmatic emphasis in public libraries. Now, library instruction has broadened into *information literacy*, and that concept holds great promise for the public library. The emphases on lifelong learning, active citizenship, and informed decision making that are part of information literacy fit closely with the historic values of public libraries and with their commitment to respond to community and societal needs. While the public library has an important role to play in fostering these concepts for all ages, the focus here will be on the out-of-school adult.

LIBRARY INSTRUCTION

Before looking more closely at information literacy, we should document the current status of instructional practice in public libraries. How deeply involved are public libraries with user instruction? Articles published in 1978, 1981, 1982, 1984, and 1989 all included comments to the effect that instructional programs other than those aimed at children had not been widely established.[1] Woods, Burns, and Barr, in 1990, observed that the instruction given in public libraries is often informal and ad hoc and given as part of the reference transaction. They suggest that a formal program of instruction helps the library maintain quality, appropriate content, and consistency and they infer that a formal program of instruction is better than instruction through the reference interview.[2]

Despite these comments on the paucity of public library instruction, interest was sufficient in 1980 to warrant publication of a book on this topic, and, in 1984, Margaret Hendley noted a growing public library instruction underground.[3] A 1989 survey of Canadian public libraries did find that over 90 percent of respondents had conducted some type of user education program and 24.2 percent said that instruction was institutionalized in their libraries to the point that a library policy on bibliographic instruction existed.[4] The most extensive statistics come from the Adult Services in the Eighties Project (ASE). This project was an attempt to document the scope of adult services in public libraries, and the data was collected in 1986. Out of the 4,213 public libraries responding to this benchmark survey, 82.9 percent did provide group instruction on library use and 93.9 percent provided instruction to individuals.[5] Considering the continuing view expressed throughout the 1980s that library instruction in public libraries was not well developed, coupled with the lack of literature on the topic, these figures are surprisingly high. Unfortunately, the picture of what goes on in these group activities is hazy. Some public libraries do have a longstanding reputation for offering well-designed, sequenced classes in library use (Denver, Seattle, and Norfolk Public Libraries, for example) but we don't hear about many of these in the literature.[6] Types of programs written about include class visits, term paper clinics, science fair workshops, and interest-focused workshops— one-shot offerings designed to meet specific community needs. Possibly, these are the kinds of activities reflected in the high percentage of libraries reporting group instruction activities in the ASE Project, but it is hard to tell. At any rate, public library instruction was not developed to the point that it warranted favorable comment from prominent figures in the library instruction movement.

In 1982, Kirkendall and Stoffle conjectured that the then-current emphasis on the adult independent learner and the growth of information would lead to an elevated role for library instruction in public libraries.[7] That has not happened. Though sporadic programs take place, no evidence exists that library instruction has been institutionalized in many public libraries the way it has been in academic and school libraries, and the Public Library Association has not adopted library instruction as a "cause." The few accounts of innovative and sustained instruction programs are more models for imitation than they are an accurate reflection of widespread practice. However, public libraries have devoted attention to a range of other audience-specific programming and educational activities for adults, and these sometimes include instructional components.[8] Key interest areas have included parent education, adult education, the aging, adult job seekers, minority groups, literacy education, and the business community.

Reports of these activities do include integrated instructional activities—for example, instruction for adult job seekers, business computer applications, skills classes for older adults, and homework help classes for parents. Beilke conjectured in 1984 that library instruction was integrated with various programming efforts, and that still seems to be the situation.[9] Because of this diffusion, public libraries as a large group do not seem to have adopted formal instruction in the way that libraries in academic institutions have. This is not necessarily negative. Tying in instruction with programming for special audiences relates it to the need of the moment and heightens motivation, which in turn heightens learning. It is the public library parallel to course-related instruction in academic libraries.

Formal instructional programs emerged from academic and school libraries where there was a real need. That need is seen even today, every day, at the reference desk, where a clearly defined and captive audience exists, sustained contact is possible, and *instruction* is in keeping with the academic enterprise. Out of this environment, the construct of library instruction developed. That construct was not adopted en masse by public libraries because the public library is a different kind of institution with a different kind of community. The need for instruction is there, but the audience is amorphous and shifting; it is difficult to find a commonality of background, and information needs are individual and unique. Library service evolves to meet community needs and fit the environment, and those needs are different in public libraries. Kathleen Heim, in her report on the Adult Services in the Eighties Project, observes that services arise from special publics, not from absolutes "conceptualized in the abstract by theoreticians."[10] Models for library instruction in the public library will have to come from the special publics that institution serves.

While formal library instruction programs have not become broad-based, the purpose of library instruction—helping people learn to find the information they need—has, and that is reflected in the inclusion of instructional activities within the framework of services to targeted audiences and through the reference desk.

Individualized Instruction

Individualized instruction through the context of the reference interview offers the best hope for public libraries to provide user education to the community at large, but organizational change and a broadened concept of the reference interview are required for this to take place on any substantive basis. Individualized instruction is suggested for many reasons. First, it is a concept that is widely endorsed by public librarians and is part of their present-day value system. Harris, in her 1989 survey of public librarians in Canada, found that although 85.6 percent of respondents agreed that the primary goal of reference librarians in public libraries is to provide users with information, 86.6 percent agreed that the best reference librarians combine information provision with bibliographic instruction.[11] The ASE Project found that individualized instruction was provided in 93.9 percent of responding libraries.[12]

Sixty-three percent of public library users in an Illinois quota sample (1989) agreed or strongly agreed that the library should offer instruction but 50.6 percent said they did not want it for themselves. Even among those who did not want instruction, a majority indicated they were interested in receiving more explanation and information about a particular service, facility, or reference source. Only 18 percent expressed a preference for a focused instructional setting such as a class. The researchers concluded that public library users may be inclined toward receiving instruction in less-structured, more personalized formats, and the majority of users who want instruction prefer it in the form of both information and instruction in the reference interview.[13] This approach is in keeping with both the historic public library focus on the individual and with adult learning theory.

A large number of adults are engaged in adult learning activities. Estimates range from 79 to 98 percent of the population, and these learners prefer to pursue their learning in an independent self-directed manner.[14] Knowles's concept of andragogy (the teaching of adults) emphasizes that adult learners prefer a comfortable informal setting that acknowledges their uniqueness and that their learning is problem oriented, practical, and relates to their particular experiences and concerns. Knowles emphasizes the role of guide or facilitator rather than teacher and an individualized, mutually respectful relationship between learner and guide.[15] Humanist psychologist Carl Rogers says, "I have come to feel that the only learning which significantly influences is self-discovered, self-appropriated learning."[16] This educational theory leads to the conclusion that the most desirable way to provide library instruction is through the one-on-one relationship that exists in libraries primarily through the reference interview. As John Swan observed in 1984, this means taking the library user in hand and walking and working through the search process.[17] The instructional aspects in the reference transaction might be very basic, such as instructing in the use of particular databases, modeling the use of the library catalog, or giving some basic pointers such as the relevancy of dates in statistical or medical material or noting article length in a bibliographic citation.[18]

Information Advising and Counseling

This type of interaction is fundamental to the public library's informational and instructional objectives, but it doesn't realize the library's full value to the community. Moving the reference interview into an information advising and counseling service is a more advanced step. Individuals with complex information should receive extensive guidance on how to meet those needs, somewhat along the lines of being led through a personalized pathfinder or library guide with connections made to other libraries, electronic databases, community agencies, government sources, referrals to experts, and additional appropriate sources. Along the way, a good bit of instruction about the production, organization, and flow of information is likely to be imparted along with more basic information concepts.

This individual counseling and advising role is labor-intensive. Most libraries try to provide this service, but it often takes place at a busy reference desk in a haphazard and inconsistent manner, depending on the amount of activity that is occurring. Historically, public libraries do not place value judgments on the uses of or types of information retrieved at the public library. Although some public libraries do have policies that restrict reference services in certain areas such as trivia contests or city directory information, the philosophy, on the whole, is that each individual and his or her request are treated with an equal level of respect and care. In a busy library, reference questions may come in at the rate of one every two or three minutes. These questions can run the gamut from sports trivia required to settle bar disputes to the request of an aspiring entrepreneur who needs to do in-depth market research before starting a new business but hasn't the slightest idea of how to begin. The five minutes that can be allotted to this second situation are not nearly enough, the librarian feels despair at the low level of service that is being given, and the entrepreneur may think less of the library as an information source. Poor public perception of the library leads to underuse, poor support of services, and a failure to consider the library as a serious information center. Penland, in his study of independent learners, found that only 14 percent use the library regularly, and he concluded that the library was not seen as a significant source of help.[19] Only about 25 percent of citizens are regular library users, and a recent Iowa study concluded that a significant portion of the population is not even aware of the information services available in libraries.[20]

Public libraries must rethink organizational structure and staffing patterns to be able to provide in-depth information counseling and guidance. Here, academic libraries do provide models. Many university libraries offer a triage approach to information services as a way to respond to multiple constituencies, with information services provided by student assistants, general reference librarians, and subject bibliographers. Husbanding professional resources in a similar manner in public libraries might help public libraries meet immediate demand, provide professional time for consultative reference, and also free up time to form links with various agencies and constituencies. Not that the sports questions or city-directory requests or car-value queries are unworthy of attention, but what about the vital information needs that are not being met due to time constraints? Some hard choices will have to be made. Responding to immediate demand at the reference desk can result in a continued cycle of answering the quickie questions and turning away those who have critical information needs that cannot be settled in five or ten minutes. If we take our role as information specialist seriously, we must be structured to make this information counseling available. This is a service that needs to be provided in the manner of a professional guiding and working with a client. Subject specialization may be required, and provisions must be made for working with the client in a consultative manner away from the reference desk. This reference and information consulting should be available by appointment and that service should be promoted despite the fact that it may generate business that is hard to handle. Such a service would be good for citizens and the community and would improve the library's image as a dynamic institution.

INFORMATION LITERACY

The information consultant role would also position the public library to support information literacy. A clear understanding of what is meant by "information literacy" provides a starting point for thinking about the library's potential contribution. In 1980, the Council of the American Library Association adopted a policy statement that read, in part, "It is essential that libraries of all types accept the responsibility of providing people with opportunities to understand the organization of information. . . . The American Library Association encourages all libraries to include instruction in the use of libraries as one of the primary goals of service."[21] This document affirmed that preparation for independent information retrieval is essential for sustaining lifelong professional and personal growth and it is basic to almost every aspect of living in a democratic society.

Three years later, *A Nation at Risk: The Imperative for Educational Reform,* a report issued by the National Commission of Excellence in Education (Washington, D.C.: U.S. Government Printing Office, 1983), cited alarming weaknesses in American public schools and dismayed members of the library profession with its failure to even mention the role of libraries in leading the United States to a learning society. *A Nation at Risk,* and the activity it generated, is considered a catalyst in attracting library attention to the concept of *information literacy.* The term was given a formal definition through the work of the ALA Presidential Commission on Information Literacy. The commission's final report, issued in 1989, "officially" defined the term: "To be information literate a person must be able to recognize when information is needed and have the ability to locate, evaluate, and use effectively the needed information. . . . Ultimately, information literate people are those who have learned how to learn."[22] This definition includes several key abilities having to do with information:

- the ability to recognize that information can be helpful in decision making and that the right information can help make things better,

- the ability to know where to go to get information and how to retrieve it,

- the ability to evaluate information as a critical information consumer,

- the ability to process information; that is, the ability to think about information, analyze it, and extrapolate what is valuable at that particular time in a person's life—all higher-order thinking skills, and

- the ability to use and communicate information.

These processes go far beyond the concept of educating library users in how to locate information or how to use specific libraries or sources. The first step in becoming information literate is having the mindset to even think about using information in decision making. Influencing attitudes and heightening awareness are a crucial element here. Then there must be the ability to find information. This step opens the way for the public library to promote itself as the place where people go to get good information or to connect with other good information sources. The ultimate goal is preparing individuals to utilize information productively in any context and from any source, whether it comes from television, newspapers, libraries, or sophisticated electronic sources.

The vision embraced in information literacy challenges libraries to make a difference in people's lives. It calls on libraries to contribute to the betterment of society through helping all citizens become "independent seekers of truth."[23] This philosophical thrust has a strong tradition in public library history, harkening back to the missionary impulse that led the founders of public libraries to see them as "the people's university" or "the arsenal of democracy."[24]

The challenge for public libraries is to translate this stirring rhetoric into meaningful, sustained programs.

What Are the Problems?

We need to think about what the public library can reasonably do in implementing information literacy and what is better left to other agencies. Most public libraries serve sprawling and untidy communities with incredibly diverse needs and wide-ranging educational, economic, and societal backgrounds. The ALA President's Report on Information Literacy talks about "independent seekers of truth" and the need for an informed citizenry with the ability to manage information successfully.[25] The reality is that twenty-three million Americans can't read above the fifth-grade level. Twenty percent of all Americans can't write a check that a bank can process.[26] Forty-three percent of working persons ages twenty-one through twenty-five do not have sufficient literacy skills to handle multistep directions, and 40 percent of all thirteen-year-olds do not have the necessary thinking skills to process the information they read in a textbook or newspaper.[27] All these people are part of the public library community. This community also includes older adults, job seekers, businessmen, new readers, and young children. Some of these people use the library, more of them don't, and most of them don't even think about the library as a valid information source.

The diversity of our communities, our lack of sustained contact with users, and our low usage have several implications for information literacy and public libraries. Rather than widespread efforts directed at teaching members of the community the mechanics of how to locate information and the higher-order thinking skills of evaluating and processing information, our strongest efforts should be spent at the beginning of the information literacy continuum—promoting the concept that information can be useful in reaching decisions in daily life and that the public library is a good place to find some of that information. Then we must follow through.

What Can We Do About It?

Collaborative efforts with other government agencies, community groups, and the private sector offer a promising approach. Libraries can actively form alliances with these organizations, find out what their information needs are, and deliver. Charles Curran believes that public libraries should force alliances with the schools and the marketplace.[28] Teachers and schools are the natural allies of libraries in promoting the concept of information as a useful good. Business and industry are taking a steadily increasing role in work force development, opening a wedge for enterprising librarians. The work force today needs more than people who are literate. It needs people who are *information* literate; as we make connections, we can communicate this vital need. Virginia State Librarian John Tyson believes that an information literate citizenry will be key to addressing many of the social and economic ills that plague our nation today: poverty, unemployment, high school dropout rates, and bleak economic development.[29] Connecting with social service agencies opens the way for libraries to respond to these societal needs. Overall, partnerships are a way to work effectively in the community, overcome institutional isolation, and promote the value of information and the library's role in making information available.

Recent research (1990) finds that public library leaders are already emphasizing constituency building, targeting services, and reaching out into the community in an active fashion. An appeal of information literacy is that it can be integrated into these existing organizational priorities, and it fits with community-based planning. Also, libraries do not seem to have limited services and concentrated roles, despite that suggestion by the Public Library Planning Project.[30] Because information literacy combines both education and a strong information component, it is in line with the interest in focusing efforts on targeted groups rather than limiting roles to an "either/or" choice.

Public libraries come in various sizes and configurations, and organizational structures will always vary. One feasible structure would be working through reference or adult services with librarians offering a continuum of services. Each librarian would be an information consultant involved in several roles: providing reference, counseling, advising on databases, and serving as liaison with specific groups or agencies in a fashion similar to the reference/bibliographer approach of some academic libraries. Establishing and maintaining contact with targeted agencies would be a high priority of this position.

The information consultant model would require librarians who are active and people oriented, and who are able to make contact, speak persuasively and knowledgeably, and listen; librarians who are comfortable in an advising and guidance capacity that goes beyond answering questions; and librarians who are interested in what people have to say and what is important to them. The learning has to go in both directions. Information consultants must be willing to listen to what people want and need and build on the way their constituents use information and perceive libraries. The result would be an active library reaching out into the community with a focus on information and services, not just the library as a building and a collection of books.

On a national level, the Public Library Association should be promoting programs on information literacy, and, hopefully, the programs and writings sponsored by the National Forum on Information Literacy, an umbrella group of national organizations, will direct greater attention to the out-of-school adult. Public librarians will have the opportunity to participate in training institutes sponsored by the America 2000 Partnership, which has been formed by the National Forum on Information Literacy, the United States Department of Education, and other groups. The thrust of the America 2000 Partnerships is to help communities achieve the National Education Goals, including goal five: adult literacy and lifelong learning.[31]

CONCLUSION

Information literacy is a broad-based concept that reflects the realities of today's world. Information does confer power, and individuals and businesses who have good information and know how to use it have an edge. Those who don't know how to get and use information are disadvantaged, and their ignorance will be costly to them as individuals and to society. The public library does have a role to play in providing information skills. The public library belongs to the community, and it is the only community agency that is concerned with the information needs of all its citizens. If we believe that information literacy is a survival skill, then the public library must become actively involved. Our work is cut out for us.

NOTES

1.   Sheryl Anspaugh, "Public Libraries: Teaching the User," in *Progress in Educating the Library User*, ed. John Lubans (New York: Bowker, 1978), 125-32; John Lubans, "Library Literacy: The Public Library and User Education," *RQ* 20 (summer 1981): 337-40; Carolyn Kirkendall and Carla Stoffle, "Instruction," in *The Service Imperative for Libraries: Essays in Honor of Margaret E. Monroe*, ed. Gail A. Schlachter (Littleton, Colo.: Libraries Unlimited, 1982), 56-57; Margaret Hendley, "User Education: The Adult Patron in the Public Library," *RQ* 24 (winter 1984): 191; and Robert E. Kaehr, "Bibliographic Instruction in the Public Library: To Have or Not to Have," *Public Library Quarterly* 9, no. 4 (1989): 5-12.

2.   Kathleen G. Woods, Helen T. Burns, and Marilyn Barr, "Planning an Instruction Program in a Public Library," in *The LIRT Library Instruction Handbook*, ed. May Brottman and Mary Loe (Englewood, Colo.: Libraries Unlimited, 1990), 49.

3.   Hendley, "User Education," 191.

4.   Roma Harris, "Bibliographic Instruction in Public Libraries: A Question of Philosophy," *RQ* 29 (fall 1989): 95.

5.   Danny P. Wallace, "The Character of Adult Services in the Eighties: Overview and Analysis of the ASE Questionnaire Data," in *Adult Services: An Enduring Focus for Public Libraries*, ed. Kathleen M. Heim and Danny P. Wallace (Chicago: American Library Association, 1990), 62.

6.   Shelly Adatto, "Helping Users Help Themselves," *PNLA Quarterly* 56 (winter 1992): 9-10; Woods, Burns, and Barr, "Planning an Instruction Program in a Public Library," 51; and Amy Louise Frey and Saul Spiegel, "Practical Librarian: Educating Adult Users in the Public Library," *Library Journal* 104 (April 15, 1979): 894.

7. Kirkendall and Stoffle, "Instruction," 57.

8. See references to these in Heim and Wallace, *Adult Services*, 273, 279, 345; and Jerrolyn M. Dietrich, "Library Use Instruction for Older Adults," *Canadian Library Journal* 41 (August 1984): 203-8.

9. Patricia F. Beilke, "Library Instruction in Public Libraries: A Dream Deferred, a Goal to Actualize," *The Reference Librarian* 10 (spring/summer 1984): 127.

10. Kathleen M. Heim, "An Overview of the Adult Services in the Eighties Project," in *Adult Services,* 5.

11. Harris, "Bibliographic Instruction in Public Libraries," 94.

12. Wallace, "The Character of Adult Services in the Eighties," 62.

13. Susan J. Dielh and Terry L. Weech, "Library Use Instruction in the Public Library: A Survey of User Preferences," *Research Strategies* 9 (winter 1991): 31, 32, 36.

14. Allen Tough, *The Adult's Learning Projects: A Fresh Approach to Theory and Practice in Adult Learning*, 2d ed. (Austin, Tex.: Learning Concepts, 1979), 18; and K. Patricia Cross, *The Missing Link: Connecting Adult Learners to Learning Resources* (New York: College Entrance Examination Board, 1978), 1.

15. Malcolm Knowles, *The Adult Learner: A Neglected Species*, 2d ed. (Houston, Tex.: Gulf, 1978).

16. Carl R. Rogers, "Personal Thoughts on Teaching and Learning," in *Selected Educational Heresies*, ed. William F. O'Neill (Glenview, Ill.: Scott, Foresman, 1969), 210.

17. John C. Swan, "The Reference Librarian Who Teaches: The Confessions of a Mother Hen," *The Reference Librarian* 10 (spring/summer 1984): 55.

18. For an excellent article on instructional aspects in the reference transaction, see Jane A. Reilly, "Library Instruction Through the Reference Query," *The Reference Librarian* 10 (spring/summer 1984): 135-48.

19. Patrick Penland, "Adult Self-Planned Learning," *Public Libraries* 17 (summer 1978): 6.

20. Charles Curran, "Dealing with User Behavior: A Prerequisite for Librarian Involvement in the Information Literacy Movement," in *Information Literacy: Learning How to Learn*, Proceedings of the Twenty-Eighth Annual Symposium of the Graduate Alumni and Faculty of the SCILS, April 6, 1990, ed. Jana Varlejs

(Jefferson, N.C.: McFarland, 1990), 41; and James Rice, "Library Awareness Survey," *Public Libraries* 31 (November/December 1992): 350.

21. American Library Association, "Policy Statement: Instruction in the Use of Libraries," Council Document no. 45 (document approved at the annual meeting of the American Library Association, New York, June 1980).

22. American Library Association, Presidential Committee on Information Literacy, *Final Report* (Chicago: American Library Association, 1989), 1.

23. For a good discussion of the role of libraries in helping individuals to independently seek information, see Hannelore B. Rader, "Bibliographic Instruction or Information Literacy," *College and Research Libraries News* 51 (January 1990): 18, 20.

24. Sidney H. Ditzion, *Arsenals of Democratic Culture: A Social History of the American Public Library Movement in New England and the Middle States from 1850 to 1900* (Chicago: American Library Association, 1947).

25. American Library Association, *Final Report.*

26. Patricia Glass Schuman, introduction to *Information Literacy: Learning How to Learn*, 4-5.

27. Clesson S. Bush, "Beyond the K-12 Curriculum: A National Look at Literacy and Implications for Information Access," *Bulletin of the American Society for Information Science* 17 (October/November 1990): 27-28; and *National Assessment of Educational Progress, the Reading Report Card: Trends in Reading Over Four National Assessments, 1971-1984* (Princeton, N.J.: Educational Testing Service, 1985), 15.

28. Charles Curran, "Information Literacy and the Public Librarian," *Public Libraries* 29 (November/December 1990): 352.

29. Patricia Senn Breivik and Barbara J. Ford, "Promoting Learning in Libraries Through Information Literacy," *American Libraries* 24 (January 1993): 101.

30. Joan Durrance and Connie Van Fleet, "Public Libraries: Adapting to Change," *Wilson Library Bulletin* 67 (October 1992): 32-34.

31. *America 2000, An Education Strategy: Source Book* (Washington, D.C.: U.S. Department of Education, 1991), 64.

6

The Instructional Role of the Library Media Specialist in the Information-Age School

Carol C. Kuhlthau

Rutgers, the State University of New Jersey
School of Communication, Information and Library Studies

What is the future instructional role of the library media specialist in elementary through secondary education? What role does the library media center have in the information age school? Underlying these questions is the critical issue of what it means to be literate in the information age. While there is no clear consensus on this issue, certainly children need to know how to read, to communicate ideas in writing and orally, and to calculate numbers. Beyond these traditional skills of literacy, however, we need to identify the unique abilities required for everyday life in an information society, particularly in the information workplace.

New technologies have drastically altered the workplace and the skills needed to be competent on the job. In the book *The Age of the Smart Machine*, Shoshana Zuboff describes her study of an automated workplace with three types of workers: executives, plant workers, and office workers.[1] She reports that all three groups are required to make more critical judgments and to apply more abstract thinking in an automated work environment. Decisions made on the job require using computer-generated information rather than information gathered from direct personal contact with the problem situation. The automated workplace also requires less individualized tasks and more team projects. She suggests that ability to make critical judgments from abstract information and ability to work as a member of a team are essential skills for the information age workplace. These abilities converge in actual work situations where critical judgments are made by teams of workers.

Portions of this paper were presented by the author in 1991 at the Annual Symposium of the Graduate Alumni and Faculty of SCILS, Rutgers University, and at the Annual Conference Program of the Educational and Behavioral Sciences Section of the Association of College and Research Libraries.

If we examine how school learning has been structured, it is not surprising that students are not prepared for the information workplace. Schools have been organized on an industrial model that, ironically, has been intensified by recent attempts to increase accountability. For one thing, most instruction has centered around predigested material in textbooks and has been directed to simple "right" answers that can be tested, measured, and compared across populations. "Teaching for the test" has become common practice in many of our schools rather than encouraging creative, innovative thinking and offering opportunities for developing ability in making critical judgments. In addition, competition between students has been emphasized rather than teaming in a cooperative process of learning.

Educating for the information age calls for restructuring schools in some very basic ways. Constructivist approaches to teaching and learning rather than the traditional transmission approach develop skills, not only for the workplace but for active participation as a citizen and as a lifelong learner.[2]

An information age school is described in the final report of the American Library Association Presidential Committee on Information Literacy as follows:

> The school would be more interactive, because students, pursuing questions of personal interest would be interacting with other students, with teachers, with a vast array of information resources, and the community at large to a far greater degree than they presently do today. One would expect to find every student engaged in at least one open-ended, long-term quest for an answer to a serious social, scientific, aesthetic, or political problem. Students' quests would involve not only searching print, electronic, and video data, but also interviewing people inside and outside of school. As a result, learning would be more self-initiated. There would be more reading of original sources and more extended writing. Both students and teachers would be familiar with the intellectual and emotional demands of asking productive questions, gathering data of all kinds, reducing and synthesizing information, and analyzing, interpreting, and evaluating information in all its forms. . . . One would expect such a school to look and sound different from today's schools. . . . On the playground, in the halls, in the cafeteria, and certainly in the classroom (and in the library media center) one would hear fundamental questions that make information literacy so important: How do you know that? and What evidence do you have for that? Who says? and How can we find out?[3]

The mission of the library media center program as stated in *Information Power: Guidelines for School Library Media Programs* is "to insure that students and staff are effective users of ideas and information."[4] This challenge goes beyond teaching library skills to the development of critical thinking and information literacy. These programs center on the process of learning from information across the curriculum with the teacher and the library media specialist working as an instructional team.

THREE CURRENT TRENDS

There are three important trends in instruction in school library media centers that indicate the wave of the future. The first is a shift from library skills to information skills and information literacy. The second is a process orientation to skill instruction rather than an exclusively source orientation. The third is increased integration of the school library media center into the curriculum, establishing an organized, cooperative, resource-based teaching between library media specialists and subject teachers. When we examine each of these more closely, patterns of future direction emerge.

Information Skills/Information Literacy

There has been a noticeable shift from library skills to information skills with attention to education for information literacy. Information skills are much broader than library skills. Where library skills center on location of sources, information skills encompass use of sources and interpretation and application of information within sources. Where library skills center on how to use a library, information skills encompass the underlying concepts and patterns in the organization of information.

The problem of transference of skills has troubled librarians for some time. Library media specialists and academic librarians have been cornered over the lack of transference of skilled library use from high school to college. Mellon's identification of "library anxiety" in undergraduates, particularly freshmen, has been borne out over and over in all types of academic libraries.[5] Goodin's study of transference of skills learned in high school has revealed the importance of a broad view of library and information skills and their application.[6]

Information skills are intended to be transferable to a vast range of situations and problems. The library media center is a laboratory for learning the concepts of information location. The concepts of organization, indexing, and access are taught using such tools as Dewey decimal classification, card catalog or online catalog systems, *Readers' Guide*, or *Magazine Index*.

The library media center also serves as a laboratory for learning how to use information after it is located, for finding out about the world, and for critical thinking.[7] Children and teenagers are guided in recognizing when they need information, in making sense of what they have found, in fitting it in with what they already know, and in seeking further information based on expanding thoughts. This type of inquiry approach prepares students for learning throughout their lives.[8,9]

The Presidential Committee on Information Literacy developed a statement of purpose centering on the process of learning from information: "Such a learning process would actively involve students in the process of 1) knowing when they have a need for information; (2) identifying information needed to address a given problem or issue; (3) finding needed information; (4) evaluating the information; (5) organizing the information; (6) using the information effectively to address the problem or issue at hand."[10] These are basic skills for learning in the information age.

Process Approach

The second trend is toward a process approach to instruction in information skills. Exclusive source orientation and excessive concern for the product of library research without any consideration for the process of learning from information seem to be at the very heart of the problem of transference. Information skills need to be applied within the context of the search process in a meaningful sequence. Often, students approach library assignments as though they had no past experience with the process. Their lack of self-awareness of the process of information use inhibits their learning in future situations of information need.

The traditional steps recommended for students to follow in library research are not likely to be helpful to them. What I call "the Warriner's model" has been in basic high school composition texts for years and is ingrained in many as the way to describe library research.[11] This model is not based on empirical research. In fact, recent studies have revealed quite a different process for learning from information. The Warriner's model recommends the following steps for library research:

1. Selecting and limiting the subject

2. Preparing a working bibliography—a list of available sources

3. Preparing a preliminary outline

4. Reading and taking notes

5. Assembling notes and writing the final outline

6. Writing the first draft

7. Writing the revised final draft with footnotes and a bibliography.

Warriner's is a transmission approach to library research rather than a constructivist approach and does not allow for individual exploration and formulation within the search process.

Over the past ten years I have conducted a series of studies of students' *actual* processes in library research, which reveal quite a different model. I found that students were confused and anxious when they first came to the library to work on a project, no matter how skilled they were at using the library or how skilled at writing a paper. Their confusion and anxiety often disrupted productive learning. An extensive qualitative study revealed a series of common experiences in the process of a search which can be articulated, learned, and transferred to other information-seeking situations.[12] The model of the information search process developed in this study has been verified in large-scale studies of different types of library users as well as in longitudinal studies and has been implemented in library programs across the country and abroad.[13]

The information search process may be described as a process of construction occurring in six stages with distinct tasks for each stage:

1. Initiation—recognizing an information need

2. Selection—identifying a general topic

3. Exploration—exploring information on a general topic

4. Formulation—formulating a specific focus

5. Collection—gathering information pertaining to the focus

6. Presentation—preparing to present the information or solve the problem

Particular thoughts, feelings, and actions are commonly experienced in each stage. Students' thoughts and feelings about what they are doing, and about themselves, change during the search process. Feelings of anxiety and confusion are common at the beginning exploratory stages. The formulation of a focus is the turning point of the students' feelings about their work. Before the focus is formed, they are commonly uncertain and anxious. After the focus, they are more confident, have a clearer sense of direction, and are more interested. Strategy for action in the first half of the process, before formulation of a focus, is exploratory, such as reading about a general topic, listing interesting ideas, reflecting, and discussing ideas. Strategy for action following focus formulation is more conclusive, such as selective reading to define and extend the focus, taking detailed notes, and documenting the focus for presentation. In contrast, the Warriner's model recommends strategies that identify and define the topic before any exploratory reading for informed formulation takes place.

Students need instruction and guidance in the constructive process of learning from the information gathered during a library search. When they understand the overall search process, they can learn specific strategies for particular stages. They begin to see that the process is experienced in a similar way each time. The process approach to information-skill instruction is becoming common practice in library media centers within a variety of different programs and approaches.[14]

Integration into the Curriculum

The third trend in instruction is full integration of the school library media center into the curriculum. Literacy in the information age requires that classroom instruction be grounded in multiple resources rather than bound to a single textbook. The library media specialist provides access to a wealth of materials rich in challenging ideas, fully integrated into the curriculum. In resource-based learning, as advocated in *Information Power*, the AASL/AECT guidelines for school library media programs, the library media specialist and the teacher work together as a team to plan instruction and to teach students in all areas across the curriculum that use resources from the library media center as well as from the wider network of library and information centers and databases and from the community at large.[15] The library media specialist's knowledge of resources combines a wide variety of wonderful books to read with both technology for instruction and technology for accessing information.

As we have noted, information skills are process skills similar to those of reading and writing. Just as children need something to read and to write about, they need a reason to use information, something to think about and to learn. Information skills are not taught as a separate course but integrated into learning experiences across the curriculum. The program is designed for all students, not just college-bound, and it is developed around the basic need of every person to find meaning and understand his or her world. A team teaching approach is employed in which the teacher brings knowledge of content and concepts and the library media specialist brings knowledge of resources and process. Strategies for integrating this approach into the curriculum and teaming with teachers have been successfully implemented in programs across the country.[16,17] One trend that has inhibited advancements in this area, however, is the practice of scheduling classes into inflexible blocks of time that are not adaptable or easily coordinated with classroom learning. In schools where administrators and teachers support and value the library media center, there are many success stories of cooperative ventures between teachers and librarians in guiding students in the constructive process of learning from information.

In the field studies I have been conducting over the past eight years, a consistent pattern of a natural sequence of information-use activities is emerging.[18] The sequence matches children's developmental stages and their need for information arising from experiences in their classrooms and in their personal lives. A sequential information environment can be planned for students, from elementary school through middle school through high school.

Children in kindergarten through fifth or sixth grade are involved in expanding their knowledge base and in learning to read, write, and communicate ideas. During this time, they need to interact with lots of books and the ideas generated in books and other materials. Electronic technology for gathering and processing ideas needs to be readily available. Activities center on developing skill in using information by having children recall (tell what they remember), summarize (tell in a capsulized form), paraphrase (tell in their own words), and extend (tell their reaction and how it relates to what they already know). Instruction centers around inquiry and discovery, with children actively involved in their own learning. As questions arise and a need for more information is apparent, students are guided in finding that information and in sharing it with their classmates. They are rewarded for paraphrasing but also are encouraged to quote the source of their information. In this way, children are continually engaged in recognizing their need for information and in locating, evaluating, and using information as a means of learning.

By middle school, these children are ready to address an extensive problem requiring an extended search for information. A personally compelling question, topic, or issue motivates their sustained attention. Their ability to recall, summarize, paraphrase, and extend are applied to the task of writing a paper or other form of presentation. Their work focuses on their own perspective, formed during a period of concentrated information use under the guidance of the team of the library media specialist and the teacher. Collaboration and cooperation among students are encouraged. Students learn the process of locating, evaluating, and using information as well as the mechanics of producing a product to report their findings. The mechanics, however, do not overshadow their primary purpose of discovering and sharing. They learn the interrelationship of information sources, such as how information gathered from interviewing an expert relates to that obtained from an organized collection. They learn ways of integrating information into what they already know and methods for documenting the origins of their emerging ideas. They use information technologies, such as databases, and become aware of vast networks of information. They are guided through the search process and are encouraged throughout to reflect on their experience. In this way, the process of seeking information, as well as the product, is assessed and evaluated.

In high school, assignments center on the process of learning from information. Students are actively involved in synthesizing, analyzing, drawing conclusions, and identifying further questions and problems. They are challenged to integrate information from mass media and everyday life experience into classroom learning. As troubling or interesting questions arise, they are expected to seek more information in the organized collection of the library. Findings are reported and presented in a variety of ways, some requiring extensive writing, others presented less formally, such as sharing an insight on a muddled point raised in class. Integrating past experience with new learning leads to evaluative analysis and critical judgments. Collaboration among students provides support in the process of information seeking as well as encouraging an exchange of ideas. A wide range of print and electronic resources are available, as well as access to networks of information outside the school.

CONCLUSION

Restructuring schools for educating a generation prepared for the information workplace, for participant government, and for enriched lives is the critical task before educators today. The library media center has the potential for dynamically contributing to restructuring schools into productive, engaging learning environments. This dynamic role can be fully realized only with the clear understanding and involvement of other key players in the school community. As library media specialists envision their instructional role more broadly to incorporate learning from information rather than instruction of a narrow range of library skills, educational planners, innovators, and administrators are beginning to comprehend the importance of the library media center in the information age school.

The media center as the information center is a critical component for preparing children for full participation in an information society where information skills are survival skills. Unfortunately, there is a very real danger of becoming a nation divided between those who have the ability to learn from information and those who do not. In these difficult economic times it is all too easy for unenlightened educators to be tempted to diminish or even eliminate library media services.

The future role of the library media specialist is to actively participate in the education of an information literate generation. In one of my recent studies, a college student remarked that he could never have too much information because he understood the process of exploring and formulating to be part of information seeking; once he had formed a focused perspective of a problem, he could sift through vast amounts of information, selecting only that information pertinent to his focus.[19] Information literacy arms a person with the skills to use information in a complex technological society for the construction of meaning. Library media specialists play a crucial leadership role in restructuring education for the information age.

NOTES

1. Shoshana Zuboff, *The Age of the Smart Machine: The Future of Work and Power* (New York: Basic Books, 1988).

2. Richard S. Prawat, "Teachers' Beliefs About Teaching and Learning: A Constructivist Perspective," *American Journal of Education* (May 1992): 354-95.

3. American Library Association, Presidential Committee on Information Literacy, *Final Report* (Chicago: American Library Association, 1989), 9.

4. American Library Association, *Information Power: Guidelines for School Library Media Programs* (Chicago: American Library Association; American Association of School Librarians; Association for Educational Communications and Technology, 1988), 1.

5. Constance A. Mellon, "Library Anxiety: A Grounded Theory and Its Development," *College and Research Libraries* 47 (March 1986): 160-65.

6. M. Elspeth Goodin, "The Transferability of Library Research Skills from High School to College" (Ph.D. diss., Rutgers University, 1987).

7. Jacqueline C. Mancall, Shirley L. Aaron, and Sue A. Walker, "Educating Students to Think: The Role of the School Library Media Program," *School Library Media Quarterly* 15 (fall 1986): 18-27.

8. Daniel Callison, "School Library Media Programs and Free Inquiry Learning," *School Library Journal* 32 (1986): 20-24.

9. Karen Sheingold, "Keeping Children's Knowledge Alive Through Inquiry," *School Library Media Quarterly* 15 (1986): 80-85.

10. American Library Association, *Final Report*, 7.

11.   J. E. Warriner and F. Griffith, *English Grammar and Composition* (New York: Harcourt, 1973).

12.   Carol C. Kuhlthau, "Developing a Model of the Library Search Process: Cognitive and Affective Aspects," *Reference Quarterly* 28 (1988): 232-42.

13.   Carol C. Kuhlthau, "Information Search Process: A Summary of Research and Implications for School Library Media Programs," *School Library Media Quarterly* 18 (fall 1989): 19-25.

14.   Michael B. Eisenberg and Michael K. Brown, "Current Themes Regarding Library and Information Skills Instruction: Research Supporting and Research Lacking," *School Library Media Quarterly* 20 (winter 1992): 103-10.

15.   American Library Association, *Information Power.*

16.   David V. Loertscher, *Taxonomies of the School Library Media Program* (Englewood, Colo.: Libraries Unlimited, 1988).

17.   Philip M. Turner, *Helping Teachers Teach: A School Library Media Specialist's Role*, 2d ed. (Englewood, Colo.: Libraries Unlimited, 1993).

18.   Carol C. Kuhlthau, "Implementation of the Process Approach to Information Skill Instruction: Longitudinal Study of a Model Program" (forthcoming).

19.   Carol C. Kuhlthau, *Seeking Meaning: A Process Approach to Library and Information Services* (Norwood, N.J.: Ablex, in press).

7

Education for the Academic Library User in the Year 2000

Virginia Tiefel

Ohio State University Libraries

What is the future of library user education in academic libraries? Does it have a future? Do academic libraries and librarians have a future? The answer is yes, and it can be an exciting, important, influential, and rewarding future. Librarians have only to envision it and seize the opportunity to create it. This chapter details how to comprehend this future through an analysis of the problem/challenge today and how librarians are meeting it. It then discusses projections for the future and how librarians are already adapting their programs to meet these projections.

GOALS OF LIBRARY USER EDUCATION

Before beginning, it is important to look at the goals set for academic library user education. What is the goal of academic library user education? The answer has remained consistent: to support the educational goals of the institution. So, to a certain extent, the goals will be institution-specific, but it is possible to look at some general, broad goals of postsecondary education that are applicable to most institutions and library user education programs.

Educational goals can be defined in a variety of ways, so a single comprehensive definition is somewhat elusive. Some examples can provide a good composite definition. John Gardner has said that the ultimate goal of education should be "to shift to the individual the burden of pursuing his own education."[1] Education has been defined as the process of turning information into knowledge. Education should facilitate students' learning of what they want and need to learn, enable them to learn more efficiently, and motivate them to learn. The purpose of education is "to educate for fifty years of self-fulfillment,"[2] which is now termed *lifelong learning*. The 1987 Boyer report defined an educated person as one who makes connections across disciplines and ultimately relates what he or she has learned effectively to life.[3] This report stressed that college should connect technology, the library, and the classroom to enable students most effectively to "engage in creative, independent learning."[4]

How well are these and similar goals being met? The National Commission of Excellence in Education issued an influential report in 1983—*A Nation at Risk: The Imperative for Educational Reform* (Washington, D.C.: U.S. Government Printing Office)—which, in being very critical of education, said that the educational foundations of our society were mired in mediocrity. In 1985 alone, national reports on education were sponsored by the National Endowment for Humanities, the National Institute of Education, and the Association of American Colleges. In examining undergraduate education in this country, the Boyer report described curricula as "disjointed," guidance to students as "inadequate," and the transition from high school to college as "haphazard and confusing." The report also charged that today's system doesn't educate for breadth and that students are given the "cafeteria style approach" to choosing courses without the guidance of knowledgeable and experienced faculty.[5]

In examining undergraduate education and what it should accomplish, a 1986 University of California task force report stated that, instead of becoming broader, education has in many instances narrowed in its application. The task force found that the heavy emphasis on vocational and science education and early specialization worked to the detriment and even exclusion of the liberal arts and humanities. Instead of educating for integrative thinking, students are departmentalized more and more as they progress in their education.

A broader approach is needed in education, one that recognizes that today's graduates must function in one world. They must have an international perspective and approach. The Boyer report refers to a global approach as necessary because "our world has undergone immense transformation." Education must "lead to a more competent, more concerned, more complete human being."[6]

In summary, an undergraduate education should motivate students to learn and to do so effectively and independently. Students need to acquire basic skills, fundamental ideas and concepts, and a broad range of knowledge. Their approach should be broad, across disciplines, and with an international perspective. They should learn to think critically and integratively and be prepared to continue educating themselves for their entire lives. Studies have shown that postsecondary education is not meeting many of these goals.

Given this broad definition of undergraduate education and the changes called for to achieve this, where do libraries and, specifically, library user education fit into the picture? How does the library support undergraduate education? What are the broad objectives of library user education? How well have librarians been meeting those objectives? What role can libraries play, based on the past and projected changes in the future of education?

In facilitating use of information, teaching has long been identified as one of the major functions of libraries, that is, teaching to support both classroom assignments and individualized learning. Library user education goes back at least 100 years, when objectives were to help students acquire the ability to judge a book and become an independent and lifelong learner. Today's programs encompass these same objectives and include teaching students how to identify, find, evaluate, and select information. Today's goal is to educate students for the information age, equipping them to function as independently as possible to meet their information needs for work and leisure, that is, equipping them to fulfill the "lifelong learning" concept.

More recently, the importance of libraries and library instruction was noted in the Boyer report, which stated, "The college library must be viewed as a vital part of the undergraduate experience." It further observed that "students should be given bibliographic instruction and be encouraged to spend as much time in the library—using its wide range of resources—as they spend in class."[7]

The goals of education are to ensure that students will

- pursue lifelong learning,

- be independent in their pursuit of learning, and

- acquire a broad education, basic skills, and the ability to think critically.

The goals of library user education are to teach students how to

- identify, locate, evaluate, and select information, and

- function effectively and independently in the information age.

THE CHALLENGE

Growth of Information

There are three major factors affecting the development of effective library user education programs: the exponential growth of information; the complications of providing and using technology; and variation in and/or lack of users' information and skills. Much has been written about the exponential growth of information. A few facts demonstrate the magnitude of the expansion:

- In 1950, only 17 percent of the work force had jobs in information, but today, 65 percent of the work force have jobs related in some way to information and only 12 percent remain in manufacturing.[8]

- The quantity of scientific and technical data doubles every 5.5 years, but that increase is predicted to jump to 40 percent a year, which means that the quantity of scientific and technical data will double every twenty months.[9]

- The federal government spends over one billion dollars a year on information-related activities.[10]

- We "mass-produce" information the way we did cars. Knowledge is the driving force of our economy.[11]

The information explosion over the last twenty-five years has reduced the percentage of available information libraries can provide. Some librarians have seen a concomitant decline in their influence. In fact, libraries are now facing competition for control of information from computer centers and vendors.

Impact of Technology

What are some of the major complications in using technology to meet the demands of the information explosion? Many believe that libraries are not structured nor suited to meet these demands. Staff time is required to help library users make good use of the equipment necessary for searching information electronically. Users must master complex databases and learn which databases are best for their needs. Users often believe that if they find something relevant, they have exhausted the library's resources and that if they find nothing, the library has nothing on the topic. These are problems endemic to print materials also, but many librarians believe that the easier accessibility provided by technology exacerbates the problem. There is a perception that libraries have used technology to continue doing what they've done in the past, and because technology is expensive, its cost has not brought proportionate benefits to library users. This certainly is debatable, but it is a viewpoint shared by some librarians and library users.

Technology has brought with it the convenience of remote access. In 1986, 48 percent of Association of Research Libraries (ARL) libraries provided remote access. A 1993 survey showed an increase of this service to 67 percent of those libraries. Public service access included such services as circulation, reference, interlibrary loan, document delivery, and photocopy service. Indications are that users need the whole range of library services. The survey indicated a shift in types of remote users from campus computer activists and local faculty to faculty, staff, and students distanced from the campus, as well as the disabled. It is predicted that Internet access will exacerbate the demand.

The library's role has traditionally been to archive, acquire, record, store, and preserve print. Libraries are now expected to provide access to information in new formats and link all types of resources while eliminating costly duplications. Whereas, many libraries have historically been quite isolated, they are now expected to provide integrated service at the local, regional, and national levels.[12]

Library Users

Part of the challenge lies with the library users whose variation in knowledge and skills tests the user-education librarians' ability to reach all users with the most useful instruction at the time of need. Technology complicates the disparity in users' capabilities. Valentine's study identified students' unfamiliarity with libraries as a major impediment to student research.

Constance Mellon, in her study of college students' abilities and attitudes, found that although students enter college with little library knowledge, educators expect their students to have library skills. (Both points are substantiated by studies and experience at the Ohio State University.) Students lack the critical thinking skills needed for evaluating and selecting information.

Mellon's two-year study showed that 75 to 85 percent of the students in composition classes were afraid or anxious and felt lost in the library. She cites four reasons: size of library (only three floors, though); not knowing where things are; not knowing what to do; and not knowing how to begin the research process. Emotional attitudes affect performance and library anxiety prevents students from approaching the problem logically or effectively. Mellon attributed the fears to students' belief that other students are competent, lack of competence is shameful and should be kept hidden, and asking questions reveals inadequacies. Mellon urges librarians to recognize students' anxieties and provide experiences that are successes, not failures.[13]

Though highly desirable for the user, remote access complicates the instruction librarian's mission. Accustomed to face-to-face communication, librarians must now anticipate, respond, and help whom Sloan calls the "invisible patron." This is further complicated by the perception that the remote user is different from the user within the library building. Remote users are less likely to be satisfied with an automated system that emulates "traditional" access.[14]

The many challenges of meeting the goals of library user education relate to

- the growth of information,

- the impact of technology, and

- the long-standing complication of library user attitudes, skills, and expectations.

LIMITATIONS OF CURRENT INSTRUCTION

Demand Outstrips Resources

Although the present approach to library user education has worked well despite some inherent shortcomings, the future impact of economics and technology will exacerbate these shortcomings. User education programs, like the one at Ohio State, have tried to exploit every opportunity to teach students, including course-integrated and course-related instruction, workshops, research clinics, and one-on-one reference instruction. A major problem with this approach is that it is labor-intensive. Whereas some classes are taught in large-group sessions, most are small groups having some follow-through with individual instruction.

To complicate this issue further, the society of the 1990s is faced with severe budget restrictions, often referred to as "downsizing." Higher education has been cited as an example of the need to reduce the size of institutions as a whole, and that includes academic libraries. Indeed, many have said that the halcyon days of steady growth and increased support for academic libraries are over. The library is going to be called on to justify its budget and expenditures and account in a measurable way for its support. This all augurs for small staff who will be expected to instruct and deliver ever-increasing quantities of information. The demand is growing as the means to meet it are diminishing.

Other Limitations

Another limitation of the present approach is that the student is usually passive during the instruction. Even though we know that students learn by doing (active learning), a good share of library instruction relies on the lecture method, which is one of the least effective teaching methods.

In addition, librarians often do not teach what is actually needed by the students, but what they assume is needed. Studies have shown that librarians don't study users' needs well enough, but make inaccurate assumptions and teach on that basis. It is imperative that librarians focus more on studies to determine user needs and how best to satisfy them. Another limitation is that the content of much instruction concentrates on research tools rather than concepts. This is a fragmented approach and does not prepare students for understanding the research process or developing the ability to search on their own. Also, electronic databases have not been well integrated with print resources in instructing students how to make the best use of all resources, not just print.

Transferability and timing of instruction are crucial factors. Present instruction doesn't enable many students to transfer instruction from one assignment to another. They see instruction as specific to a single need and not applicable to future needs. Many studies have demonstrated that students must have the instruction at the time of need, that is, when they are ready to work on the assignment. This is difficult to accomplish because students start at different times on an assignment. Often, the instruction can't be given at the same time as the assignment, thereby decreasing the relevance and effectiveness of the instruction for the students. Even when given at the time of the assignment, the instruction is often forgotten by the students by the time they begin.

Repetition of instruction is another limitation that is virtually impossible to eliminate for all students. Frequently, classes are mixes of students; some have had instruction in other classes and others have not. In this case, the librarian must begin with the lowest skill level, so the instruction is repetitious for some students. Students find this monotonous and tedious and become impatient with the librarian and the instruction.

The current status of instruction for remote users also needs improvement. Studies have shown that remote users are frustrated with the lack of help. Sally Kalin has found that technical assistance is the most frequent request made by remote users, followed by a need for help in how to search. Kalin identifies three kinds of invisible users: the techie, who often comes from the sciences; the user, who is looking for new applications; and the frightened or untutored user, who is the most common and the hardest to deal with—this one, Kalin asserts, needs a "reference psychotherapist." [15]

Kalin observes that after mastering the technical skills, users need to develop searching skills. With more humanists and social scientists joining scientists in searching, complications arise. Scientists are often proficient at searching, but faculty from the other disciplines generally need more help. Kalin encourages the use of online help for users but urges caution about overwhelming the users with too much documentation. To improve instruction, librarians must

- find more efficient, cost-effective ways of teaching students,

- study user needs more carefully,

- focus their instruction on concepts and the transfer of instruction beyond the one assignment,

- make instruction more interactive,

- provide instruction at the time of need,

- integrate the use of print and electronic information,

- reduce repetitive instruction, and

- provide the special instruction needed for remote users.

Many librarians have been reactive rather than anticipatory and slow to integrate technology into planning and priorities. This lack of action keeps libraries in a reactive role.

THE FUTURE OF LIBRARY USER EDUCATION

The Future of Technology

"Sweeping technological changes" are coming in the next few years.[16] Television sets will be replaced by television/computers called "smart TV" or "telecomputers." Over the fiber optic cables, access will be available to any television station, theatre, film, classroom, sports event, church, library, or conference attached to the network. The migration from analog to digital waves will make this possible.

Analog, which is the current technology of television, recorders, cassettes, telephone, and so on, is application-specific; it must be sent and played at the same pace and can't be easily edited or manipulated. Digital, which is used for computers, microprocessors, compact discs, and so on, is homogeneous and can be easily stored, compressed, corrected, edited, and manipulated. Digital television doesn't send the picture, but information about the picture: the image is formed and controlled in the telecomputer, not at the station. Fully digitized networks with sufficient capacity will make it possible to send digitized information anywhere, in almost any format.

The future will be measured in gigabits—one billion bits will move across the country in one second. It has been estimated that the average person processes 27,000 written words in a day. At the age of seventy years, that person will have processed 20 billion bits of information. It is predicted that there will soon be networks that can send 100 billion bits a second.[17]

In December of 1991, a three-billion-dollar bill, "High-Performance Computing Act," was passed by the U.S. Congress. It will fund the development of a fiber optics cable on existing fiber optics laid by centers, telephone companies, and government agencies. This cable is much faster than conventional wire. The connected centers that will form the first parts of the National Research and Education Network (NREN) is predicted to replace the Internet (covers 35 countries) and to increase speed 100 times. The federal government has since named the information superhighway the National Information Infrastructure (NII) and appointed a task force and council to develop policies and plans for implementation. It is predicted that the development of NII will bring a true information revolution that will permeate people's lives in dramatic ways.

The electronic book Smartcard, which is already being designed, will probably be mass-produced. The size of a credit card, it could hold a twenty-four-volume encyclopedia in digital form. This book card could be played on a portable eight-by-ten-inch screen. It would have color and provide sound options for reading and music, and a port for attaching a printer. One card with the capacity of eight megabytes could hold 200 books and would be inexpensive. Some predict that the electronic book will become the standard.[18]

The Future of Academic Libraries

It is important to remember that libraries are tied to their institutions, which are in turn tied to society, its trends, and attitudes. Libraries must adopt information literacy as their goal. Certainly, technology will be a major factor in the academic library's future. It is predicted that by the end of this decade, supercomputers will be affordable and on everyone's desk. Everything will be linked by fiber optics, so there will be no interlibrary loan or missing books, journals, and so on. The electronic library will be one massive database, and some say libraries will have to choose between the print and the digital medium. Everything will be accessible remotely. Librarians may lose control to computer people and for-profit vendors. If that happens, only those who can afford to pay will have access to information.

In addition to new technology and the information environment, Harold Shull notes a third factor, social change. Shull identifies ten issues that will affect higher education, which must be addressed if libraries are to meet the challenges of the future. A major issue is population, which will decline in the number of college-age students and increase in nontraditional students, raising ethnic and racial issues. Other factors are the variation from state to state in support of information and the mergers in the information industry structure. In technology and access, the issue of print resources versus online information is a major one. Public libraries will be patterned after the Pike's Peak District Library with its strong emphasis on outreach and technology. Scholarly communication patterns will become increasingly informal.

Shull identifies four of these factors that will transform higher education. One is the increase in nontraditional and foreign students. Another is the increased use of computers and telecommunications for teaching, research, and service. He also predicts expanded vocational curricula and development of academic-industrial partnerships. These changes will require flexible scheduling, off-site service, and so on. Shull believes that instruction librarians must teach the capabilities and deficiencies of the new information technologies. There will need to be closer communication with public libraries to prepare students for life after graduation. He believes if the library adopts a passive stance, it will fade into obscurity.

Libraries now contain a smaller percentage of recorded information than in the past. The information age is focused less on the printed word and more on images, sounds, and facts. Some have observed that this shift from books as information storage and dissemination to computer will result in the disappearance of libraries. The library will no longer be the main information source for many. Libraries must decide how to adjust to continuous change.

The library will be without walls and will have to respond to a wider and more diverse clientele. We must rethink the library and coordinate print and electronic sources and create local databases. Some believe we must stop gross additions to information and develop systems to make the information we have more useful. The changes called for will make libraries more expensive, but if the changes are not forthcoming, libraries will have less import and influence.

However, some believe that libraries will become more access oriented, that document delivery will become more important, and that the size of libraries will become less important. These beliefs are based on the observation that technology has changed how faculty identify, locate, and use information. They say there are two myths addressed in these predictions: bigger libraries are better and researchers and scholars are skilled users of research libraries. The important issue isn't size, but how easy the library is to use.[19]

These changes will encourage librarians to become more active participants in the scholarly/communication process. Librarians will work more closely with faculty in developing services. Libraries will need flexibility, collaboration, diversity, and fluidity. There will be a heavy stress on users' needs. Libraries will need to develop and implement services tailored to student needs. Libraries' role in teaching will expand. Most of the staff will be working with users and developing artificial intelligence applications for libraries. Librarians will provide "expert systems that help define needs, facilitate information access, and tailor the information packages to suit individuals or groups of people."[20]

Access to almost all information will be available at the user's workstation. There will be faster, more convenient delivery of information regardless of location. The emphasis will be on access, not collection. Acquisition will be demand-driven. The library will be seen as a facilitator of access, not a storage house. Technology will be transparent to the user.

Librarians must focus on mission, not method, and become proactive. They must create a vision of the electronic library. Peter Lyman has stated that librarians' dominant role in the digital library will be a teaching one that will develop a new form of information literacy. Innovation will be required and staff will need to acquire new technical skills. New gateways to vendor products will be developed, document delivery will be networked, and there will be significant changes in national bibliographic control. There will be a growing simplicity of the interface between the user and the complex systems we build. An interface using common searching techniques will be created and more electronic databases and courseware will be developed. Full-text retrieval and interactive imaging will increase.

Issues determining the future of academic libraries will encompass

- technological changes that will provide faster access to greater quantities of information, with impact on almost every library operation,

- social change that will bring different types of students,

- coming to terms with the issues of print and electronic information,

- determining who will provide the leadership and, thereby, control the use of information, and

- how the information industry develops.

Responding to these issues, the academic libraries of the future will need to

- teach the capabilities and deficiencies of electronic information,

- place a strong emphasis on research,

- work with public library librarians to provide continuity to students' pursuit of lifelong learning,

- be flexible and able to adjust to change,

- be prepared to respond to a more diverse clientele,

- develop systems to make information more useful and easily used,

- provide document delivery,

- de-emphasize acquisition and increase interlibrary cooperation,

- emphasize user assistance,

- develop artificial intelligence applications for libraries, and

- provide more instruction to ensure information literacy.

Some assumptions for the future are the continuing diversity of interdisciplinary information requirements and improved national networking. There will be more inter-vendor cooperation and the rate of technological change will accelerate. Innovation will be vital to the future of libraries and their institutions.

Describing the Program of the Future

What is needed in the library instruction program of the future? There have been many theories put forth about this topic. A look at some of these theories might be useful. A summary of the elements of such a program will follow with examples of what some libraries are currently doing toward achieving the projected library instruction program of the future.

W. David Penniman cites Harry Goodwin's 1950s description of the ideal information system.[21] As relevant today as it was forty years ago, Goodwin said the ideal information system would allow the user to receive the desired information at the time required, in the briefest form, and in order of importance. Necessary auxiliary information would be provided with reliability indicated (implies critical analysis), source identified automatically (little effort required), without undesired or untimely information, and with the assurance that no response means that it doesn't exist.

The role and needs of faculty and remote users must be a part of any program. Libraries are seen as complex and bureaucratic and most faculty are reluctant to ask for help. Some means of assisting faculty that allows them a degree of anonymity needs to be offered. Results of a user-needs study by Patricia Candless and others at the University of Illinois showed that users had a strong interest in dial-up capability to the library's online systems, training on how to search databases independently, and twenty-four-hour reference service.

Gary Marchionini and Danuta Nitecki, in writing about supporting users of automated systems, advise that users be able to use systems with little help and that education focus on generic information strategies, not on the mechanics of indexes or systems. Emphasis should be placed on both local and remote databases. Strategies for using the system to perform such functions as narrowing and broadening topics should be included. Instruction should be short, intensive units and self-directed with a variety of media. Users must be encouraged to do complete searches. Libraries should provide settings and tone that set a sense of comfort and control, provide basic instruction on search techniques, and encourage the perception that the process isn't difficult and that the system is moving toward one that is more efficient, effective, and easy to use.

Over six years ago, Joel Rudd and Mary Jo Rudd prophesied that "future instruction in bibliographic and library skills . . . will be more efficient and effective when presented on computer."[22] David Lewis cites rising user expectation as an important factor in the future of libraries. Libraries aren't easy to use and, if tools are available outside the library that are more easily used, students will bypass the library. Lewis believes that librarians will need to provide all kinds of instructional tools.

In 1988, Evan Farber, in a perceptive prediction of the future of instruction, said that basic instructional needs will ultimately be taken care of by computers. Whereas automation will change how bibliographic instruction operates, it will not change its basic purpose, which is to enhance the teaching/learning process. Farber predicted that automation might help librarians do a better job. As users can make direct use of information online, librarians may be much more involved in teaching system search strategies, interpreting information, and helping users decide which online resources to access. Farber said that libraries are going to have to combine the new technology with traditional materials. Librarians will increasingly be regarded as partners in the teaching/learning process, as well as experts in searching for information.

To develop any instruction program requires a few key elements. According to a study done by Nancy Gwinn of CLR-funded instruction programs, the extent of commitment of the library director is the most important factor in a program's success. Library instruction must be integrated with other educational experiences. Gwinn found that major obstacles to the development of successful programs were staff turnover and indifferent institutional administrations.

Planning the program of the future requires keeping in mind the shortcomings of today's bibliographic instruction (BI) programs. Programs must reach users with needed information at the time of need, teach at various skill levels, and ensure that students know how to apply critical thinking skills. Librarians must deal with student anxiety, which, according to Mellon, includes the intimidating size of the library (even when not very large) and students not knowing where things are, what to do, or how to begin the research process. Additional pressure is on librarians to ensure that students have the successful experience that Mellon and many others point out as being so important for a program to be effective. Remote access presents its own special problems as already outlined. Kalin urges help for the remote user, but cautions that the amount of instruction should be limited.

The labor-intensive nature of the present approach to instruction is complicated by the reduction in budgets faced by most libraries in the immediate and long-range future. Libraries are expected to meet increasing demands with fewer resources. Even though the instruction is expensive to administer, it is not, in many cases, the most effective. The lecture method is the most common means of teaching, but it is also one of the least effective. Instruction should focus on concepts, not tools, and should better integrate the use of electronic sources.

Another observation of current instruction is that most students do not transfer the instruction from one assignment to another. Repetition of instruction is a common criticism by students. Current practice frequently fails to teach students independence in their information seeking. There also must be more emphasis on the capabilities and deficiencies of the new information technology.

Academic librarians need to seek closer ties with public librarians to help students better make the transition to public libraries after graduation. Librarians must place more emphasis on systems that make information useful and less on increasing the quantity of available information. Access and document delivery are very important issues. The size of the library is no longer as important as its ease of use. Academic librarians should make information literacy their goal.

The library user education program of the future should ensure that

- the user receives the information at time of need, in as succinct a form as possible, and in the order of importance, with a minimum amount of effort or help required,

- faculty are included and involved in the program,

- dial-up access with some brief help is readily available,

- instruction focuses on strategies, not tools,

- instruction is brief, self-directed, and at various skill levels,

- users are encouraged to do complete searches and apply critical-thinking skills,

- the process isn't perceived as difficult, but the system is efficient, effective, easy to use, and leads to success,

- instruction makes maximum use of technology,

- the use of print and electronic information is efficiently combined,

- the library director is committed to the program,

- the program is as cost-effective and as student-interactive as possible, and

- instruction is not repetitious for the students and carries over to other assignments.

MOVING TOWARD THE PROGRAM OF TOMORROW

By the year 2000, supercomputers will be widely available and the electronic library will be one massive database. Everything will be accessible remotely. Social and technological changes will require flexibility and off-site service. The emphasis will be on the user, who will need to be able to select and evaluate information. With heavy emphasis on user needs, librarians will need to develop and implement services tailored to these needs. In accomplishing this, librarians need to concentrate on mission, not method, and develop a growing simplicity in interface between the user and the systems. Librarians will need to take a very proactive role.

Future emphasis will be on users. Gerry Campbell has urged the profession to focus on its primary mission of enabling people to get information. He believes the survival of the library profession will rest on its ability to make the necessary changes from paper to electronic information quickly. A system is needed that is user friendly and enables the users to identify their information needs; determine how to meet those needs; and locate, evaluate, and select the information. This will have to be developed according to the emerging technology, based on information changes and budget constraints, and meeting as effectively as possible the basic principles of library instruction, while eliminating the negative aspects of today's programs.

In a study of innovative applications of technology to public services done by the author in 1991, many of the thirteen libraries studied had identified and even developed a number of the elements predicted for the program of the future.

Perceptions of needs, existing programs, and the future plans of the thirteen libraries examined, revealed some common concerns and issues. There was an emphasis on users and their behavior, a recognition of the need for question negotiation, and a strong need for more help for the user in selecting and using information. The changes in curriculum that are common to many institutions were perceived as increasing the demand for more instruction. Users' awareness of more available information will also increase the need for more instruction and help. Complicating these needs was the issue of lack of money, which was a factor in almost every institution.

Issues common to every library were increased pressure for more dial-up access and campuswide information delivery. Users want more materials faster and the ability to scan tables of contents. Most librarians interviewed were planning to create more of their own databases. In terms of the technology to deliver these services, there was a definite shift from mainframe to distributed systems. Services must be compatible with both Macintosh and IBM computers and most campuses found CD-ROMs to be useful.

Many aspects of the program projected for the future were already available at one or more of the sites visited. For example, full text in some disciplines is available online at Carnegie-Mellon in the LIS II project, which also provides access to several databases and the catalog on computer. The Inspec project provides the online text of four publications in the sciences, as well as user-initiated interlibrary loan and photocopying. The CARL System's UnCover II provides citations to articles and tables of contents to 10,000 multidisciplinary journals and will supply photocopied articles within twenty-four hours of request. Both Carnegie-Mellon and CARL furnish online versions of full-text CHOICE reviews.

The Pike's Peak District Library has provided dial-up access for more than fourteen years. This library has produced a number of locally developed databases. USC Info at the University of Southern California provides access to fourteen databases operating on Macintosh computers and available on VT100 dial-up access. For Project Jefferson, librarians have created special databases to help freshman students with their English assignments.

The University of Cincinnati has created MIQ, which is a special search tool for MEDLINE that simplifies and speeds up searching. The IAIMS project combines patient and hospital records with journal databases to provide online information for doctors that would largely go unseen in that format. Arizona State University, a member of CARL, provides its users access to the entire system, including UnCover and many Wilson databases. They are working on a database of the most frequently asked questions.

The University of Houston has developed the Intelligent Reference Information System (IRIS), which combines their Reference Expert and networked CD-ROMs. The University's libraries are continuing to develop the Expert System and expand the CD-ROM network. Texas A&M has focused on making its catalog more user friendly by developing MacNOTIS. It also provides access to several Wilson indexes and dial-up access. Inmagic is an expert system designed for a technical writing class and includes a database specially created by the librarians.

San Diego State University has several Reference Advisory Systems (RAS) that are subject specific. In creating these, the librarians have emphasized brevity. The University of California, San Diego, has RoboRef and Remote Access Interface Design (RAID). The former provides basic library information and some instruction on how to use certain reference tools. RAID provides dial access to the local and statewide catalogs.

At Northwestern University, the library has taken a leadership role in developing an online campuswide information system. The information varies from library hours to local events. The library is planning the Curriculum Innovation Project, which will integrate computing technologies into faculty research promoting the library's information on computers. They plan to foster faculty interest in the Library of Congress Memory Project.

Pennsylvania State University library staff are providing course-related instruction in several lower-level courses. They want to move these activities to computers so the librarians will have time to meet the increased demands for instruction at the upper level. They are developing a CAI program for their instruction of a business course that had been somewhat ineffective. The librarians discovered that students were not doing the assignment at the time they received the library instruction, so they decided to create a CAI program to enable students to have access to library instruction whenever they started their assignment. These librarians are also creating their own databases and they have developed Ask Fred, which is a stand-alone terminal that provides basic library information. They are working on making their catalog interface more user friendly.

Ohio State's Gateway to Information

It is apparent from the brief summary of projects above (and there are many more) that librarians are already developing programs to meet the needs of users now and in the future. One final example of librarians' responses to these present and future needs is a program that has been under development at Ohio State for six years.

Ohio State's Gateway to Information project has been developed to meet many of the immediate user needs and to be able to adapt to change as the future demands. The Gateway is linked to a computer-based catalog and CD-ROMs and incorporates the use of traditional (print) sources. The system strives to lead users to the best information for their needs, regardless of format. The Gateway takes users far beyond the catalog, providing instruction and guidance in identifying which materials will likely best meet their information needs, where the materials are, and how to evaluate and use them. The Gateway is designed to make the users independent in searching for information; no handouts or help screens are needed to use the system. Though initially designed to meet the needs of lower-level undergraduate students, The Gateway has always included plans for the expansion of the content to meet the needs of upper-level undergraduate and graduate students.

The Gateway not only provides ready access to the text of relevant CD-ROM-based encyclopedia articles and journal indexes, but presents these sources on screens that have a common appearance and are accessed by simple commands. By providing users with a common front end for the electronic indexes, The Gateway removes the requirement to learn a number of different protocols. In this way, it introduces students to searching new sources of information, regardless of the format, origin of the database, or their computer experiences.

The search strategy concept, which is applicable to most information searching, has been widely used by instruction librarians to teach students how to organize and implement an information search. The search strategy is a step-by-step process moving from the general to the specific, considering all the relevant areas of the library, and uses continuous evaluation to promote selection of the best information.

The Gateway's design is based on this *search strategy* concept. Users begin with a broad information source, such as an encyclopedia, to help define and narrow their topics. Following the search strategy map, they are presented with resource options such as periodical indexes, books, biographies, and statistical sources. The search strategy map guides a researcher from the broad information sources to the more specific. Or, users can go directly to any single source, bypassing the steps that are irrelevant to their needs. By providing these services, The Gateway offers a high degree of independence to researchers and can assist or instruct large numbers of users with specific research questions at their time of need.

The Gateway has a notebook section that allows users to save any parts of their searches to a special file that can be printed at any time. Integral to The Gateway is an evaluation section that guides users in applying critical thinking skills to evaluating their information. Reminders to use this section appear on most screens to try to instill in users the concept of evaluation and the need to evaluate almost all information.

The Gateway has been funded by an initial grant from the Fund for the Improvement of Postsecondary Education, two grants from the Department of Education's College Library Technology and Cooperation Grants Program, HEA Title IID program, and a fourth grant from the William Randolph Hearst Foundation. The University Libraries provided leadership and support as did the University's Academic Computing Center and the Instructional Development and Evaluation Unit.

The Gateway has been continuously evaluated and then revised and developed according to evaluation results. Student evaluations indicate that most students really do like using The Gateway and it has acquired a loyal following of users. Of 4,693 evaluation forms recorded between July 16, 1990, and November 30, 1993, 79 percent of them indicated a completely or mostly successful search. Use of The Gateway was considered very or generally easy by 81 percent. From 3,937 evaluations, 83 percent said that they would use The Gateway again, only 5 percent said they wouldn't, and 12 percent were either unsure or had no opinion. Comments are generally positive with many suggestions about how to expand the system, usually by adding databases or providing remote access to residence halls, offices, and homes.

CONCLUSION

Thus, libraries are moving into the future and librarians have already seized many of the opportunities provided by technology. Programs have been implemented (or are in development) that focus heavily on making information more widely available and easier to use. More instruction is being offered, artificial intelligence systems are being developed, document delivery is becoming more common, and electronic information is being integrated. In developing these programs, librarians have demonstrated vision, flexibility, and responsiveness to change.

Library user education does have a future—a very bright and important one. In fact, that is where forward-thinking libraries are placing their emphasis. Keeping the goals of information literacy and lifelong learning in mind, libraries need to develop programs that make good use of technology in educating users. Library user education programs must address the issues of user attitudes, skills, and expectations, as well as the costs and shortcomings of existing programs. Librarians must keep current with developing technology and even be anticipatory about its future. Emphasis must continue to be placed on ease of use and document delivery. Librarians must become more proactive and increase outreach activity. Much of the above has already been implemented by librarians and libraries. It simply remains for librarians to expand and accelerate their activity.

NOTES

1. Gardner, *Self-Renewal*, 12.

2. Cleveland, "Education for Citizenship," 14.

3. Boyer, *College*, 259.

4. Ibid., 292.

5. Ibid., 90.

6. Ibid., 292.

7. Ibid., 164-65.

8. Naisbitt, *Megatrends*, 4.

9. Ibid., 16.

10. Dowling, *The Electronic Library*, 11.

11. Naisbitt, *Megatrends*, 7.

12.   Battin, "The Library," 27.

13.   Mellon, "Attitudes," 137-39.

14.   Sloan, "High Tech/Low Profile," 6.

15.   Kalin, "The Invisible Users of Online Catalogs," 589.

16.   Gilder, "Now or Never," 188.

17.   Govan, "Ascent or Decline?" 24-44.

18.   Lande, "Toward the Electronic Book," 28-30.

19.   Dougherty, "Needed: User Responsive Research Libraries," 62.

20.   Allen et al., "The Model Research Library," 134-35.

21.   Penniman, "New Developments and Future Prospects for Electronic Databases," 16.

22.   Rudd and Rudd, "Coping with Information Overload," 320.

BIBLIOGRAPHY

Allen, Nancy, Irene Hoadley, June Lester, Pat Molholt, Danuta Nitecki, Lou Wetherbee, and Anne Woodsworth. "The Model Research Library: Planning for the Future." *Journal of Academic Librarianship* 15, no. 3 (1989): 132-38.

Battin, Patricia. "The Library: Center of the Restructured University." *Current Issues in Higher Education*, no. 1 (1983-84): 25-31.

Boyer, Ernest L. *College: The Undergraduate Experience in America.* New York: Harper & Row, 1987.

Campbell, Jerry D. "Choosing to Have a Future." *American Libraries* 24, no. 6 (June 1993): 560-66.

————. "It's a Tough Job Looking Ahead When You've Seen What's Dragging Behind." *Journal of Academic Librarianship* 17, no. 3 (1991): 148-51.

Cleveland, Harlan. "Education for Citizenship in the Information Society." *EDUCOM Bulletin* (fall 1985).

Dougherty, Richard M. "Needed: User Responsive Research Libraries." *Library Journal* 115 (January 1991): 59-62.

Dowling, Kenneth E. *The Electronic Library: The Promise and the Process.* New York: Neal-Schuman, 1984.

Edgerton, Russell. "Entering the Information Society: An Introduction." *Current Issues in Higher Education*, no. 1 (1983-84): 1-2.

Farber, Evan Ira. "Guest Editorial: Bibliographic Instruction." *Library Times International* (January 1988): 52-54.

Feletti, Grahame, and LuAnn Wilkerson. "Problem-Based Learning: One Approach to Increasing Student Participation." *The Department Chairperson's Role in Enhancing College Teaching*, no. 37 (spring 1989): 51-60.

Gardner, John W. *Self-Renewal: The Individual and the Innovative Society.* New York: Harper & Row, 1987.

Gilder, George. "Now or Never." *Forbes* 148, no. 8 (October 14, 1991): 188-94.

Govan, James F. "Ascent or Decline? Some Thoughts on the Future of Academic Libraries." Paper presented at The Future of the Academic Library Conference, University of Wisconsin, September 1989.

Gwinn, Nancy E. "Academic Libraries and Undergraduate Education: The CLR Experience." *College and Research Libraries* 41, no. 1 (January 1980): 5-16.

Haynes, Craig, comp. *Providing Public Services to Remote Users.* Ed. C. Brigid Welch. Washington, D.C.: Association of Research Libraries Office of Management Studies, June 1993.

Kalin, Sally Wayman. "The Invisible Users of Online Catalogs: A Public Services Perspective." *Library Trends* 35, no. 4 (spring 1987): 587-95.

Lande, Nathaniel. "Toward the Electronic Book: A Proposal for a System That Would Introduce Readers Electronically to Mountains of Material Is Currently Making the Rounds." *Publishers Weekly* 238 (September 20, 1991): 28-30.

Lewis, David W. "Inventing the Electronic University." *College and Research Libraries* 489, no. 4 (July 1988): 291-304.

Lyman, Peter. "Library of the (Not-So-Distant) Future." *Change* 20 (January/February 1991): 34-41.

Marchionini, Gary, and Danuta A. Nitecki. "Managing Change: Supporting Users of Automated Systems." *College and Research Libraries* 48, no. 2 (March 1987): 104-9.

McCandless, Patricia. "The Invisible User: A User Needs Assessment for Library Public Services." Paper presented at the Meeting of Association of College and Research Libraries, Science and Technology Section, Dallas, June 1984.

Mellon, Constance A. "Attitudes: The Forgotten Dimension in Library Instruction." *Library Journal* 113 (September 1, 1988): 137-39.

Naisbitt, John. *Megatrends.* New York: Warner Books, 1984.

Nelson, Nancy Melin. "Library Technology: RLG's Document Transmission Workstation: LIR Is First Electronic Library." *Information Today* (March 1991): 55-56.

Penniman, W. D. "New Developments and Future Prospects for Electronic Databases." *Bulletin of American Society for Information Science* 16 (August/ September 1989): 16-17.

Robinson, Louis. "The Computer: An Enabling Instrument." *Current Issues in Higher Education*, no. 1 (1983-84): 3-13.

Rudd, Joel, and Mary Jo Rudd. "Coping with Information Overload: User Strategies and Implications for Librarians." *College and Research Libraries* 47, no. 4 (July 1986): 315-22.

Schwartz, John. "The Highway to the Future." *Newsweek* 119 (January 13, 1992): 56-57.

Seiler, Lauren, and Thomas Suprenant. "When We Get the Libraries We Want, Will We Want the Libraries We Get?" *Wilson Library Bulletin* 65 (June 1991): 29-31, 152, 157.

Sheridan, Jean. "The Reflective Librarian: Some Observations of Bibliographic Instruction in the Academic Library." *Journal of Academic Librarianship* 16, no. 1 (1990): 22-26.

Shill, Harold B. "Bibliographic Instruction: Planning for the Electronic Information Environment." *College and Research Libraries* 48, no. 5 (September 1987): 433-53.

Sirato, Linda. "Dialogue and Debate: Asking Some Basic Questions." *Research Strategies* 8, no. 4 (summer 1990): 150-52.

Sloan, Bernard G. "High Tech/Low Profile: Automation and the 'Invisible' Patron." *Library Journal* 3, no. 18 (November 1, 1986): 4-6.

Stewart, Thomas A. "Boom Time on the New Frontier." *Fortune* 128, no. 7 (autumn 1993): 153-61.

Valentine, Barbara. "Undergraduate Research Behavior: Using Focus Groups to Generate Theory." *Journal of Academic Librarianship* 19, no. 5 (November 1993): 300-304.

Wand, Patricia A. "Launching the National Information Infrastructure." *College & Research Libraries News* 54, no. 10 (November 1993): 550.

8

Library Instruction in Special Libraries: Present and Future

Mignon Strickland Adams

Director of Library Services
Philadelphia College of Pharmacy and Science

The art museum library, the public law library, the academic science library, the marketing firm library, the veterinary school library—all fall within the grouping of special libraries. The term covers libraries with very different collections, very different services, and very different clientele. Those who work in special libraries often use as a definition that they work in "organizations that use or produce specialized information."

THE PARENT INSTITUTIONS' INFLUENCE

Special libraries are usually classified according to the nature of their collections. The Special Libraries Association has twenty-six divisions, representing those who may work with newspapers, maps, pharmaceutical, educational, or other materials. In addition, the *Encyclopedia of Associations* (Detroit: Gale, 1993) lists twenty additional organizations that represent librarians who work with subject collections ranging from theology to recorded sound. However, their patterns of instruction are most often determined by the patterns of their parent institutions rather than by the nature of their collections.

College and university branch libraries consider themselves to be special libraries and may provide services to unaffiliated researchers on a regional or national level, yet their major user-education efforts, like those of their main library counterparts, are aimed at students. Not only are students usually available to come in groups, they often have assignments that force them to use the library.

Public libraries also may have special library branches. Some of the branches are well known, such as the Performing Arts Library of New York or the Fleisher Music Collection of the Free Library of Philadelphia. Instructional activities in these libraries are usually individualized, because public library patrons seldom come in groups.

Corporate or agency libraries are those most often thought of as "special libraries." They exist to serve exclusively the needs of that organization, rather than the wider needs of society that most other libraries serve. Their existence depends upon their being able to define the needs of the parent organization and meet those needs as efficiently as possible. These libraries tend to be small, limited collections staffed often by only one librarian. Corporate librarians may seldom think of themselves as being involved in "library instruction" and their users may be resistant to group instruction. However, they are often involved in activities they may call "marketing" or "public relations," which are, in reality, educational activities.

Scattered across the country are private research libraries, which exist because they contain a unique collection. They are often the product of a wealthy individual's private collection, and may be endowed by that individual. These librarians typically do little instruction, and for what they see as very good reasons. Their clientele seek them out because of a special need for these special collections. The librarians do not see a need to market their services or instruct those who come to see them.

THE CURRENT STATE OF INSTRUCTION IN SPECIAL LIBRARIES

A broad range of instructional activities in special libraries exists, all the way from none at all to full-blown formal programs. Many special librarians, particularly those in small libraries, maintain that they do no training or outreach because they are short-staffed and could not handle any increased activity. Others with large and famous collections see no need; their highly motivated users know what they want and how to find it. In general, libraries in subject areas with little computer access tend to have less instruction and see less need for it. Those in areas with heavy computer dependence tend to have developed much more instruction. Health sciences libraries and law libraries are examples of these areas.

Health sciences libraries focus on the health sciences and include those at hospitals, research centers, and medical and other health sciences schools (osteopathy, dental, pharmacy, nursing, among others). These libraries were among the first to provide online searching, end-user searching, and CD-ROM stations. Their searching is concentrated on MEDLINE and a handful of other databases, so much of their teaching is aimed at producing proficient searchers in these databases. Many health sciences libraries have added positions (with titles such as "trainer" or "educational services manager") within the last ten years. In addition to identifying, locating, and using medical literature, health sciences librarians may also teach skills called "personal information management," which are aimed at helping professionals organize and access their own collection of information.

Law libraries are divided into three groups, according to the institutions they serve: law schools, law firms, and court/county libraries. Those in law schools have long been involved in instruction, because they often teach or help teach the legal research course generally required of all first-year law students. Law firms, where instruction has traditionally been one-to-one, have had a recent surge in general instruction and in instruction that is more substantive. In addition to orientation of new members, law firm librarians may now give group sessions on basic sources in particular areas of the law as well as instruction in end-user searching. (Like health practitioners, lawyers have long been performing their own searches; and again, as in medicine, law has few databases, though they are major databases.) Court/county libraries are usually open to the public, so librarians there are accustomed to introducing laypeople to legal sources as well as helping attorneys.

Current Exemplary Programs

In talking to a number of special librarians, I was able to identify six instructional programs, described below, that illustrate the directions special libraries are taking. Taken together, these libraries point the way to the future of instruction in special libraries.

Integrating Databases

The Columbia University Health Sciences Library is one of the sites that is developing an Integrated Academic Information Management System (IAMS), funded by the National Library of Medicine. Included on one system are MEDLINE and other relevant bibliographic databases; a document delivery system; the library's catalog, including (in addition to books and journals) CAI programs and audiovisual software; an online textbook of medicine, with hypertext ability to browse; and clinical records.

A user may access the system through a menu, or through the built-in links. For example, if a physician prescribes aspirin for a hospitalized patient whose condition contraindicates aspirin, the physician is alerted when the order is entered into the computer and may, if he or she chooses, read the relevant section in the online textbook, see the journal references that support the textbook section, and have the references automatically updated through a MEDLINE search.

Such a complicated system requires a great deal of instruction. Because Columbia librarians have found that their users are very reluctant to come to the library or even to attend classes within their departments, most instruction is embedded in the system, with very easy access and very simple help screens. Handouts and flash cards supplement the online information.

Another IAMS site, Georgetown University Medical Center, has developed a four-year sequence in medical information for medical students. The curriculum includes basic computer literacy, use of educational software, bibliographic searching of the medical literature, and the use of expert systems to help in diagnosis and treatment decisions. Librarians are responsible for teaching the mechanisms of information management, access, and retrieval.

Creating an Internal Database

A number of years ago, Philadelphia Newspapers, Inc. (which includes both the *Philadelphia Inquirer* and the *Daily News* and is a subsidiary of Knight-Ridder) began a database first consisting only of its own articles, then forming the foundation of Vutext, which transmits the database to DIALOG. The library staff is responsible for two crucial activities: tagging stories on their way from typesetting to the computer; and training all users of the database, both orientation and advanced training, for those who want it. The library is also responsible for the upkeep of a new database of digitized photographs. Keyword searches allow a user to retrieve thumbnail photos, which are then used to call up a production-ready image.

In its educational role, this special library serves as the gatekeeper to databases of extreme importance to its users. The library staff's expertise in searching and training makes them essential to their users. In conjunction with the newsroom staff, the library staff is responsible for the training program in personal computer skills. The library also provides orientation for newly hired executives and those transferred from other newspapers in their chain. This outreach to executives—those with the ultimate power—puts the library in a special place in the company.

Surveying Information Needs

Very often librarians assume that they know best what their users need, and they may make these assumptions based on very little data. Librarians at McNeil Consumer Products—the makers of Tylenol, among other drugs—have determined to find out what their users themselves think.

The library sends questionnaires to the 1,200 employees to survey what information they need, where they're presently getting their information, and whether or not they're pleased with it. Based on the surveys, recent educational efforts have included seminars on patent literature and how to find information about competitors. Librarians have also decided that their users need to be educated in asking better questions and in understanding the kind of information they should expect to get. In addition to the needs of its researchers, the library also has determined the needs of the company's financial executives and presents seminars on various financial tools available.

Specifying Lifelong Information Needs

Every student at the Philadelphia College of Pharmacy and Science is a science major, and thus needs to be completely comfortable with the scientific literature and the process of identifying and locating it. Biology majors at the college go through a progressive program designed to make them proficient in their use of literature. In the first semester of their first year, these students are introduced to Biological Abstracts and must locate and analyze ten articles on a given topic; in their second semester, they use these articles to update their bibliographies through Science Citation Index. They do not write a "research paper" until they thoroughly understand how and why scientific research is written. By the end of their four years, they have used other science indexes, gone to other libraries, and had considerable experiences in end-user online searching. Most of these students go on to graduate school, and they arrive there with research skills that put them years ahead of many of their peers.

Serving Remote Users

The Hay Group is an international human resources consulting firm with seventeen U.S. locations and about fifty more around the world. The librarian at the home office is the information consultant for the U.S. locations and serves as a backup to international ones. She estimates that 80 percent of her clientele are remote users, most of whom she communicates with only by fax or phone. She sees as her major roles consulting on the kinds of information available, advising on the best sources of information, and referring users to others in the company who may have the information they seek. This library no longer buys books, because it is more cost-effective, when a book is needed, to tell the inquirer where the book may be *purchased*. Document delivery is done primarily through vendors.

Given this pattern of use, it is impossible to bring people together in a group for instruction. In a marketing effort, the librarian sends a flier to each field office that introduces the library's services and encourages users to examine their information needs. She also promotes end-user searching, often coaching individuals over the phone in their use of dial-in CD-ROMs. Hay has just completed a client-server network, and wide-area links are expected within a year. This librarian sees her future role as one of helping to decide what goes on a desktop computer and designing a course of action to get it there.

Training Virtual Library Users

The library of the Virginia Campus of the George Washington University opened in the fall of 1991. Major efforts go to serve graduate students in specialized executive business programs. All students are currently employed, and, for some education programs, are drawn from all over the country. The library has only 1,600 volumes and 100 periodical subscriptions, but the world of information is open to its students through online searching, unlimited document delivery, and direct access to the main campus library in the District of Columbia.

Though mediated searches can be performed, the goal is to train students to be end-users. If they have a computer and modem, and little time on campus (which describes most of these students), they are given a disk with George Washington University's communication software, along with passwords to the online catalog of the Washington Research Librarians Consortium and selected periodical databases; in the near future, they will also be given full-text databases.

Intensive workshops are offered to classes at the beginning of each semester. These workshops focus on remote access to the catalogs and databases available, and on the support services. In between the courses, librarians provide individualized instruction by phone or fax, advising on research strategies or the mechanics of searching.

LOOKING AHEAD:
TRENDS IN SPECIAL LIBRARIES

Even in the diversity of special libraries, certain trends are apparent. New computer technology is having a profound impact. As access to information becomes more important than owning it, the collections of most special libraries are shrinking to an even smaller size than before. Integrated databases—online systems that link together bibliographic databases with hypercard access to abstracts, with document delivery systems, and with local databases of, for example, patient records or marketing information—are now appearing. Computers also allow remote use in a way not previously possible.

The clientele of special libraries is also changing. Corporations are finding that their employees may have reading difficulties, and library services to these employees may need to be very different. Though ten years ago few if any library users were comfortable with computers, now almost all of them have at least had their hands on a keyboard. Special libraries that serve the public find that many people are no longer satisfied with access to the library only during traditional work hours.

Special libraries are also finding that they need to justify their roles. Academic, public, and school libraries have a traditional role, one often buttressed by the expectations of accreditors. Special libraries exist only because they fill special needs, and, in a downsizing economy, those needs may be questioned.

EFFECTS OF INSTRUCTION

Certainly, the rise of the computer means that information seekers need a whole new set of skills. Many special librarians—especially in health science and legal libraries—are taking an initiative in teaching these skills: basic skills, search strategies, information management, reaching users, keeping up with changes in professional curricula, and marketing and research strategies.

Basic skills, depending on the setting, may mean knowing how to boot up a computer, or learning how to read. If librarians assume, as many have, that they should teach whatever skills are necessary to use their materials, then their teaching will need to be diverse. At least one leader in special libraries (Guy St. Clair) advocates the involvement of librarians in literacy programs.

Search strategies are necessary for the clientele of special libraries. By and large, they know their own subject areas. What they often do not know is the specific information available in their areas or the best way to go about finding it. Special librarians in the future will need to educate their users in how to ask questions and how to determine what information might be available.

Information management skills are necessary for the users of special libraries, who need to know how to manage the vast amount of information they find. Health sciences librarians have taken a lead in personal information management: how to organize information on a hard disk so that it's easily retrievable, for example, or how to deal with reprints. Health sciences librarians have also taken the lead in helping to create integrated databases. Those presently being developed in medicine foreshadow future efforts in other disciplines. For example, a user of an in-house corporate system could read an article on a competing company in a newspaper database, go from there to a linking database of company information, and then to local e-mail, which lists recent internal memos on the company. Librarians are the logical instructors in the effective development and use of these systems.

Reaching users is an essential skill. Unless their library is in an academic setting, special librarians often have difficulty forming groups for instruction. In the past, they have resorted to fliers and a great deal of one-on-one instruction. As many organizations move into an online environment, librarians will have another way to reach their users, and much instruction will need to occur more readily on electronic mail. Some of the most avid library users may be people the librarians have never seen or even heard.

Librarians must be attuned to changing professional curricula. Many professions have been criticized because their practitioners appear to be too specialized. In response, professional schools are broadening their curricula to include problem-solving skills and the perspectives of other disciplines. This move from lecture and textbook-based courses toward more active learning means that the library will be used differently. Teaching skills of librarians will be called upon to foster independent learning.

Marketing and research strategies are already being used by many special librarians. Though they may not think of these strategies as instructional, they are; one instruction librarian who subsequently received a degree in public relations felt that she had already learned all she needed to know as an instruction librarian. If the fate of a library depends on whether or not it is filling the needs of its constituency, then those who work there had better be sure they know what those needs are. Surveys, interviews, and focus groups are all techniques that will yield this knowledge.

Those in a "downsizing" organization also need to determine that those who make budget decisions are fully informed as to the nature and effectiveness of the library. Educational efforts such as newsletters or presentations to those in power can help in this process. Special librarians who have met and ascertained the information needs of executives have "positioned" themselves within the organization.

SUMMARY

Many special librarians have never thought of themselves as doing much instruction, even though in reality they have. In the past, this instruction took place most often on a one-to-one basis, with a librarian responding to the information needs of one user at a time. In the future, successful librarians will need to be more creative. When complex integrated information systems are set up, librarians—those who know how users approach finding information—need to reach out to remote users, recognizing that this group may in the future make up a large proportion of their clientele.

Though demonstrating their worth is of most importance to corporate libraries, all special libraries should be in the process of identifying the information needs of the organization they serve and determining whether or not the library is meeting those needs. They need to make sure they have positioned themselves so that those making budget decisions recognize the contributions of the libraries.

Special libraries are moving toward the twenty-first century. Their instructional activities reflect, and will continue to reflect, this movement.

BIBLIOGRAPHY

Brecht, Albert. "Changes in Legal Scholarship and Their Impact on Law Library Reference Services." *Law Library Journal* 77 (winter 1984): 157-64.

Broering, Naomi C., and Helen E. Bagdoyan. "The Impact of IAMS at Georgetown: Strategies and Outcomes." *Bulletin of the Medical Library Association* 80, no. 3 (July 1992): 263-75.

Hubbard, Abigail, and Barbara Wilson. "An Integrated Information Management Program . . . Defining a New Role for Librarians in Helping End-Users." *Online* 10, no. 2 (March 1986): 15-23.

Moore, Mary. "Innovation and Education: Unlimited Potential for the Teaching Library." *Bulletin of the Medical Library Association* 77, no. 1 (January 1989): 26-32.

Rankin, Jocelyn A., et al. "Highlighting Problem-Based Learning and Medical Libraries." Special section. *Bulletin of the Medical Library Association* 81, no. 3 (July 1993): 293-315.

St. Clair, Guy. "The 'New' Literacy: Do Special Librarians Have a Role?" *Special Libraries* 82, no. 2 (spring 1991): 99-105.

Self, Phyllis C. "User Education in Academic Health Sciences Libraries: Results of a Survey." *Medical References Services Quarterly* 9, no. 4 (winter 1990): 101-7.

Sirkin, Arlene Faber. "Marketing Planning for Maximum Effectiveness." *Special Libraries* 82, no. 1 (winter 1991): 1-6.

Spaulding, Frank H. "Special Librarian to Knowledge Counselor in the Year 2002." *Special Libraries* 79, no. 2 (spring 1988): 83-91.

Zachert, Martha Jane. *Education Services in Special Libraries*. Chicago: Medical Library Association, 1990.

———. "The Information Manager as Provider of Educational Services." *Special Libraries* 80, no. 3 (summer 1989): 193-97.

9

Information Literacy

American Library Association

Presidential Committee
Final Report, January 1989

No other change in American society has offered greater challenges than the emergence of the Information Age. Information is expanding at an unprecedented rate, and enormously rapid strides are being made in the technology for storing, organizing, and accessing the ever-growing tidal wave of information. The combined effect of these factors is an increasingly fragmented information base, large components of which are only available to people with money and/or acceptable institutional affiliations.

Yet in an information society, all people should have the right to information that can enhance their lives. Out of the superabundance of available information, people need to be able to obtain specific information to meet a wide range of personal and business needs. These needs are largely driven either by the desire for personal growth and advancement or by the rapidly changing social, political, and economic environments of American society. What is true today is often outdated tomorrow. A good job today may be obsolete next year. To promote economic independence and quality of existence, there is a lifelong need for being informed and up-to-date.

How our country deals with the realities of the Information Age will have enormous impact on our democratic way of life and on our nation's ability to compete internationally. Within America's information society, there also exists the potential of addressing many long-standing social and economic inequities. To reap such benefits, people—as individuals and as a nation—must be information literate. To be information literate, a person must be able to recognize when information is needed and have the ability to locate, evaluate, and use effectively the needed information. Producing such a citizenry will require that schools and colleges appreciate and integrate the concept of information literacy into their learning programs and that they play a leadership role in equipping individuals and institutions to take advantage of the opportunities inherent within the information society.

Ultimately, information literate people are those who have learned how to learn. They know how to learn because they know how knowledge is organized, how to find information, and how to use information in such a way that others can learn from them. They are people prepared for lifelong learning, because they can always find the information needed for any task or decision at hand.

THE IMPORTANCE OF INFORMATION LITERACY TO INDIVIDUALS, BUSINESS, AND CITIZENSHIP

In Individuals' Lives

Americans have traditionally valued quality of life and the pursuit of happiness; however, these goals are increasingly difficult to achieve because of the complexities of life in today's information- and technology-dependent society. The cultural and educational opportunities available in an average community, for example, are often missed by people who lack the ability to keep informed of such activities, and lives of information illiterates are more likely than others to be narrowly focused on secondhand experiences of life through television. But life is more interesting when one knows what is going on, what opportunities exist, and where alternatives to current practices can be discovered.

On a daily basis, problems are more difficult to solve when people lack access to meaningful information vital to good decision making. Many people are vulnerable to poorly informed people or opportunists when selecting nursing care for a parent or facing a major expense such as purchasing, financing, or insuring a new home or car. Other information-dependent decisions can affect one's entire lifetime. For example, what information do young people have available to them when they consider which college to attend or whether to become sexually active? Even in areas where one can achieve an expertise, constantly changing and expanding information bases necessitate an ongoing struggle for individuals to stay in control of their daily information environments, to keep up-to-date with information in their fields as well as with information from other fields that can affect the outcomes of their decisions.

In an attempt to reduce information to easily manageable segments, most people have become dependent on others for their information. Information prepackaging in schools and through broadcast media and print news media, in fact, encourages people to accept the opinions of others without much thought. When opinions are biased, negative, or inadequate for the needs at hand, many people are left helpless to improve the situation confronting them. Imagine, for example, a family that is being evicted by a landlord who claims he is within his legal rights. Usually they will have to accept the landlord's "expert" opinion, because they do not know how to seek information to confirm or disprove his claim.

Information literacy, therefore, is a means of personal empowerment. It allows people to verify or refute expert opinion and to become independent seekers of truth. It provides them with the ability to build their own arguments and to experience the excitement of the search for knowledge. It not only prepares them for lifelong learning, but, by promoting successful quests for knowledge, it also creates in young people the motivation and excitement for pursuing and experiencing learning throughout their lives.

Moreover, the process of searching and interacting with the ideas and values of their own and others' cultures deepens people's capacities to understand and position themselves within larger communities of time and place. By drawing on the arts, history, and literature of previous generations, individuals and communities can affirm the best in their cultures and determine future goals.

It is unfortunate that the very people who most need the empowerment inherent in being information literate are the least likely to have learning experiences that will promote these abilities. Minority and at-risk students, illiterate adults, people with English as a second language, and economically disadvantaged people are among those most likely to lack access to the information that can improve their situations. Most are not even aware of the potential help that is available to them. Libraries, which provide the best access point to information for most U.S. citizens, are left untapped by those who most need help to improve their quality of life. As former U.S. Secretary of Education Terrell Bell once wrote, "There is a danger of a new elite developing in our country: the information elite." [1]

In Business

Herbert E. Meyer, who has served as an editor for *Fortune* magazine and as vice-chairman of the National Intelligence Council, underscores the importance of access to and use of good information for business in an age characterized by rapid change, a global environment, and unprecedented access to information. In his 1988 book, *Real World Intelligence,* he describes the astonishment and growing distress of executives who "are discovering that the only thing as difficult and dangerous as managing a large enterprise with too little information is managing one with too much." [2]

While Meyer emphasizes that companies should rely on public sources that are available to anyone for much of their information, it is clear that many companies do not know how to find and use such information effectively. Every day, lack of timely and accurate information is costly to American businesses. The following examples[3] describe cases of such losses or near losses:

A manufacturing company had a research team of three scientists and four technicians working on a project and, at the end of a year, the team felt it had a patentable invention in addition to a new product. Prior to filing the patent application, the company's patent attorney requested a literature search. While doing the search, the librarian found that the proposed application duplicated some of the work claimed in a patent that had been issued about a year before the team had begun its work. During the course of the project, the company had spent almost $500,000 on the project, an outlay that could have been avoided if it had spent the approximately $300 required to complete a review of the literature before beginning the project.

A manufacturing company was sued by an individual who claimed that the company had stolen his "secret formula" for a product that the company had just marketed. An information scientist on the staff of the company's technical library found a reference in the technical literature that this formula was generally known to the trade long before the litigant developed his "secret formula." When he was presented with this information, the litigant dropped his $7 million claim.

When a technical librarian for an electronics firm was asked to do a literature search for one of its engineers, four people had already been working to resolve a problem for more than a year. The literature search found an article that contained the answer the engineer needed to solve his problem. The article had been published several years before the project team had begun its work. Had the literature search been conducted when the problem was first identified, the company could have saved four man-years of labor and its resulting direct monetary costs.

The need for people in business who are competent managers of information is important at all levels, and the realities of the Information Age require serious rethinking of how business should be conducted. Harlan Cleveland explores this theme in his book, *The Knowledge Executive*.

> Information (organized data, the raw material for specialized knowledge, and generalist wisdom) is now our most important, and pervasive resource. Information workers now compose more than half the U.S. labor force. But this newly dominant resource is quite unlike the tangible resources we have heretofore thought of as valuable. The differences help explain why we get into so much trouble trying to use for the management of information concepts that worked all right in understanding the management of things—concepts such as control, secrecy, ownership, privilege and geopolitics.
>
> Because the old pyramids of influence and control were based on just these ideas, they are now crumbling. Their weakening is not always obvious, just as a wooden structure may look solid when you can't see what termites have done to its insides. Whether this "crumble effect" will result in a fairer shake for the world's disadvantaged majority is not yet clear. But there is ample evidence that those who learn how to achieve access to the bath of knowledge that already envelops the world will be the future's aristocrats of achievement, and that they will be far more numerous than any aristocracy in history.[4]

In Citizenship

American democracy has led to the evolution of many thousands of organized citizen groups that seek to influence public policy, issues, and community problems. Following are just a few examples:[5]

A local League of Women Voters has been chosen to study housing patterns for low-income individuals in its community. It must inform its members of the options for low-income housing and, in the process, comment publicly on the city's long-range, low-income housing plans.

In an upper midwestern city, one with the highest unemployment rate in fifty years, a major automobile company offers to build a new assembly plant in the central city. The only stipulation is that the city condemn property in a poor ethnic neighborhood of 3,500 residents for use as the site of its plant. In addition, the company seeks a twelve-year tax abatement. Residents of the neighborhood frantically seek to find out how they might save their community from the wrecker's ball but still improve their tax base.

A group of upper-middle-class women in the Junior League has read about increased incidences of child abuse. They want to become better informed about the elements of child abuse: What brings it on? What incidents have occurred in their own community? What services are available in their community? What actions might they take?

To address these problems successfully, each of these groups will have to secure access to a wide range of information, much of which—if they know how to find it—can be obtained without any cost to their organizations.

Citizenship in a modern democracy involves more than knowledge of how to access vital information. It also involves a capacity to recognize propaganda, distortion, and other misuses and abuses of information. People are daily subjected to statistics about health, the economy, national defense, and countless products. One person arranges information to evidence one point, another arranges the same information to evidence a different, even opposite, point. One political party says the social indicators are encouraging, another calls them frightening. One drug company *states* that most doctors prefer its product, another "proves" doctors favor its product. In such an environment, information literacy provides insight into the manifold ways in which people can all be deceived and misled. Information literate citizens are able to spot and expose chicanery, disinformation, and lies.

To say that information literacy is crucial to effective citizenship is simply to say it is central to the practice of democracy. Any society committed to individual freedom and democratic government must ensure the free flow of information to all its citizens in order to protect personal liberties and to guard its future. As U.S. Representative Major R. Owens has said:

Information literacy is needed to guarantee the survival of democratic institutions. All men are created equal but voters with information resources are in a position to make more intelligent decisions than citizens who are information illiterates. The application of information resources to the process of decision-making to fulfill civic responsibilities is a vital necessity.[6]

OPPORTUNITIES TO DEVELOP INFORMATION LITERACY

Information literacy is a survival skill in the Information Age. Instead of drowning in the abundance of information that floods their lives, information literate people know how to find, evaluate, and use information effectively to solve a particular problem or make a decision, whether the information they select comes from a computer, a book, a government agency, a film, or any number of other possible resources. Libraries, which provide a significant public access point to such information, usually at no cost, must play a key role in preparing people for the demands of today's information society. Just as public libraries were once a means of education and a better life for many of the over twenty million immigrants of the late 1800s and early 1900s, they remain today as the potentially strongest and most far-reaching community resource for lifelong learning. Public libraries not only provide access to information, but they also remain crucial to providing people with the knowledge necessary to make meaningful use of existing resources. They remain one of the few safeguards against information control by a minority.

Although libraries historically have provided a meaningful structure for relating information in ways that facilitate the development of knowledge, they have been all but ignored in the literature about the information society. Even national education reform reports, starting with *A Nation at Risk*[7] in 1983, largely exclude libraries. No K-12 report has explored the potential role of libraries or the need for information literacy. In the higher education reform literature, Education Commission of the States President Frank Newman's 1985 report, *Higher Education and the American Resurgence*, only addresses the instructional potential of libraries in passing, but it does raise the concern for the accessibility of materials within the knowledge explosion.[8] In fact, no reform report until *College*,[9] the 1986 Carnegie Foundation Report, gave substantive consideration to the role of libraries in addressing the challenges facing higher education. In the initial release of the study's recommendations, it was noted that

> The quality of a college is measured by the resources for learning on the campus and the extent to which students become independent, self-directed learners. And yet we found that today, about one out of every four undergraduates spends no time in the library during a normal week, and 65 percent use the library four hours or less each week. The gap between the classroom and the library, reported on almost a half-century ago, still exists today.[10]

Statistics such as these document the general passivity of most academic learning today, and the divorce of the impact of the Information Age from prevailing teaching styles. The first step in reducing this gap is making sure that the issue of information literacy is an integral part of current efforts at cultural literacy, the development of critical thinking abilities, and school restructuring. Due to the relative newness of the information society, however, information literacy is often completely overlooked in relevant dialogues, research, and experimentation. Moreover, most current educational and communication endeavors—with their long-standing history of prepackaging information— militate against the development of even an awareness of the need to master information-management skills.

The effects of such prepackaging of information are most obvious in the school and academic settings. Students, for example, receive predigested information from lectures and textbooks, and little in their environment fosters active thinking or problem solving. What problem solving does occur is within artificially constructed and limited information environments that allow for single "correct" answers. Such exercises bear little resemblance to problem solving in the real world, where multiple solutions of varying degrees of usefulness must be pieced together, often from many disciplines and from multiple information sources such as online databases, videotapes, government documents, and journals.

Education needs a new model of learning—learning that is based on the information resources of the real world, learning that is active and integrated, not passive and fragmented. On an intellectual level, many teachers and school administrators recognize that lectures, textbooks, materials put on reserve, and tests that ask students to regurgitate data from these sources do not create an active, much less a quality, learning experience. Moreover, studies at the higher education level have proven that students fail to retain most information they are "given."

> The curve for forgetting course content is fairly steep: a generous estimate is that students forget 50 percent of the content within a few months. . . . A more devastating finding comes from a study that concluded that even under the most favorable conditions, "students carry away in their heads and in their notebooks not more than 42 percent of the lecture content." Those were the results when students were told that they would be tested immediately following the lecture; they were permitted to use their notes; and they were given a prepared summary of the lecture. These results were bad enough, but when students were tested a week later, without the use of their notes, they could recall only 17 percent of the lecture material.[11]

Because of the rapidly shrinking half-life of information, even the value of that 17 percent that students do remember must be questioned. To any thoughtful person, it must be clear that teaching facts is a poor substitute for teaching people how to learn, that is, giving them the skills to be able to locate, evaluate, and effectively use information for any given need.

What is called for is not a new information studies curriculum but, rather, a restructuring of the learning process. Textbooks, workbooks, and lectures must yield to a learning process based on the information resources available for learning and problem solving throughout people's lifetimes—learning experiences that build a lifelong habit of library use. Such a learning process would actively involve students in the processes of

- knowing when they have a need for information,

- identifying information needed to address a given problem or issue,

- finding needed information,

- evaluating the information,

- organizing the information, and

- using the information effectively to address the problem or issue at hand.

Such a restructuring of the learning process will not only enhance the critical thinking skills of students but will also empower them for lifelong learning and the effective performance of professional and civic responsibilities.

AN INFORMATION-AGE SCHOOL

An increased emphasis on information literacy and resource-based learning would manifest itself in a variety of ways at both the academic and school levels, depending upon the role and mission of the individual institution and the information environment of its community. However, the following description of what a school might be like if information literacy were a central, not a peripheral, concern reveals some of the possibilities (though the description is focused on K-12, outcomes could be quite similar at the college level).

The school would be more interactive, because students, pursuing questions of personal interest, would be interacting with other students, with teachers, with a vast array of information resources, and with the community at large to a far greater degree than they presently do today. One would expect to find every student engaged in at least one open-ended, long-term quest for any answer to a serious social, scientific, aesthetic, or political problem. Students' quests would involve not only searching print, electronic, and video data, but also interviewing people inside and outside of school. As a result, learning would be more self-initiated. There would be more reading of original sources and more extended writing. Both students and teachers would be familiar with the intellectual and emotional demands of asking productive questions, gathering data of all kinds, reducing and synthesizing information, and analyzing, interpreting, and evaluating information in all its forms.

In such an environment, teachers would be coaching and guiding students more and lecturing less. They will have discovered that the classroom computer, with its access to the libraries and databases of the world, is a better source of facts than they could ever hope to be. They will have come to see that their major importance lies in their capacity to arouse curiosity and guide it to a satisfactory conclusion, to ask the right questions at the right time, to stir debate and serious discussion, and to be models themselves of thoughtful inquiry.

Teachers would work consistently with librarians, media resource people, and instructional designers within both their schools and their communities to ensure that student projects and explorations are challenging, interesting, and productive learning experiences in which they all can take pride. It would not be surprising in such a school to find a student task force exploring an important community issue with a view toward making a public presentation of its findings on cable television or at a news conference. Nor would it be unusual to see the librarian guiding the task force through its initial questions and its multidiscipli-nary, multimedia search, all the way through to its cable or satellite presentation. In such a role, librarians would be valued for their information expertise and their technological know-how. They would lead frequent in-service teacher workshops and ensure that the school was getting the most out of its investment in information technology.

Because evaluation in such a school would also be far more interactive than it is today, it would also be a much better learning experience. Interactive tutoring software that guides students through their own and other knowledge bases would provide more useful diagnostic information than is available today. Evaluation would be based upon a broad range of literacy indicators, including some that assess the quality and appropriateness of information sources or the quality and efficiency of the information searches themselves. Assessments would attend to ways in which students are using their minds and achieving success as information consumers, analyzers, interpreters, evaluators, and com-municators of ideas.

Finally, one would expect such a school to look and sound different from today's schools. One would see more information technology than is evident today, and it would be important to people not only in itself but also in regard to its capacity to help them solve problems and create knowledge. One would see the fruits of many student projects prominently displayed on the walls and on bookshelves, and one would hear more discussions and debate about substan-tive, relevant issues. On the playground, in the halls, in the cafeteria, and certainly in the classroom, one would hear fundamental questions that make information literacy so important: How do you know that? and What evidence do you have for that? Who says? and How can we find out?

CONCLUSION

This call for more attention to information literacy comes at a time when many other learning deficiencies are being expressed by educators, business leaders, and parents. Many workers, for example, appear unprepared to deal effectively with the challenges of high-tech equipment. There exists a need for better thinkers, problem solvers, and inquirers. There are calls for computer literacy, civic literacy, global literacy, and cultural literacy. Because we have been hit by a tidal wave of information, what used to suffice as literacy no longer suffices; what used to count as effective knowledge no longer is adequate.

The one common ingredient in all these concerns is an awareness of the rapidly changing requirements for a productive, healthy, and satisfying life. To respond effectively to an ever-changing environment, people need more than just a knowledge base, they need techniques for exploring it, connecting it to other knowledge bases, and making practical use of it. In other words, the landscape upon which we used to stand has been transformed, and we are being forced to establish a new foundation called "information literacy." Now *knowledge*, not minerals nor agricultural products nor manufactured goods—is this country's most precious commodity, and people who are information literate, people who know how to acquire knowledge and use it, are America's most valuable resource.

COMMITTEE RECOMMENDATIONS

To reap the benefits from the Information Age by our country, its citizens, and its businesses, the American Library Association Presidential Committee on Information Literacy makes the following recommendations:

1. *We all must reconsider the ways we have organized information institutionally, structured information access, and defined information's role in our lives at home, in the community, and in the workplace.*

To the extent that our concepts about knowledge and information are out of touch with the realities of a new, dynamic information environment, we must reconceptualize them. The degrees and directions of reconceptualization will vary, but the aims should always be the same: to communicate the power of knowledge; to develop in each citizen a sense of his or her responsibility to acquire knowledge and deepen insight through better use of information and related technologies; to instill a love of learning, a thrill in searching, and a joy in discovering; and to teach young and old alike how to know when they have an information need and how to gather, synthesize, analyze, interpret, and evaluate the information around them. All of these abilities are equally important for the enhancement of life experiences and for business pursuits.

Colleges, schools, and businesses should pay special attention to the potential role of their libraries or information centers. These should be central, not peripheral; organizational redesigns should seek to empower students and adults through new kinds of access to information and new ways of creating, discovering, and sharing it.

2. *A Coalition for Information Literacy should be formed under the leadership of the American Library Association, in coordination with other national organizations and agencies, to promote information literacy.*

The major obstacle to promoting information literacy is a lack of public awareness of the problems created by information illiteracy. The need for increased information literacy levels in all aspects of people's lives—in business, in family matters, and civic responsibilities—must be brought to the public's attention in a forceful way. To accomplish this, the Coalition should serve as an educational network for communications, coalescing related educational efforts, developing leadership, and effecting change. The Coalition should monitor and report on state efforts to promote information literacy and resource-based learning and provide recognition of individuals and programs for their exemplary information literacy efforts.

The Coalition should be organized with an advisory committee made up of nationally prominent public figures from librarianship, education, business, and government. The responsibilities of the advisory committee should include support for Coalition efforts in the areas of capturing media attention, raising public awareness, and fostering a climate favorable for information literacy. In addition, the advisory committee should actively seek funding to promote research and demonstration projects.

3. *Research and demonstration projects related to information and its use need to be undertaken.*

To date, remarkably little research has been done to understand how information can be more effectively managed to meet educational and societal objectives or to explore how information management skills impact on overall school and academic performance. What research does exist appears primarily in library literature, which is seldom read by educators or state decision makers.

For future efforts to be successful, a national research agenda should be developed and implemented. The number of issues needing to be addressed are significant and should include the following:

- What are the social effects of reading?

- With electronic media eclipsing reading for many people, what will be the new place of the printed word?

- How do the characteristics of information resources (format, length, age) affect their usefulness?

- How does the use of information vary by discipline?

- How does access to information impact on the effectiveness of citizen action groups?

- How do information management skills affect student performance and retention?

- What role can information management skills play in the economic and social advancement of minorities?

Also needed is research that will promote a "sophisticated understanding of the full range of the issues and processes related to the generation, distribution, and use of information so that libraries can fulfill their obligations to their users and potential users and so that research and scholarship in all fields can flourish."[12]

The Coalition can play a major role in obtaining funding for such research and for fostering demonstration projects that can provide fertile ground for controlled experiments that can contrast benefits from traditional versus resource-based learning opportunities for students.

4. *State Departments of Education, Commissions on Higher Education, and Academic Governing Boards should be responsible to ensure that a climate conducive to students' becoming information literate exists in their states and on their campuses.*

Of importance are two complementary issues: the development of an information literate citizenry and the move from textbook and lecture-style learning to resource-based learning. The latter is, in fact, the means to the former as well as to producing lifelong, independent, and self-directed learners. As is appropriate within their stated missions, such bodies are urged to do the following:

> To incorporate the spirit and intent of information literacy into curricular requirements, recommendations, and instructional materials. (Two excellent models for state school guidelines are Washington's *Information Skills Curriculum Guide: Process Scope and Sequence* and *Library Information Skills: Guide for Oregon Schools K-12.*[13])

> To incorporate in professional preparation and in-service training for teachers an appreciation for the importance of resource-based learning, to encourage implementation of it in their subject areas, and to provide opportunities to master implementation techniques.

> To encourage and support coordination of school/campus and public library resources/services with classroom instruction in offering resource-based learning.

> To include coverage of information literacy competencies in state assessment examinations.

> To establish recognition programs of exemplary projects for learning information management skills in elementary and secondary schools, in higher education institutions, and in professional preparation programs.

5. *Teacher education and performance expectations should be modified to include information literacy concerns.*

Inherent in the concepts of information literacy and resource-based learning is the complementary concept of the teacher as a facilitator of student learning rather than as presenter of ready-made information. To be successful in such roles, teachers should make use of an expansive array of information resources. They should be familiar with and able to use selected databases, learning networks, reference materials, textbooks, journals, newspapers, magazines, and other resources. They also should place a premium on problem solving and see that their classrooms are extended outward to encompass the learning resources of the library media centers and the community. They also should expect their students to become information literate.

To encourage the development of teachers who are facilitators of learning, the following recommendations are made to schools of teacher education. Those responsible for in-service teacher training should also evaluate current capabilities of teaching professionals and incorporate the following recommendations into their programs as needed.

New knowledge from cognitive research on thinking skills should be incorporated into pedagogical skills development.

Integral to all programs should be instruction in managing the classroom, individualizing instruction, setting problems, questioning, promoting cooperative learning—all of which should rely on case studies and information resources of the entire school and community.

Instruction within the disciplines needs to emphasize a problem-solving approach and the development of a sophisticated level of information management skills appropriate to the individual disciplines.

School library media specialists need to view the instructional goals of their schools as an integral part of their own concern and responsibilities and should actively contribute toward the ongoing professional development of teachers and principals. They should be members of curriculum and instructional teams and provide leadership in integrating appropriate information and educational technologies into school programming. (For further recommendations regarding the role of library media specialists, consult *Information Power: Guidelines for School Media Programs* prepared by the American Association of School Librarians and the Association for Educational Communications and Technology, 1988.)

Exit requirements from teacher education programs should include each candidate's ability to use selected databases, networks, reference materials, administrative and instructional software packages, and new forms of learning technologies.

A portion of the practicum or teaching experience of beginning teachers should be spent with library media specialists. These opportunities should be based in the school library media center to promote an understanding of resources available in both that facility and other community libraries and to emphasize the concepts and skills necessary to become a learning facilitator.

Cooperative, or supervising, teachers who can demonstrate their commitment to thinking skills instruction and information literacy should be matched with student teachers, and teachers who see themselves as learning facilitators should be relied upon to serve as role models. Student teachers should also have the opportunity to observe and practice with a variety of models for the teaching of critical thinking.

6. *An understanding of the relationship of information literacy to the themes of the White House Conference on Library and Information Services should be promoted.*

The White House Conference themes of literacy, productivity, and democracy will provide a unique opportunity to foster public awareness of the importance of information literacy. (The conference will be held sometime between September 1989 and September 1991.) The American Library Association and the Coalition on Information Literacy should aggressively promote consideration of information literacy within state deliberations as well as within the White House Conference itself.

BACKGROUND TO REPORT

This report was released on January 10, 1989, in Washington, D.C. Partial funding for printing of this report is provided by the H. W. Wilson Foundation. The American Library Association's Presidential Committee on Information Literacy was appointed in 1987 by ALA President Margaret Chisholm with three expressed purposes: 1) to define information literacy within the higher literacies and its importance to student performance, lifelong learning, and active citizenship; 2) to design one or more models for information literacy development appropriate to formal and informal learning environments throughout people's lifetimes; and 3) to determine implications for the continuing education and development of teachers. The committee, which consists of leaders in education and librarianship, has worked actively to accomplish its mission since its establishment. Members of the Committee include the following:

Gordon M. Ambach, Executive Director
Council of Chief State School Officers

William L. Bainbridge, President
School Match

Patricia Senn Breivik, Chair, Director
Auraria Library
University of Colorado at Denver

Rexford Brown, Director
Policies and the Higher Literacies Project
Education Commission of the States

Judith S. Eaton, President
Community College of Philadelphia

David Imig, Executive Director
American Association of Colleges for Teacher Education

Sally Kilgore, Professor
Emory University
(former Director of the Office of Research, U.S. Department of
    Education)

Carol Kuhlthau, Director
Educational Media Services Program
Rutgers University

Joseph Mika, Director
Library Science Program
Wayne State University

Richard D. Miller, Executive Director
American Association of School Administrators

Roy D. Miller, Executive Assistant to the Director
Brooklyn Public Library

Sharon J. Rogers, University Librarian
George Washington University

Robert Wedgeworth, Dean
School of Library Science
Columbia University

For Further Information

Further information on information literacy can be obtained by contacting:

Information Literacy and K-12
c/o American Association of School Librarians
American Library Association
50 East Huron Street
Chicago, Ill. 60611

Information Literacy and Higher Education
c/o Association of College and Research Libraries
American Library Association
50 East Huron Street
Chicago, Ill. 60611

NOTES

1. Terrell H. Bell, communication to University of Colorado President E. Gordon Gee, September 1986.

2. Herbert E. Meyer, *Real World Intelligence: Organized Information for Executives* (New York: Weidenfeld & Nicholson, 1987), 29.

3. James B. Tchobanoff, "The Impact Approach: Value as Measured by the Benefit of the Information Professional to the Parent Organization," in *President's Task Force on the Value of the Information Professional* (Anaheim, Calif.: Special Libraries, 1987), 47.

4. Harlan Cleveland, *The Knowledge Executive: Leadership in an Information Society* (New York: Dutton, 1985), xviii.

5. Joan C. Durrance, *Armed for Action: Library Response to Citizen Information Needs* (New York: Neal-Schuman, 1984), ix.

6. Major Owens, "State Government and Libraries," *Library Journal* 101 (January 1, 1976): 27.

7. United States National Commission on Excellence in Education, *A Nation at Risk: The Imperative for Educational Reform* (Washington, D.C.: U.S. Government Printing Office, 1983).

8. Frank Newman, *Higher Education and the American Resurgence* (Princeton, N.J.: Princeton University Press, 1985), 152.

9. Ernest L. Boyer, *College: The Undergraduate Experience in America* (New York: Harper & Row, 1987).

10. "Prologue and Major Recommendations of Carnegie Foundation's Report on Colleges," *Chronicle of Higher Education* 33 (November 5, 1986): 10-11.

11. K. Patricia Cross, "A Proposal to Improve Teaching, or What Taking Teaching Seriously Should Mean," *AAHE Bulletin* 39 (September 1986): 10-11.

12. Edward Connery Lathem, ed., *American Libraries as Centers of Scholarship* (Hanover, N.H.: Dartmouth College, 1978), 58.

13. State Superintendent of Publication, *Information Skills Curriculum Guide: Process Scope and Sequence* (Olympia, Wash.: State Superintendent of Public Instruction, 1987); and Oregon Department of Education, *Library Information Skills: Guide for Oregon Schools K-12* (Salem: Oregon Department of Education, 1987).

BIBLIOGRAPHY

Breivik, Patricia Senn. "Making the Most of Libraries in the Search for Academic Excellence." *Change* 19 (July/August 1987): 44-52.

Breivik, Patricia Senn, and Robert Wedgeworth. *Libraries and the Search for Academic Excellence.* Papers from a National Symposium sponsored by Columbia University and the University of Colorado, New York, March 15-17, 1987. Metuchen, N.J.: Scarecrow Press, 1988.

Hardesty, Larry, Nicholas P. Lovrich Jr., and James Mannon. "Library Use Instruction: Assessment of the Long-Term Effects." *College & Research Libraries* 43 (January 1982): 38-46.

Hyatt, James A., and Aurora A. Santiago. *University Libraries in Transition.* Washington, D.C.: National Association of College and University Business Officers, 1987.

Lewis, David W. "Inventing the Electronic University." *College & Research Libraries* 49 (July 1988): 291-304.

"The Literacy Gap." *Time* (December 19, 1988): 56-57.

Moran, Barbara B. *Academic Libraries: The Changing Knowledge Center of Colleges and Universities.* Asheeric Higher Education Research Report, no. 8. Washington, D.C.: Association for the Study of Higher Education, 1984.

10

Avoiding the Cereal Syndrome;
or, Critical Thinking in
the Electronic Environment

Cerise Oberman

Advances in technology have allowed the "supercatalog" to move from an idea to a reality. With its multiple databases and integrated structures, the supercatalog offers access to more information more easily than ever before. For all the advantages that this new technology offers, there are also serious problems that must be recognized and confronted. The most serious of these is that users must choose from a multitude of possibilities in order to fulfill their information needs. Research about consumer tolerance for making choices, whether about cereals or databases, suggests that "more is less," not "more is more." Thus, it is imperative that librarians adequately prepare users with the critical thinking skills that are necessary to take advantage fully of the new electronic environment. More than ever, critical thinking must become the core of bibliographic instruction.

When George Orwell (1949) penned his now famous phrase "Freedom is Slavery," he was not thinking about the emergence of a sophisticated integrated information retrieval system. Yet, his dystopian vision of a world where choice results in individual confusion and anxiety presages at least one of the critical issues emerging from our increased abilities to provide access to a wide range of information easily and transparently (i.e., making choices).

This problem is not limited to online information systems. Indeed, it is becoming a growing area of concern in our everyday lives. Perhaps an illuminating, if mundane, example of this problem is evident in the extraordinary increase of items available in the supermarket. Not surprisingly, the overwhelming availability of competing items to choose from in the supermarket, according

---

to one study, results in increased anxiety among shoppers (Williams 1990). This was borne out recently by a story a friend relayed to me. He had gone to the grocery store to pick up his favorite cereal. The endless aisles of different types of cereals so overwhelmed and frustrated him—he could not find his favorite brand—that he abandoned his cart mid-aisle and went to a small corner grocery that had far fewer choices. He was a victim of the "cereal syndrome." Much to the dismay of hypermarkets everywhere, all indications seem to support the conclusion of David A. Gosline, president of the American Institute for Research, that "Choices do not make life easier; they make it more difficult for all of us" (Williams 1990, C1).

The problems of choice facing consumers in the grocery store are not that different from the problems of increasing choice that face students and faculty in the emerging online library environment. Libraries, armed with the latest technological breakthroughs, have begun to reshape access patterns to information. The one pattern that has become the sine qua non of libraries is the building of the "supercatalog." The supercatalog, according to Shaw (1988): 1) is distant-dependent, 2) contains multiple collections residing on one computer (or accessible via a network), and 3) has access points only limited by content of record. The idea of the supercatalog is attractive: a single access point, available from any microcomputer, which can provide the user with information about local library holdings, and electronic gateways to other library holdings, periodical abstracts and indexes, national bibliographic utilities, encyclopedias, and so on.

This online library, well advanced beyond the online catalog, opens opportunities for the user unimagined as recently as twenty-five years ago. Shaw (1988) asserts that this new catalog offers "nothing short of improving the quality of both learning and research." But he hastens to add that "we do not yet understand either learning or research well enough to know much about how to approach the task" (p. 143). Clearly this new supercatalog presents a number of interesting and challenging problems, not the least of which is the overwhelming number of choices presented to the user. Users may soon be confronting the library equivalent to the "cereal syndrome." More important, perhaps, is the question that the situation provokes: How do we ensure that students are equipped to harness the extraordinary powers of this new online environment? The answer to this question lies in bibliographic education.

The emergence of the supercatalog is one of the most important consequences of computer and telecommunication technologies. Shill (1987) was correct when he suggested that the wiring of the university is "the most significant area for library administrators and instruction librarians to monitor" (p. 443). The wiring of the university and the concomitant emergence of new information structures are indeed two of the most influential environmental elements influencing higher education. Furthermore, their impact on instruction librarians and the design of instruction has been, and will continue to be, acute.

The online public access catalog, the first major component in the new online library, spurred much discussion and experimentation in teaching methods and formats. What was instantly apparent was that "the mere presence of an online catalog often create[d] a false sense of confidence concerning the comprehension of its content and the knowledge required to use it effectively" (Baker 1986, 36). Borne out by a number of other studies, the online catalog was viewed as a panacea by users, regardless of their success in locating relevant materials. The lure of technology had made itself felt. The conclusion of a study of user information-seeking behavior at Bowling Green State University, for instance, indicates that "automation (i.e., online public access catalog, OCLC, optical discs) attracts—and it attracts even the user who has infrequently used library reference sources" (York 1988, 16).

Perceived user happiness, though a desirable by-product, is not acceptable from an instruction librarian's perspective (nor should it be acceptable to researchers). Users must understand the online environment. Specifically, as Baker (1986) asserts, the user must be able to 1) understand the function and purpose of the online catalog; 2) define the scope of the catalog; 3) understand selected concepts of an online information retrieval system; 4) structure an online catalog search by choosing, entering, and manipulating search vocabulary; and 5) interpret the results of a search and identify information from it that is pertinent to the user's information needs. By adopting the database itself as the conceptual model for teaching online retrieval, Baker and Sandore (1988) have concentrated on identifying and teaching concepts that are unique to the online environment (e.g., Boolean searching, command structure, controlled vocabulary versus free-text searching, command language). The articulation of concepts unique to the electronic library underscores the additional skills that students must possess to operate successfully in this new environment.

A number of studies at academic libraries illustrate the dismal abilities of students, at the most basic level, of being able to match their subject needs with appropriate computer retrieval systems. At the Undergraduate Library of the University of Illinois at Urbana-Champaign for instance, eighty-two searches conducted on CD-ROM databases were reviewed and analyzed by three judges for suitability and appropriateness of database in relation to the subject content. Users had a selection of sixteen CD-ROM databases to choose from; only 22 percent of the searchers selected databases deemed appropriate for their search topic. Almost 20 percent of the users selected databases considered to be not even one of the three most suitable databases (Allen 1990). At the University of North Carolina's Undergraduate Library a series of interviews with InfoTrac users revealed that 9 percent of those interviewed were trying to use InfoTrac for researching such topics as Graham Greene, Spanish American War, and Kierkegaard (Momenee 1987).

In other words, if these studies are typical of other user groups, the most basic critical thinking skills required for matching subject relevance with appropriate sources of information are sorely missing in the vast majority of undergraduates. These are not revolutionary findings. Quite the contrary. The same statistics would no doubt be duplicated in an examination or selection of print indexes and/or abstracts. What is significant, however, is that unlike print reference tools, which for the most part remain singular in form and format, the online environment is hurtling toward a totally integrated information network in the form of a supercatalog. This integration, which promises transparency of access to millions of information bits, has several possible outcomes: 1) it will be embraced warmly and enthusiastically for bringing the information to the user, not the user to the information; more than likely, this reaction will be from knowledgeable informed users who can easily distinguish which, among many information retrieval options, are appropriate; 2) it will be embraced enthusiastically from a misguided perception that all information is dispensed through the supercatalog (a misperception already evidenced in studies of online public catalogs and InfoTrac); and 3) it will be a replication of the "cereal syndrome," which results in increased anxiety and avoidance.

It is interesting to note that in Huston and Oberman's (1989) study of information-seeking novices, there is a marked contrast between their affective behavior in searching for information outside the database environment and in the database environment itself. When gathering information to support a project outside the online environment, students represented their efforts as "alive" and "happening." This is attributed to the "living, human nature of the information providers who were functioning, as 'interfaces' between the bodies of knowledge and the requesters of information" (p. 205). When the same students were asked to use manual and online methods to gather information, their mental state was significantly changed and they expressed either qualified success or dissatisfaction. These findings seem to support Mellon's (1986) qualitative study of students' reactions to library use. Through an extensive sampling of students' experiences in using the library, Mellon concluded that "when confronted with the need to gather information in the library for their first research paper, many students become so anxious that they are unable to approach the problem logically or effectively" (p. 163). The addition of electronic access may indeed serve to magnify students' anxieties.

The most extensive examination of students' affective behavior in conducting library-based research was done with elementary and secondary school students. In a series of longitudinal studies over a five-year period, Carol Kuhlthau (1987) plotted the library research process of these students. Her research revealed six stages that these students progressed through in their process of gathering information:

1. task initiation characterized by feelings of uncertainty and apprehension,

2. topic selection characterized by optimism,

3. prefocus formulation characterized by confusion and frustration and strong doubts about individual ability to complete the task,

4. focus formulation characterized by the emergence of a central theme,

5. information collection characterized by a sense of direction and increased confidence, and

6. search closure characterized by relief, satisfaction, and accomplishment.

Kuhlthau's (1988) research-process model offers some interesting insights into student emotional behavior when pursuing the unknown. The third and fifth stages of the model in particular—prefocus exploration and information collection—offer a unique insight into the problems of choice and selection. It is in these two stages of the search process that students confront a series of choices; their reactions are telling. In the prefocus exploration stage, students seek a focus for their topics. According to Kuhlthau, their feelings are characterized by "confusion, doubt, sometimes threat, uncertainty" (p. 238). Yet the actions and strategies identified to overcome their feelings include finding and reading additional information, identifying relevant descriptors, and taking notes.

In the initial information collection stage, students must locate materials that support their focused topics. Their feelings are characterized by "realization of extensive work to be done, confidence in ability to complete the task, and increased interest" (p. 240). Their actions and strategies directly involve using the library for conducting a successful search for materials, using a variety of reference tools, and seeking assistance from a reference librarian.

What is of particular interest is that students in the Kuhlthau study exhibit an increased sense of confidence once they have completed the focus stage of their research—that is, once they have completed making their choices. The information collection stage, marked by confidence and increased interest on the part of the students, may, at best, be illusory. Kuhlthau is not studying the quality of the student products, rather their affective and cognitive processes. But if the studies cited earlier are general indicators of students' inability to understand the online environment—its complexities and its dimensions—then perhaps, in that domain too, their ignorance will be fueled by a naive confidence.

The significance of Kuhlthau's work is that it provides a road map of student thinking at each stage of the research process. Additionally, it provides a potential yardstick by which students can gauge their state of mind and recognize that as each stage is completed a growing sense of confidence and accomplishment will emerge. Among other things, Kuhlthau's study suggests that the process of research is often filled with ambiguities and uncertainties. Finally, she proposes that once students understand that research is not a linear process, they can proceed with reassurance and security. By understanding the process, students will be better prepared to be successful.

This affective study, limited as it is to elementary and secondary students, is precisely the type of study that needs to be conducted for the electronic information environment.[1] Investigation, particularly during the information collection stage, might yield some important insights into whether the networked environment is the seductive creature it is currently perceived as, or whether, as the networked environment becomes more intricate and interwoven, students will recognize its complexities and feel overwhelmed rather than comforted by it.

It is too presumptuous to assume that we are creating an online library environment that will result in a higher level of anxiety and confusion for users. This is borne out by a recent study of user persistence in scanning references. Wiberley and Daugherty (1988) conclude that "maximizing retrieval . . . can lead to [information] excess" (p. 154). Information excess can lead to intellectual distress. It was found that end-users preferred to receive limited search results (between thirty and seventy citations). It was also found that end-users would commonly abandon the search for information entirely if provided with more references than they were willing to scan.

Even skeptics about the impact of information overload recognize its potential problems. Rudd and Rudd (1986), for instance, assert that the issue of information overload is much overrated and there is little empirical evidence to suggest that increased amounts of information have an effect on the quality of the decision-making process. However, they do take time to suggest a four-point model to prevent users from possible information overload; limiting information by type, date, and so on; minimizing time users spend in locating desired materials; developing and refining users' skills through instructional programs; and, finally, selecting and evaluating information.

These skills demand significant critical thinking skills on the part of the user. And indeed, it is these new skills that are the heart and soul of the conceptual movement of bibliographic instruction. They have been embraced by an ever-increasing number of practitioners and, most recently, have been codified by the Association of College & Research Libraries (ACRL) Bibliographic Instruction Section (BIS) in their *Statement of Model Objectives for Academic Bibliographic Instruction* (1987). The ACRL BIS "Statement of Model Objectives" is not specifically written for the electronic environment. The statement is, however, intended to cover all concepts that are essential for students to understand and to handle effectively the ever-growing system of information opportunities, including the electronic environment.

Recognition of the importance of concepts to bibliographic instruction has been a rite of passage for the instructional movement. It has released library instruction from a limited tool-bound and preset formula approach to an unlimited information-based and realistic approach. Theoretically, this new approach should introduce students to the vagaries of research and equip them to handle the unlimited choices of information sources and search possibilities available to them in the expanding information universe. But does it?

Concepts alone do not seem to be the answer. Anecdotal evidence from instruction librarians across the country suggests that, though practitioners are eager to incorporate conceptual approaches into their instruction, they are often disappointed in the response of their students.[2] Frequent complaints are that "They don't seem to understand," that "They need the basics before they are ready for concepts," and that "They cannot apply the concepts once they are in the library."

The teaching of concepts (including, for example, evaluation of materials, publishing cycles for disciplines, selection of information sources, development of a database search strategy) can only be successful if it is recognized, as Rudd and Rudd (1986) did in their discussion of information overload and the decision-making process, that concepts inherently require students to use critical thinking skills. Most importantly, critical thinking skills cannot be taken for granted, even among college students.[3]

If instruction librarians examine the concepts that have been articulated as important to instructional efforts (e.g., Oberman and Strauch 1982; Beaubien et al. 1982; Reichel and Ramey 1987; and Baker 1986b; among others), it is clear that most of these concepts demand that students operate in the world of abstraction. McInnis's (1982) use of metaphors to discern the relationship of publications to one another, Keresztesi's (1982) description of the growth of a discipline and its parallel bibliographic structure, and Baker's (1986a) database as a conceptual model are all exemplary conceptual approaches to library instruction. In every instance, however, students must engage in what is most likely unfamiliar cognitive territory. As such, library instructors' expectations may exceed students' cognitive abilities.

Library instruction, over the years, has slowly shifted its focus. Its initial concerns were with the lowest cognitive objectives, as classified by Bloom (1984), of knowledge (representing lowest level of learning outcomes, such as recalls of specifics and universals), and comprehension (representing the lowest level of understanding, which does not require establishing relationships to other material). Emphasis is now, appropriately, on the highest cognitive objectives of analysis (ability to break down materials into their component parts so that their organizational structure can be understood), synthesis (ability to reassemble elements or parts to formulate new patterns or structures), and evaluation (ability to judge the value of materials on definite criteria). Analysis, synthesis, and evaluation are all cognitive objectives that demand that students think.

The cognitive skills of analysis, synthesis, and evaluation are nowhere more obviously needed than when students encounter the online information environment. Numerous studies (see earlier discussion) suggest that some students view the online environment as a means of circumventing traditional mechanisms for understanding the relationships between their information needs and information resources. Others face the online environment with trepidation and confusion. Both of these problems may only become exacerbated by the emergence of the supercatalog.

Thus, it is more critical than ever that we recognize the complexity of information concepts and the limited abilities of our students to adequately understand and apply them. The networked environment, the supercatalog, and the proliferation of microcomputers are moving us toward a "disembodied" library. If the future does indeed take the form of "a single, unified electronic record of scholarship," as Eldred Smith (1990, 67) suggests in his recent essay, *The Librarian, the Scholar, and the Future of the Research Library*, then students need to understand more than what they see on the computer screen. They also must understand a combination of the "how, who, why, and where" of bibliographic concepts and how to search and select from a vast repository of information. If they do not understand the concepts, if they cannot critically apply them, we may be faced with the paradox of building a marvelously sophisticated information apparatus that only a limited few can fully understand and use.

What then is the proper educational response to the online information environment? It must be a new combination of methodology and pedagogy. Methodologically, instruction librarians must place the online environment in the broader context of the information world. As such, the online environment, and the concepts that are unique to its manipulation, must not exist in an information vacuum. The relationship between the concepts unique to information systems must be interwoven and connected to the broader concepts of information generation, access, and evaluation. The ACRL BIS "Model Statement of Objectives" specifically (and rightfully) ignores singling out the online information environment in hopes of encouraging instruction librarians to approach information as an entire package of interrelated concepts. This methodological approach should provide users with all the important concepts that must be understood and applied in or out of an electronic environment.

Perhaps more radical is the pedagogical implication. Though the world of information may be becoming more complicated, the cognitive skills necessary to successfully operate within it remain the same. What needs to change are the teaching methods that instruction librarians use to prepare students to face the contemporary world of information. The complexity of the online environment has given new impetus to this need. It is time to recognize that concepts of bibliographic instruction are complex and abstract. It is time to recognize that most students are not formal thinkers and, therefore, cannot automatically translate abstract concepts into practical applications. It is time to recognize that the cognitive objectives of analysis, synthesis, and evaluation must be overt educational goals. Finally, it is time to experiment with teaching methodologies, such as active learning, which places primary importance on promoting thinking.

Active teaching, which results in active learning, offers an opportunity for students to discover the concepts that they will need to operate in an information-rich environment. Active teaching is a pedagogical tool that assists students in drawing on their own experiences as a bridge to new experiences. It is a tool that allows students to discover and apply concepts to the problem at hand. Most importantly, it is a tool that explicitly demands that students think critically and act creatively.

There are many forms of active learning, all of which are aimed at stimulating abstract and critical thinking.[4] But all of these active learning models rely on four key components that are necessary to create an active learning environment. The four components to active learning are equilibration, group activity, reinforcement and feedback, and application. Each of these components contributes directly to the learning environment. However, the most critical component is equilibration.

Equilibration is a mental process that, according to noted child psychologist Jean Piaget, contributes directly to the cognitive growth of individuals. Taking his cue from Piaget, Robert Karplus (1976), a leader in developing active learning models for science teaching, describes equilibration as "the internal mental process in which new experiences are combined with prior expectations and generate new logical operations" (p. 2). In order to initiate the process of equilibration, or self-regulation as it is sometimes referred to, a situation that provokes disequilibrium must be introduced. The presentation of a situation that requires students to draw on familiar experiences to solve a problem to which the solution may be unfamiliar is upsetting to their equilibrium. The mental discomfort of disequilibrium challenges students to think actively and constructively.

For example, in Oberman's (1983) active learning model designed for question analysis, students are asked to sort packets of questions into two piles and label those piles. The questions are benign so students are not puzzled over jargon. They must, however, determine the distinctions between questions (i.e., short or long; fact or research; objective or subjective). This is an exercise in disequilibrium. It is designed specifically so that students can draw on their familiar experiences with such questions, while forcing them to create and test hypotheses about how the questions should be categorized.[5] The result is that they are forced to think about the types of answers these questions require and the differences between these answers.

The purpose of disequilibration is to create a situation that demands active thinking on the part of students, active thinking that requires them to discover, on their own, a new pattern or new idea. This self-discovery, as is true with most "learning by doing" activities, has the added benefit, at its best, of students remembering what they discovered and transferring the principle to a new problem.

The creation of disequilibrium in a classroom, however, must be well managed. Nothing is more counterproductive than giving students an exercise that results in frustration and ends in despair. Thus it is critical to the success of any self-regulation exercise to ensure (and control) the level of frustration. One of the easiest ways to reduce anxiety among students when asking them to solve an unfamiliar problem is to have them work in groups. Group activity, the second key component to active learning, is a powerful technique in a learning environment.

The worth of group activity behavior in learning activities (Bouton and Garth 1983) has been well documented. Four important advantages are consistently ascribed to group activity. First, in any group a natural leader emerges from within the group. This ensures that the group will perform the task at hand with minimum intervention from the teacher. Second, quicker learners in the group will assist slower learners. Peers are responsive to one another and demonstrate a patience in explaining problems and processes to one another. Third, students feel more comfortable in offering ideas, exchanging thoughts, and contributing to discussion in small groups. Interaction in small student groups is more often lively and free of the constraints of public exposure. Finally, group activity usually results in an increased interest in the learning activity at hand because it eliminates the potential for individual frustration.

Active learning, however, is not wholly dependent on group activity by students. Active learning requires the teacher, or leader, to assume the roles of manager, expert, consultant, and interpreter. These roles are best played by providing appropriate reinforcement and feedback to students at critical junctures in the active learning sequence. Reinforcement and feedback can take either an oral or written form. During group activity, the leader is actively engaged in visiting each group, listening, offering advice, answering questions, and even gently guiding groups in their discovery process. Again, this active role reduces the potential for frustration by making the leader available during the exploring and thinking process. Written reinforcement and feedback are also a powerful teaching tool. They allow the teacher, in the role of expert, to confirm the solution or solutions to a disequilibrium activity in a positive and constructive manner. They also enable the expert to expand upon the solution of the problem through additional explanation or illustration.

Finally, the active learning model must incorporate an application stage. The application stage ensures that the discovery of a concept or skill through group activity can be generalized to a new problem. Application reinforces the concept being taught, while at the same time, it may involve further cognitive challenges. For instance, in the question analysis example, the sorting of cards into two distinct piles was a prelude to introducing the concept that different types of questions require different research approaches. The next step is taking one of the "research-like" questions and narrowing it by a set of criteria (time, place, interest groups, etc.). The exercise ends with an application that requires students to use what they have learned and apply it to a new and different question.

Active learning, then, is built on the assumption that critical thinking is, perhaps, even more important than subject content. In other words, if students can think critically about broad general principles, then they are more likely to be able to apply those principles to new and different problems. (For further information on the importance of critical thinking to education, see Paul 1990.)

Providing students with the cognitive tools to make informed decisions must become a keystone of library instruction. Students unable to cope with the overwhelming number of choices available to them will be further disenfranchised from the information structure. The allure of the online environment, whether in its singular CD-ROM format or its more complicated networks of databases, is powerful. Intelligent use of these new tools is essential to maximize efficiency and reduce frustration. Equally important is the emphasis that must be placed on the relationship of other information sources and their structures to the online environment.

The information world, particularly the electronic information world, is like a supermarket stocked with limitless varieties of resources. In this environment it is imperative that students face the choices on the "shelves" with the ability to discern which of the available products are appropriate. The alternative is that students, much like my friend facing the endless shelves of cereal, will turn and walk away.

NOTES

1. Carol Kuhlthau is currently working on a study with Rutgers University students.

2. The author has conducted numerous instructional workshops on conceptual approaches and active learning for bibliographic instruction across the United States and Canada over the past ten years. The anecdotal evidence is drawn from hundreds of conversations from practitioners in the field.

3. According to Inhelder and Piaget (1958), there are four stages of cognitive development: sensorimotor, pre-operational, concrete, and formal (abstract). The earliest stages, sensorimotor and pre-operational, are cognitive growth stages, which mature from infancy to age six. The concrete-thinking stage, which is characterized by being able to use known experiences to solve problems through simple associations and step-by-step instruction, is complete by age eleven. By age thirteen, a concrete learner begins the transformation to a formal or abstract learner. The formal/abstract learner is able to think in theoretical terms, can reason with concepts, relationships, and abstractions, and can plan lengthy procedures given overall goals and resources. Studies, such as Tomlinson-Keasey (1975), refute Piaget's belief in a natural and inevitable development of

cognition and suggest that most college students are not formal/abstract thinkers.

4. For examples of active learning models adapted for library instruction, see Oberman (1983) and Oberman and Linton (1982).

5. For a more detailed explanation of equilibration see Oberman (1983), pp. 24-25.

REFERENCES

Allen, G. 1990. Research Notes: Database Selection by Patrons Using CD-ROM. *College & Research Libraries* 51, no. 1: 69-75.

Association of College & Research Libraries, Bibliographic Instruction Task Force on Statement of Objectives. 1987. Model Statement of Objectives for Academic Bibliographic Instruction: Draft Revision. *College & Research Libraries News* 48, no. 5: 256-61.

Baker, B. 1986a. A Conceptual Framework for Teaching Online Catalog Use. *The Journal of Academic Librarianship* 12, no. 2: 90-96.

————. 1986b. A New Direction for Online Catalog Instruction. *Information Technology and Libraries* 5, no. 1: 35-41.

Baker, B., and B. Sandore. 1988. *Effective Information Retrieval: A Model for Teaching and Learning.* Unpublished paper presented at the Library and Information Technology Second National Conference, Boston, October.

Beaubien, A. K., S. A. Hogan, and M. W. George. 1982. *Learning the Library.* New York: R. R. Bowker.

Bloom, B. S., ed. 1984. *Taxonomy of Educational Objectives: The Classification of Educational Goals.* New York: Longman.

Bouton, C., and R. Y. Garth, eds. 1983. *Learning in Groups.* New Directions in Teaching and Learning, vol. 14. San Francisco: Jossey-Bass.

Huston, M. M., and C. Oberman. 1989. Making Communication: A Theoretical Framework for Educating End-Users of Online Bibliographic Information Retrieval Systems. *The Reference Librarian* 24: 199-211.

Inhelder, B., and J. Piaget. 1958. *The Growth of Logical Thinking: From Childhood to Adolescence.* New York: Basic Books.

Karplus, R. 1976. *Science Teaching and the Development of Reasoning.* San Francisco: National Association for Research in Science Teaching. (ERIC Document Reproduction Service No. ED123128.)

Keresztesi, M. 1982. The Science of Bibliography: Theoretical Implications for Bibliographic Instruction. In *Theories of Bibliographic Education: Designs for Teaching,* ed. C. Oberman and K. Strauch. New York: R. R. Bowker.

Kuhlthau, C. C. 1987. An Emerging Theory of Library Instruction. *School Library Media Quarterly* 16, no. 1: 23-28.

———. 1988. Developing a Model of the Library Search Process: Cognitive and Affective Aspects. *RQ* 28, no. 2: 232-42.

McInnis, R. 1982. Do Metaphors Make Good Sense in Teaching Research Strategy? In *Theories of Bibliographic Education: Designs for Teaching,* ed. C. Oberman and K. Strauch. New York: R. R. Bowker.

Mellon, C. A. 1986. Library Anxiety: A Grounded Theory and Its Development. *College & Research Libraries* 47, no. 2: 160-65.

Momenee, G. 1987. Asking the Right Question: Why Not InfoTrac? *Research Strategies* 5, no. 4: 186-90.

Oberman, C. 1983. Question Analysis and the Learning Cycle. *Research Strategies* 1, no. 1: 22-30.

Oberman, C., and R. A. Linton. 1982. Guided Design: Teaching Library Research as Problem-Solving. In *Theories of Bibliographic Education: Designs for Teaching,* ed. C. Oberman and K. Strauch. New York: R. R. Bowker.

Oberman, C., and K. Strauch, eds. 1982. *Theories of Bibliographic Education: Designs for Teaching.* New York: R. R. Bowker.

Orwell, G. 1949. *1984.* New York: Harcourt Brace Jovanovich.

Paul, R. 1990. *Critical Thinking: What Every Person Needs to Survive in a Rapidly Changing World.* Rohnert Park, Calif.: Center for Critical Thinking and Moral Critique, Sonoma State University.

Piaget, J. 1972. Intellectual Evolution from Adolescence to Adulthood. *Human Development* 15, no. 1: 1-12.

Reichel, M., and M. A. Ramey, eds. 1987. *Conceptual Frameworks for Bibliographic Education: Theory into Practice.* Littleton, Colo.: Libraries Unlimited.

Rudd, M. J., and J. Rudd. 1986. The Impact of the Information Explosion on Library Users: Overload or Opportunity? *The Journal of Academic Librarianship* 12, no. 5: 304-7.

Shaw, W. 1988. Technology and Transformation in Academic Libraries. In *Libraries and the Search for Academic Excellence,* ed. P. S. Breivik and R. Wedgeworth. Metuchen, N.J.: Scarecrow Press.

Shill, H. B. 1987. Bibliographic Instruction: Planning for the Electronic Information Environment. *College & Research Libraries* 48, no. 5: 433-53.

Smith, E. 1990. *The Librarian, the Scholar, and the Future of the Research Library.* New York: Greenwood Press.

Tomlinson-Keasey, C. 1975. *A Search for the Component Operations of Formal Operations.* Unpublished paper presented at the Society for Research in Child Development Convention, Denver, Colorado.

Wiberley, S. E., Jr., and R. A. Daugherty. 1988. Users' Persistence in Scanning Lists of References. *College & Research Libraries* 49, no. 2: 149-56.

Williams, L. 1990. Decisions, Decisions, Decisions: Enough! Too Many Choices in the Marketplace. *New York Times*, February 14: C1.

York, C. C., L. Sabol, B. Gratch, and J. Pursel. 1988. Computerized Reference Sources: One-Stop Shopping or Part of a Search Strategy? *Research Strategies* 6, no. 1: 8-17.

ESSAYS

Introduction

To celebrate its first fifteen years, LIRT sponsored a writing contest open to anyone with something to say about library instruction in the information age. That competition reflected LIRT's operating philosophy: library instruction is truly a generic with principles common to all types of libraries. Therefore, everyone interested in library instruction has much to give to and take from the other, thus encouraging "a real dialog around the issues, problems, and opportunities of library user education" (LIRT membership brochure, 1993).

The contest planners chose to focus the essays on the effects of electronic technology; first on the way people obtain and use information and then on how this, in turn, affects library instruction. The committee produced the following statement to guide the contestants:

Information for a New Age: Redefining the Librarian?

The Information Age has seen rapid growth both in the volume of data and of information, both published and unpublished. Technologies employed to manage this growing volume require changes in the skills needed to find and evaluate information. Acquiring information literacy skills will enable people to master change rather than allowing change to master them.

What is the instructional role of libraries and librarians in this Information Age? Library service needs to be examined in light of the exponential growth in information and in the changing technology of accessing it. Among areas affected by these changes are meeting the needs of remote users, providing a full range of the variety of information sources that become more and more complex, addressing the widening gap between the information rich and the information poor, and serving an increasingly diverse user population.

Information users try to find meaning in vast amounts of data while struggling to learn new technological skills which will transfer to their next contact with Information Age technology. But many lack the critical thinking skills requisite to defining a problem, choosing the best strategies for identifying and obtaining data, and then evaluating found data to decide which items best address the problem.

Information Age data and technologies impact librarians too. Librarians have traditionally viewed face-to-face interaction with library users as the ideal model of service. With the advent of new technology, librarians also must assist remote users, who may be technologically illiterate or may be more sophisticated technologically than most librarians. Librarians will also continue to serve users who have a great deal more subject knowledge than they do, but now they are faced with a rapidly increasing number of bibliographic and nonbibliographic databases in many subject fields, and the subject specialists needing assistance with these databases may also be remote users.

Given this situation, it is vital to clarify the instructional role of libraries and librarians in the 1990's and beyond. How will it change? What aspects will stay the same? How should librarians address the dichotomy between the ideal model and rapidly changing reality? Are the concepts of bibliographic instruction too narrow for the significant role of information instructors and mediators in the 1990's and on into the 21st century?

The responses were as varied as the committee had hoped. Entrants expressed differing approaches and issues within our broad topic. The peer review process was begun by practicing library instruction librarians selected by the committee. Three librarians reviewed each paper on the basis of topic, writing style, mastery of the literature, originality, and clarity. These reviews became the basis on which the committee chose the four winning essays that comprise this volume.

Although the concept of a new "information age" shaped the contest theme with many specific references to technology as a driving force of such newness, the authors chose to address issues that downplay technology and emphasize critical thinking skills. These authors featured libraries as theaters where patrons acted out the transference of information needs from data, to knowledge, to solutions. As you read, we believe you will find this common thread connecting the essays: "library instruction" has as much to do with human mental processes as it has to do with libraries and the information they organize and hold. Thus "Redefining the Librarian" has served to revalidate the role many of us have sought to play during these first fifteen LIRT years.

Abigail Loomis (First Place Platinum), Janice A. Sauer (Second Place Gold), Daniel Callison (Third Place Silver), and Leigh Kilman (Fourth Place Bronze) all address the challenges facing librarians involved with library instruction as we enter the twenty-first century. These four authors were honored with presentations at the 1992 Annual ALA Conference in San Francisco during the LIRT program. We're pleased to share their enthusiasm, insight, and expertise with you.

11

Building Coalitions
for Information Literacy

Abigail Loomis

The paradigm of information literacy has had a profound impact on instruction programs in libraries across the country and, even more fundamentally, on the perceived mission of the libraries that support these programs, whether they be academic, public, or school.[1] It has led many of us who are instruction librarians to reassess and redefine both our own roles and those of our programs and services by giving us a broader and more socially meaningful context in which to develop them. Much of the attention given to this paradigm both in the literature of librarianship and in its conference programs and workshops focuses on how information literacy as a goal has transformed not only *what* we teach but *how* we teach. But the influence of this paradigm extends—or can extend—far beyond pedagogical concerns and issues for it also provides librarians and, in particular, instruction librarians with a powerful tool for building new coalitions and redefining old ones outside the library. Such coalitions are critical if we are to succeed in empowering students with the knowledge and skills they will need not just to survive but to thrive in a world driven more and more by information. The need for these coalitions, their nature, and the skills that we as instruction librarians need in order to build them are the focus of this paper.

That a variety of coalitions is needed if information literacy programs are to have the broad, integrated base of support they need to be successful has become increasingly apparent, particularly to those directly involved in developing such programs. Even more apparent, however, is that at some levels, particularly administrative ones, these coalitions often are woefully weak, if not, for all practical purposes, nonexistent. If one is an academic librarian, one need look no further for evidence of this deficiency than in the spate of reports on higher education written during the last decade in response to increasingly forceful calls for educational reform from legislators, parents, students, educators—the nation at large.[2]

A modified version of this paper was presented at the annual conference of the South Carolina Library Association in Columbia, S.C., October 18, 1990.

These reports share several important themes that relate implicitly to information literacy instruction. First, their underlying premise is that undergraduate education in the United States is seriously deficient and that major reforms are needed in order to empower students with the skills and knowledge they need to succeed in an increasingly complex society. Second, these reports all focus on the curricular reforms that, it is unanimously agreed, are the key to getting higher education back on track. Finally, all of these reports take a general back-to-basics stance in articulating these curricular reforms, though this common position is divided between those that define "basics" in terms of core courses and those that define them in terms of proficiencies.

In reading these reports, we discover much common ground between those on campus who are concerned with reforming and revitalizing undergraduate education and those of us in libraries who are committed to promoting information literacy. The issues by both are often strikingly similar, if not quite identical. For example, active learning and critical thinking are cornerstones of the curricular reforms proposed in most of the reports. Even the most cursory glance through the literature on library instruction published during the past five years indicates that these two approaches are central to many information literacy programs. Authors of these reports on higher education deplore the paralyzing effects on students of what one calls "those invitations to passivity and pencil-pushing," namely the lecture/textbook/reserve reading approach to teaching so prevalent in many universities and colleges.[3] Librarians repeatedly voice a similar concern about the emphasis placed—not just in education, but in society at large—on spoonfed, prepackaged information. In response, they have developed resource-based learning programs that emphasize critical thinking approaches to information no matter how it is packaged.

Like those of us in library instruction, educators interested in reform are concerned with shifting the almost exclusive concentration on subject content in the current educational experience to a process-oriented focus on the learning experience itself. As one report argued, curriculum structure should not be based on content—factual matter—but on _how_ that subject matter is absorbed or assimilated.[4] Learning in an information society cannot stop with the awarding of a diploma; in order to prepare students to survive and, indeed, thrive in such a world they must be able to re-educate themselves over and over again throughout their lives. Thus the focus in the educational process must shift from solely teaching content to also teaching students _how_ to learn. Obviously such a process-oriented, lifelong learning approach lies at the heart of many information literacy programs as well.

As are many information literacy librarians, educational reformers are concerned with teaching students basic skills or proficiencies such as communication and critical thinking skills. An urgent theme in every one of these reports is the crucial importance of teaching students the skills they need to use information, knowledge, and ideas critically although, unfortunately, this theme is all too seldom expressed in terms of information literacy.

Like us, the authors of these reports understand the need for teaching these basic skills across the curriculum. They, too, understand that the process of learning these basic proficiencies must be one of cumulative and repetitive acquisition rather than a "one-shot" occurrence. They would wholeheartedly agree with Patricia Schuman that "our mission is to facilitate understanding through knowledge," though they would expand "our" to include not just libraries but all the resources—human and material—of the campus and the community at large.[5] They, too, would agree that in order for students to give meaning to today's glut of information, all of us in academe have a responsibility to teach students the integrative skills that will transform data into knowledge, and information into ideas.

Educators share our awareness that in order for these reforms to be realized there is a critical need to re-examine the roles of some of the key players. In this redefinition, faculty—and, we would add, librarians—would serve as facilitators or guides rather than founts of information in the learning process, while students, rather than acting as passive vessels in a Dickensian classroom into which information is indiscriminately poured, will become co-inquirers, assuming active co-responsibility for their own learning. And finally, the authors of these reports describe the desired fruits of their educational labors in terms that are strikingly similar—and some might say, equally idealistic—to those found in the final report of the ALA Presidential Commission on Information Literacy, as well as other recent library publications.[6] Like us, they hope to prepare students for a lifetime of independent, self-motivated learning. The ideal educational process defined by these reports is one that develops in students attitudes of continuous inquiry, analysis, and discovery that are essential for success in the multitude of roles they will have to play in this information age. The ideal educational process is described as one that teaches the skills and knowledge needed to nurture this attitude long after these students have graduated. Again, one is struck by the parallels between this description and the goals of many information literacy programs!

After reviewing these reports one would assume that information literacy librarians have strong allies in those who set the goals and standards for higher education and in those administrators who try to realize these goals on campuses across the country. But this is not the case. The vast majority of the links between the educational concerns of "them and us" just described are nowhere to be found in the reports themselves. Teaching students to find, evaluate, and use information is indeed a major goal of the educational mission outlined in these reports, but the role of the library in achieving that goal is all too painfully absent. In fact the majority of the reports actually make no mention of libraries at all. The few that do view libraries along traditional lines, as repositories that passively support the learning process by storing materials that some students may use sometime. These proponents of the "library as warehouse" tend to lump libraries and computer labs together as support facilities that must be "healthy" in order to provide quality education.[7]

In only two of these reports are libraries discussed in any detail. In Frank Newman's *Higher Education and the American Resurgence*, librarians themselves are mentioned, but, unfortunately, as the following passage indicates, it is much to our detriment: "Library personnel, though now fully competent to handle the library automation that has taken place, have neither the education nor the emotional commitment to prepare for the shift in outlook required to change from owning, cataloging, and lending, to becoming electronic data sleuths ready to link a student or faculty member to someone else's data bank."[8]

Since Newman wrote this in 1985, he has become a strong champion of the role not just of libraries but of librarians in the educational mission of the university,[9] but such conversions have been lamentably infrequent. Only one of these six reports, Ernest Boyer's *College*, sponsored by the Carnegie Foundation, fully recognizes the active teaching role of the library and the significant contributions that libraries can make in helping a campus achieve educational reforms.[10]

Boyer's work is very much the exception. All the rest make it clear that "the educational establishment and its leaders . . . [see] no role for librarians or libraries in issues related to quality education."[11] Richard Dougherty's response nearly a decade ago to the omission of libraries from the recommendations for primary and secondary education in *A Nation at Risk* applies equally to these more recent reports. The absence of library involvement in these proposals for reform reflects, as he then said, "the reality that libraries are not judged central to the current problem"—a perception that might be cause for celebration except that neither are they perceived to be central to the solution.[12] It is indeed ironic, as Patricia Breivik notes, that libraries "which are the primary access point to information in all disciplines" on campus should be excluded from reform agendas in which a priority is preparing students to succeed in the Information Age.[13]

This relegation of the teaching role of the library to the periphery or, more often, to oblivion is mirrored in varying degrees on individual campuses. Though many campus administrators and faculty may bemoan the minimal or near-minimal information literacy skills of their students (though they usually do not label these skills as such), a goodly number do not connect the library with the solution to this problem. Though many campus administrators and faculty call for "revitalizing" education to prepare students for success in our complex, information-dominated society, few think to include librarians on the committees and task forces planning these reforms. Or, if they do include librarians, more often than not it is as spokespersons not for library instruction but for the collections to ensure that the library's physical resources will be able to support the reforms—the traditional perspective of the library as static repository. For many, the active educational role played by librarians is still unknown. Where that role is known, it often translates in the minds of many on campus as just "doing a tour" or showing students how to use *Readers' Guide*.

The reality both on the national level as reflected in the reports and on the campus level, as Breivik observes, is that very often "even among educators committed to change, there is little or no understanding that librarians have any contribution to make to learning besides their traditional warehouse role." And she goes on to put a large part of the blame squarely on the shoulders of librarians: "Despite all that we [librarians] have to offer within the search for educational excellence, we seem [though unintentionally] to have successfully managed to keep it a secret."[14]

To many on campuses and in communities at large, our instructional programs are invisible or, if visible, their link to broader educational issues outside the library is unclear. It is clear that this condition of invisibility must change, and it is equally clear that responsibility for making these changes must lie with front-line librarians, not just with library administrators. Those of us who are directly involved in information literacy instruction need to promote aggressively not just our programs but, more importantly, the rich and active potential of the library to help the campus realize educational reforms. To do so new coalitions between librarians and administrators and between librarians and faculty will have to be built and old ones redefined. And they will have to be built at all levels of higher education—not just on the individual campus level, but on state and national levels as well. In addition, instruction librarians will have to look beyond the world of academe to the community at large and build stronger coalitions with its providers of information, particularly school and public libraries. Building these partnerships places new demands on librarians, demands that require fresh attitudes and new skills.

The first coalition-building task to which we librarians must turn our attention involves no one else but us. Before doing anything else, we must recognize and define the role that librarians can and should play in the educational mission of our institutions. We also must recognize and accept that our contribution to that educational mission involves much more than making information resources available on demand. It also involves teaching—teaching students how to find, select, evaluate, and use that information effectively and efficiently.

Only after we have accepted and clearly defined our instructional role can we begin to build coalitions with potential partners outside the library by going out and "selling" our instructional role to the campus and to the community. The term "selling" is being used very deliberately here, even though attaching marketing concepts to what is essentially a service-oriented organization may not be a comfortable fit for all of us. The fit may be even less comfortable when I add that the kind of selling we need to do requires strong political skills.

Many librarians feel uneasy attaching the word "politics" to what they do. It carries sinister connotations of backroom deals made on the basis of self-interest and power rather than from any altruistic principles. But the uneasiness has other roots as well. Even when stripped of its more negative connotations, the notion of politics when juxtaposed with what we do in libraries and, in particular, in our information literacy programs seems incongruous. The association seems to diminish what we do. Libraries disinterestedly provide services whose value to the whole academic community should be obvious. We should not have to "sell" them, to justify their existence, or to negotiate for their rightful place in academic life and, more particularly, in the teaching life of the campus.

But if politics is defined more positively as the art of negotiation, persuasion, compromise, and strategizing in order to achieve certain objectives, then politics is most definitely and most necessarily involved in building coalitions for information literacy. Most educators agree that campus governance structures and decision-making processes are extremely political—"Byzantine" is the description one report uses. Woodrow Wilson confessed that he left Princeton to go to Washington in order to find a less complicated political system.[15] In *Academic Librarianship in a Transformational Age*, Allen Veaner suggests that, though the public may persist in its stereotype "of academe as the ivory tower and the professoriate as a service enterprise peopled by a self-sacrificing intellectual nobility," the reality is more like "organized anarchy," "a precariously balanced hotbed of conflicting interests and warring powers—centralization and decentralization ever battling but in constant stalemate."[16] One faculty member recently assured me that "You're expected to be political on campus; if you're not, they wonder what's wrong with you." It is essential then that we, too, recognize and accept the political nature—sometimes manifested in the positive sense of the word—of the campus environment and learn to work within it.

In advocating the integration of information literacy into the curriculum we are, in essence, being political, competing with a number of other worthwhile programs for a portion of the campus budget as well as a portion of a student's time during his or her years in school. We need to make the case campuswide that it is essential for students to spend part of that time learning the skills they need to become information literate. And we need to make that case, not in a vacuum talking to each other, but at the level of department and college curriculum committees, where new programs are regularly proposed—often very persuasively. Our success may depend on how effectively we define the role of information literacy not only as a set of skills important in and of themselves but also as a set of skills that are important because they can help other programs achieve their goals. Information literacy gives us a strong advantage in making a case because, like other basic proficiencies, its value cuts across all disciplines and covers a wide range of needs.

Successfully championing such a cause in this politically charged environment undoubtedly requires skillful politicking! Information literacy librarians must not only recognize and accept politics as an academic fact of life but develop the political skills and sensitivity needed to be strong, effective negotiators for their programs. Regrettably, the problem for many of us in user education is that the opportunities for fine-tuning our political skills in such a context often are still very limited. In many cases our immediate challenge both on campus and on the national level is simply to create opportunities to become part of the reform debate.

A final but all-important point on this question of "politics" needs to be made. Most of us who are information literacy librarians have necessarily become adept in the politics of building coalitions with faculty. After all, the faculty/librarian partnership is the cornerstone of most of our programs and much has been written in the literature about ways to develop and nurture these relationships. What is newer for us, however, is the need to develop coalitions with campus administrators. Because information literacy is a proficiency that cuts across the disciplines and is dependent on cumulative acquisition through a building-block approach, it needs to be integrated throughout the curriculum. Broad programs call for broad coalitions and, in the case of information literacy, for administrative as well as individual faculty support. So, while we need to continue to build our traditional coalitions from the bottom up by working with individual faculty, we also need to learn to build new coalitions from the top down with campus administrators and campuswide planning committees.

The important word here is "learn." There is still much for us to learn in developing these new partnerships. For it is one thing to knock on the door of a faculty member to talk about our instructional program and quite another to advocate that proposal at a campuswide curriculum committee meeting made up largely of faculty members, a number of whom see little if any relationship between the library's instructional program and the committee's charge and who, therefore, may have no idea why we are even there. We must develop the skills needed to work confidently within this broader political environment.

What do we need to learn or to keep in mind when building these coalitions? The first two points need to be addressed together for they are closely interrelated. First, it is important for information literacy librarians to understand what the issues and problems of concern are for those with whom we are building our coalitions whether they be faculty or campus administrators. Second, it is essential that we make the case for information literacy programs within the context of their goals, their needs, and their concerns, not ours. To elaborate on this a bit, it is important to understand administrators' and faculty's perspective in order to present the case for information literacy in a context that is meaningful and, therefore, attractive to them. In order to understand administrative perspectives, we need to keep current with national issues in higher education and with the ways those issues get translated into campus concerns. It is not enough simply to be aware of reports such as those mentioned earlier in this paper. We must be familiar with their details and with the issues—both explicit and implicit—that they raise. We also need to understand campus governance structure and where in it the real power for making decisions about the curriculum reposes. We need to be aware of and be a part of campus communication channels so that we can become proactively involved in the curricular decisions that will inevitably have an impact on our educational role. At the faculty level we need to understand how faculty respond to demands for educational reform; what constraints, such as faculty evaluation systems, may prohibit them from experimenting with the changes in pedagogy called for by these reforms; and what perceptions they have of the library and of its role—or non-role—in revitalizing their students' learning experiences.

Such a broad understanding is essential if we are to "package" our information literacy proposals in ways that are meaningful not just for our own library administrators but for campus administrators and faculty outside the library. We need to show both faculty and administrators how the library's instructional programs can help them solve their problems and achieve their goals. As Frank Newman—the reformed Frank Newman—noted in a paper he presented several years ago at a joint conference of librarians and university administrators:

> Remember that presidents, faculties, deans, legislators and governors pay attention when someone proposes to solve their problems. They do not pay attention much when you propose to solve your problems. The need for libraries then can be couched in terms of solving the major problems on the desks of the president, faculty or others, and you will find a ready willingness to listen.[17]

Here the term *information literacy* has powerful potential, for it links our programs to many of the goals spawned by the current movement for reform in higher education. Terms like *bibliographic* or *library instruction* may be less effective selling points for, as Breivik suggests, they tend to "reinforce the perception of something which stands alone from the curriculum and that is useful only within the libraries."[18] I would also add that such a perception can and often does throw an adversarial element into these relationships that is both unnecessary and counterproductive. The power of the information literacy paradigm is that it is relevant to any number of campus priorities—assessments of students' learning achievements, recruitment and retention of minorities, writing-across-the-curriculum, and so on. It is a powerful tool for making the links that too often, as we have seen, have been conspicuous only by their absence between the agenda of higher education and that of the library.

Finally, in building coalitions within academe it is essential that we aggressively seek out new forums for making a case for our instructional role in higher education both on the campus level and on the state and national levels. Information literacy librarians have always targeted individual faculty who seem sympathetic to the library and open to innovation for program expansion. Obviously we need to continue to do so, for such partnerships lie at the heart of our programs. But in reality, faculty/librarian partnerships can and often do prove to be shaky foundations for our programs in terms of long-term planning, for they most frequently are personality, not program, dependent.[19] We also need, therefore, to put greater emphasis on seeking out broader departmental, college, or campuswide initiatives—for example, the development of a new department or campuswide program—that hold more long-term promise for our programs. In order to do this, we and our library administrators need to be more aggressive in making sure that we are plugged into the right communication networks on campus so that we know when new programs are first being discussed and can campaign to become a part of the planning/implementation team at this initial stage rather than at the end, when the plan is a *fait accompli* and we can do no more than react.

The same outreach efforts must be implemented on state and national levels as well. Librarians spend too much time talking to each other and not enough time talking to non-librarian groups with similar educational concerns. Had librarians been on the committees that wrote the reports mentioned earlier, there is no doubt libraries would have figured as key players in the educational team. These national committees have made and will continue to make recommendations that have an impact on our campuses and, therefore, on our libraries. The voice of libraries needs to be heard in their deliberations. We also need to dramatize the link between information literacy and quality education for the organizations that determine accreditation standards so that more of them become like the Middle States Commission on Higher Education, which considers the quality of a library's instructional program as well as the size of its collection in its evaluation criteria.[20] We also need to champion information literacy in academic journals outside our profession and at conferences of higher education associations.[21] In turn we need to invite more non-librarians interested in higher education issues to participate in our own conferences.[22] Such dialogues can only serve to build the national coalitions essential both to information literacy programs and to the reform efforts of higher education.

Finally, information literacy librarians need to build coalitions off-campus as well as on. Much attention has been given in library instruction to the need to build "bridges" between primary and secondary school library education programs and those in college and university libraries. The need for such a continuum, though it is not always realized, largely because of inadequate resources, is obvious to both school and academic librarians and has been discussed frequently in the literature. But another important component of the information literacy continuum is the public library and that has until quite recently been largely ignored by academic librarians. While we speak of the information literacy continuum as taking a person from childhood through adulthood, far too often discussion seems to terminate abruptly with the graduation of a student from college. And yet the whole purpose of information literacy programs from the beginning of the continuum through its secondary and postsecondary phases is to prepare students to become lifelong learners. Where do these lifelong learners continue to learn once they graduate? More often than not, in the public library. A more active dialogue and partnership between those of us in the middle of the continuum and those at this end could benefit all. Academic instruction librarians certainly would gain from such communication in a number of ways.

First, it is clear that many public librarians have already had to come to terms with the political nature of their work. The success of their libraries' programs depends greatly on their political skills—their ability to persuade policy-making, fund-allocating legislators of the value of their services to the community. Those of us front-line instruction librarians in academe who are new to this political role can learn much about these skills from our colleagues in public libraries. For both groups, information literacy is a powerful selling point for our programs, whether to state and city legislators, campus administrators, or grant-giving agencies. In exploring together our different perspectives of information literacy, perhaps we can discover rich, new meanings in the paradigm and, more importantly, find new ways to "sell" our educational programs to our respective communities.

Second, because we in academic user education programs try to prepare our students to succeed as adults in an information age, what better "post-test" to find out how we are doing than to talk to the librarians who work with our students once they have graduated? Are the information skills we teach students in our instructional sessions applicable only to their "academic" pursuits? Or do these skills have the broader applications we hope they have—applications that will empower our students by enabling them to find and to use information effectively and efficiently in their personal, civic, and professional lives? Certainly, coalitions between academic and public librarians will provide us with some answers to these questions and help us to design instructional programs that will address the varied information needs of students in the multitude of roles they must play as adults after they graduate. Multi-type library organizations such as ALA's Library Instruction Round Table nurture such coalitions by providing public and academic, as well as school and special librarians, with forums for this much-needed dialogue.

Information literacy provides a rich context within which to develop our programs. It also is a powerful tool for strengthening existing coalitions and for building new ones. In order for us to exploit the full potential of this paradigm, librarians, especially those of us in academe, must learn new skills as well as continue to refine old ones. The effort is well worth it, however, for this combination of old and new skills may make it possible for the value of libraries and their educational potential—both in academe and in the community at large—to at long last become fully realized. Perhaps then the traditional contention that "the library is the heart of the university" to which so many on campus pay lip service will become more than a mere platitude.

NOTES

1.   There are, of course, those who question the basic concept of information literacy. See, for example, Connie Miller and Patricia Tegler, "In Pursuit of Windmills: Librarians and the Determination to Instruct," *Reference Librarian*, no. 18 (summer 1987): 119-34. Most well known, perhaps, among those who recently have challenged the value of the information literacy bandwagon is Tom Eadie who raises the old "instruction vs. information" debate in "Immodest Proposals," *Library Journal* 115 (October 15, 1990): 42-45; and in "Redefining BI for a New Information Environment: A Symposium," *Research Strategies* 10 (summer 1992): 104-21. Lawrence J. McCrank takes a different tack in this debate, suggesting that in taking up the cause of information literacy, librarians may have taken on far more than they can—or should—handle in "Information Literacy: A Bogus Bandwagon?" *Library Journal* 116 (May 1, 1991): 38-42. He continues his thoughtful exploration of the implications of the term in "Academic Programs for Information Literacy: Theory and Structure," *RQ* 31 (summer 1992): 485-97.

2.   The most notable calls for reform in higher education appear in the following reports: U.S. National Institute of Education, *Involvement in Learning* (Washington, D.C.: National Institute on Education, 1984); William Bennett, *To Reclaim a Legacy: Report on the Humanities in Higher Education* (Washington, D.C.: National Endowment for the Humanities, 1984); Association of American Colleges, *Integrity in the College Curriculum: A Report to the Academic Community* (Washington, D.C.: Association of American Colleges, 1985); Frank Newman, *Higher Education and the American Resurgence* (Princeton, N.J.: Princeton University Press, 1985); Ernest L. Boyer, *College: The Undergraduate Experience in America* (New York: Harper, 1987); and Association of American Colleges, *A New Vitality in General Education* (Washington, D.C.: Association of American Colleges, 1988). Brief summaries of these reports and of librarians' responses to some of them can be found in Shirley Ulferts Black, "Educational Reform and Libraries: A Report and Bibliography," *RQ* 28 (spring 1989): 321-24.

3.   Association of American Colleges, *Integrity in the College Curriculum: A Report to the Academic Community* (Washington, D.C.: Association of American Colleges, 1985), 16.

4.   Ibid., 24-26.

5.   Patricia Glass Schuman, "Reclaiming Our Technological Future," *Library Journal* 115 (March 1, 1990): 38.

6. American Library Association, Presidential Committee on Information Literacy, *Final Report* (Chicago: American Library Association, 1989).

7. In 1989, *Liberal Education*, a journal published by the Association of American Colleges, published an article in which "leaders in higher education" were asked to envision a curriculum for the year 2000. Of the thirteen interviewed, though several mentioned that special skills would be needed to survive in our complex information society, only one, David Riesman of Harvard, mentioned libraries and the need for students to do more library work. See "Curriculum in the Year 2000: Perspectives," *Liberal Education* 75 (January/February 1989): 26-35.

8. Newman, *Higher Education*, 152.

9. See, for example, Frank Newman, "Academic Libraries and the American Resurgence," in *Libraries and the Search for Academic Excellence*, ed. Patricia Senn Breivik and Robert Wedgeworth (Metuchen, N.J.: Scarecrow Press, 1988), 173-86.

10. Boyer, *College*, 160-67.

11. Patricia Senn Breivik, "Politics for Bridging the Gap," *Reference Librarian*, no. 24 (1989): 6.

12. Richard M. Dougherty, " 'Stemming the Tide' of Mediocrity: The Academic Library Response," in *Libraries and the Learning Society: Papers in Response to a Nation at Risk* (Chicago: American Library Association, 1984), 5.

13. Breivik, "Politics," 6.

14. Ibid., 7.

15. Irving Spitzberg, "It's Academic: The Politics of the Curriculum in American Higher Education," in *Libraries and the Search for Academic Excellence*, ed. Patricia Senn Breivik and Robert Wedgeworth (Metuchen, N.J.: Scarecrow Press, 1988), 153.

16. Allen B. Veaner, *Academic Librarianship in a Transformational Age: Program, Politics, and Personnel* (Boston: G. K. Hall, 1989), 32-33.

17. Newman, "Academic Libraries," 175.

18. Breivik, "Politics," 8.

19. For a thought-provoking exploration of these "shaky foundations," see Eugene A. Engeldinger, "Frustration Management in a Course-Integrated Bibliographic Instruction Program," *RQ* 31 (fall 1992): 20-24.

20. See Mignon Adams interview with Howard L. Simmons, the executive director of the Commission on Higher Education of the Middle States Association of Colleges and Schools: Mignon Adams, in "The Role of Academic Libraries in Teaching and Learning," *College & Research Libraries News* 53 (July/August 1992): 442, 444-45.

21. Patricia Breivik is one of a small but growing number of instruction librarians who not only publish in journals outside the library field but often coauthor these publications with faculty and campus administrators from outside the library profession. For a recent example of her cooperative efforts, see Patricia Senn Breivik and Dan L. Jones, "Information Literacy: Liberal Education for the Information Age," *Liberal Education* 79 (winter 1993): 24-29.

22. In the past several years, both the Library Instruction Round Table (LIRT) and the Bibliographic Instruction Section (BIS) of ALA have moved in this direction, including nonlibrarian educators in several of their annual ALA conference programs. For example, LIRT's 1992 program "Information for a New Age" included several nonlibrarian speakers, and Howard Simmons was the keynote speaker at BIS's 1993 program "Coping with Chaos, Thriving on Change."

12

Conversation 101:
Process, Development, and
Collaboration

Janice A. Sauer
University of South Alabama Library

As civilized human beings we are the inheritors, neither of an inquiry about ourselves and the world, nor of an accumulating body of information, but of a conversation, begun in the primeval forests and extended and made more articulate in the course of centuries. It is a conversation which goes on both in public and within each of ourselves. . . . Education, properly speaking, is an initiation into the skill and partnership of this conversation in which we learn to recognize the voices, to distinguish the proper occasions of utterance, and in which we acquire the intellectual and moral habits appropriate to conversation. And it is this conversation which, in the end, gives place and character to every human activity and utterance.[1]

Michael Oakeshott

At about the time I was finishing my thirtieth slide show and tour of freshmen through a university library as a graduate assistant in Bibliographic Instruction, I read Tom Eadie's article "Immodest Proposals," which expressed thoughts lurking in my mind that I was afraid to articulate.[2] How could I dare consider the obviously heretical position that I was just wasting my time doing bibliographic instruction? I had learned early in the MLS program to mouth the accepted wisdom that library literacy is essential for every undergraduate and that bibliographic instruction is the most efficient way to instill library literacy. If I actually believed this, why then did I so often feel that I was wasting my time with students who weren't interested in my lectures ingeniously designed to present all of this valuable information? I had entered the library degree program thinking that by learning as much as I could about libraries I would be able to help students access the information they need—but by granting the validity of this frustration I knew I would have to reconstruct bibliographic instruction's raison d'être or accept Eadie's view.

135

Now after two years as the Instructional Services Librarian of a large, comprehensive university, I know that Tom Eadie is wrong. I do still have a few, but it is no longer one about the value of my role in the educational process. Two years of teaching and providing reference service has made it very clear that what academic libraries and university students need now, more than ever, are real teachers, not just more information organizers and fact servers.

Eadie is right only if we accept his definition of bibliographic instruction built on his paradigm of library and librarian. To be meaningful, bibliographic instruction must be understood differently from his commonly accepted definition. This essay would be a very immodest proposal indeed if it attempted to refute all the definitions of library, librarian, learning theory, and bibliographic instruction objectives prevalent in library literature today. But there are three major ideas that this paper will address in order to clarify exactly why bibliographic instruction, as it is so often taught, falls short of what it must be in order to be successful. And at the same time, solutions for these failings will be proposed. As a result this paper will not be a nice, tight study but instead an overview of three areas that are essential to the definition and justification of bibliographic instruction: the change in understanding of the structure of knowledge in the twentieth century, the change in the understanding of the developmental levels of eighteen to twenty-two year olds, and finally the change in pedagogy that is necessitated by these first two changes.

The first issue involves *what* the library has to offer: facts or knowledge. For if it is knowledge, then one must recognize the revolution in thinking about how scientific knowledge is constructed. This change has affected our conception of all knowledge and therefore it should affect the paradigm we have for library. If absolute truth is ultimately unknowable, then the library can no longer be the warehouse for storing the books in which such truth resides. It is the place that allows "conversations" about ideas to occur across time and cultures. Therefore the library's mission is to allow and encourage the questions and not to dispense answers. As long as the paradigm is in dispute, librarians will talk at cross-purposes about their roles and that of bibliographic instruction.

The second vital issue concerns our understanding of the *audience* of bibliographic instruction. No one would write a speech without knowing their audience. And yet undergraduate library educators constantly decry their lack of results while doing just that. It is time that the message is geared to the audience. William Perry's study of undergraduates' developmental processes gives librarians, as it has given undergraduate educators in other academic fields, an insight into the mind of an eighteen year old and what happens over the four years of college.

The third section will show that by using the new library paradigm and William Perry's discoveries, it is possible to postulate new *methods* of doing bibliographic instruction that are viable, relevant, and actually creative. By developing objectives that are much more clearly defined and having a theoretical basis it should also be possible to evaluate the success of the effort. Collaborative learning is beginning to be recognized as a means by which students can become active participants in the exploration of knowledge instead of just passive recipients.

None of these concepts is new but they seem to have hit a substantial barrier at the library door; however, they are beginning to filter into the library from other fields. As a result, the librarian will no longer be able to limit him/herself to the role of collector, organizer, and disseminator of information. The librarian must become involved in the educational and developmental processes that begin and end outside of the library door in the structure, use, and especially the creation of knowledge.

Each year Hannelore B. Rader presents in the winter issue of *Reference Service Review* an annotated bibliography of articles published that year on library orientation and instruction. Of the over 100 articles relating to academic libraries in recent bibliographies, the vast majority have to do with ways to teach library retrieval skills effectively, efficiently, and in a variety of ways including slide presentations, computerized lessons, and interactive video.[3] There is a generally accepted recognition that library skills are important; that they are not self-evident; that they are becoming more complex as the library becomes more automated, and that they can be taught in more and more painless ways. However, only a handful of the articles deal with the theoretical bases of bibliographic instruction or any broader understanding of the function of the library in the overall learning process.

The 1981 Think Tank on Bibliographic Instruction, the first of its kind designed to explore future directions for user education, was soundly criticized in its time for the narrowness of its recommendations and its confusion of means and end.[4] Lori Arp in 1990, discussing the newly coined term "information literacy," concurred that there still has been little progress in our understanding. "Neither term [information literacy or bibliographic instruction] is particularly well defined by theoreticians or practitioners in the field, and so a great deal of confusion will occur unless we continue to articulate the parameters of this question."[5]

All this is to say that much is written in library literature about the role of learning in the library, and very little about the role of the library in learning. Substituting the first concept for the second causes the controversy about the legitimacy of user instruction. This confusion also degrades bibliographic instruction by substituting the means for the end. Only a clear understanding of the real purpose of library user education will end this controversy. The philosophical and theoretical conceptions necessary to define the role of library in learning do exist, but have found only minimal elucidation in the professional literature.

It is certain that Tom Eadie, who has been involved with BI programs, is not just speaking for himself when he discusses user education. "I think user education is a special service of questionable value that arose not because users asked for it, but because librarians thought it would be good for them."[6] He elaborates on the reasons that librarians use to justify BI: libraries are difficult to use, BI is more cost-efficient than reference service, it is effective, it provides an argument for faculty status. When Eadie sums up his stance against BI his position is clear:

> I'm not sure we should be "educating" students but I am sure we should answer their questions. I think (to echo Radford) that we should

dismantle barriers rather than train people to climb over them. I believe that a good system of signage is worth several hundred library tours, that succinct printed guides to topical areas in the reference collection are worth hundreds of ill-attended specialized workshops. In many ways we should go back to the 1960's: not to closed stacks, but to setting things up to be as simple as possible for the majority of students, and providing personal service to those who need more.[7]

There are several implications in his accusations. If what a library user needs is correct answers to questions of fact and historical truth, then the librarian's job is simple—organize that information so that it is as accessible as possible and, when asked, retrieve the correct information.

Eadie's vision of library instruction holds that since librarians find it harder to provide answers than to teach users to find their own, librarians choose the easier path—instruction. For Eadie supplying the answers fulfills his definition of the role of library. It is a position often and loudly held. but such a definition is the crux of the problem.

If a library is a place that a student goes to collect discrete bits of facts, to collect baskets full of accepted truths, or to gather the aphorisms of the collective cultural experience, then yes—there are simple answers and also better methods for teaching someone how to go about finding the desired fact, truth, and answer. There is no argument but that signage and guides can always be improved, and that barriers can and should be brought down. But barriers to what? Eadie's approach to library is an approach to authority—the library becomes a building housing the Encyclopedia of Definitive Knowledge and Absolute Truth. The librarian is then just the page turner and truth server, the Vestal Virgin in the service of this truth. The same mindset is manifested in the studies that use the percentage of right answers found at a reference desk as a gauge for the adequacy of the service. This simplistic paradigm of a library, librarian, and the user's relationship to the library is reiterated often in the literature of BI, and also in articles anguishing over whether librarianship is really a profession.

However, what if the library is a more complex concept than this? The library has indeed collected facts and statistics that should be available to its patrons as ready reference answers. But this service is not essential to the ultimate purpose of an academic library. Its primary function is as a window onto the arguments and questions of the past that have not defined truth, but which are constantly in the process of searching for it in different areas and in different ways. In this case the answers are no longer simply facts to be dispensed. Susanne Langer says, "The 'technique' or treatment of a problem begins with its first expression as a question. The way a question is asked limits and disposes the ways in which any answer to it—right or wrong—may be given."[8] Recently Jane Keefer echoed and extended Langer's statement to the information process:

When we move from an emphasis on getting the right answer to finding out the right question, we enter into the realm of the second view of information as a process. In this model, there are no wrong or right answers, only steps that move the seeker closer to the goals and purposes of a given quest.[9]

CONVERSATIONS:
KNOWLEDGE AS PROCESS

In the twentieth century there has been a radical change in the way the question is asked, and as a result our conception has changed of what knowledge is, and how it is constructed. Once we believed that the more knowledge was like what we believe scientific knowledge to be, the more true it was. Jacob Bronowski states it this way:

> Now, are the atoms real or are they not? And if the atoms are real, are the electrons real or are they not? When we do this decoding, are we discovering something which is in nature, or are we not? Are we creating the concepts out of which we make science, or are they there hidden all the time? Now this is a tremendous intellectual bifurcation. And also a fairly emotional one. For example, the world is pretty well divided into people who are proud of being machines and people who are outraged at the thought of being machines. And the world is, therefore, pretty well divided into people who would like to think that our analysis of nature is a personal and highly imaginative creation and those who would like to think that we are simply discovering what is there.[10]

Clearly it is Bronowski's position that we are not discovering "what is there," but rather are "creating the concepts out of which we make science." Thomas Kuhn, in *The Structure of Scientific Revolutions*, defines a scientific theory as a paradigm that is constructed and accepted by the authority of the scientific community and that is constantly tightened and delineated by this community until it can no longer answer new questions that arise, at which time the whole metaphor is changed and process begins again. In just this way Einstein's universe overthrew the Newtonian metaphor. When theories become strained by experiments that don't fit, the theory changes, not just incrementally and closer to the reality but by radical revolution of thought and imagination. The new paradigm is one that answers more of the old questions but also contains limitations of its own because any one paradigm is restricted by the limitations of vision and viewpoint of the minds that create it.[11]

Isaiah Berlin, a contemporary historian of ideas, has examined the origins of the earlier view of knowledge:

> The ideal that Berlin is so apprehensive of is the Platonic ideal which was reaffirmed, he says, by the Enlightenment and which is still the dominant tradition of Western political thought. This ideal is based on three promises: that all genuine questions have only one true answer, that those answers are knowable and that the answers, all compatible with one another, together form a single coherent whole. Berlin believes these premises are fallacious because they do not take account of "the crooked timber of humanity," and dangerous because they contribute to a kind of philosophical dogmatism that can only result in political tyranny.[12]

How do Bronowski's imaginative creation, Kuhn's paradigm, and Berlin's history of ideas relate to the argument about the validity of bibliographic instruction? The very essence and definition of library is dependent upon how the culture views the structure of knowledge. The change to a multiplistic and process view of knowledge radically alters how teaching academics, librarians among them, view their function. It may not have been possible to give a single correct answer. Now it is not so simple, because each answer is seen as only part of a truth that has a multiplicity of possible answers depending upon the particular social construction given at a particular time and in a particular place. If knowledge is an imaginative construct that changes with time and from culture to culture, who is it that can provide the simple right answers? We have learned through this revolution in science that knowledge is not made up of hierarchical accretions that extend what we know closer to a knowable unitary truth.

Joan M. Bechtel offers a different paradigm for the library:

> To be sure, libraries have traditionally collected the documents of human imagination and action. In doing so they have preserved the ideas and events of history and have become the centers for ongoing conversations in which people speak their opinions, criticize others', and enlarge or restrict the scope of the discussion. Scholars state their thesis in writing, add information to the topic, argue with each other, and even change the direction of the conversation. The primary task, then, of the academic library is to introduce students to the world of scholarly dialogue that spans both space and time and to provide students with the knowledge and skills they need to tap into conversations on an infinite variety of topics and to participate in the critical inquiry and debate on those issues.[13]

Bechtel's metaphor for libraries as "centers for ongoing conversation" fits the concept of knowledge as process. Hearing one side of an argument does not lead to understanding. Listening to different views existent across time and space and using these views to construct one's own vision is a much harder concept to grasp. The library presents a conversation between people with different viewpoints, different referents, different contexts for truth. If the point of reference service is to get a student into the right conversation, then the point of bibliographic instruction is to explain the nature of the library in terms of the different possible conversations going on, the historical and geographical and ideological diversity and the possibilities for these within the various subject areas.

The nature of librarianship in this new paradigm is then to serve as a facilitator and occasionally as a narrator in this library conversation. We must know what is going on where and how to get patrons to the right place. We can teach them all we know about this and the tools to get there but it is essential that we realize that the tools are just tools and that what they access is in constant flux. The ultimate goal of education, as well as for library instruction, is for every student to learn to amalgamate, internalize, and create a viewpoint of their own that adds to and enriches this conversation.

DEVELOPING THE
CONVERSATIONAL AUDIENCE

To understand how students go about internalizing such a viewpoint, how-ever, one must turn to developmental psychology, and the study of how college students learn. Because learning substantially differs between first-year students and seniors, views of the library and needs change, and so require alternate approaches to bibliographic instruction for different audiences.

In 1968, William G. Perry Jr. published his study of college students that extended the range of developmental psychology to the ages of eighteen through twenty-two. Up to that time, opinion generally had been that intellectual maturity was reached by the time a student entered college, not only that it was completely developed, but also that intellectual capacity was probably at its highest level in a lifetime. Perry did his research by interviewing students during their four years at Harvard, and then with independent judges he carefully analyzed the free responses of these students to his open-ended questions. This is accepted as a quality study crucial to the development of any kind of instructional approach to this age group. In this seminal research Perry identifies nine positions of intellectual and ethical development, which can be simplified into four fairly discrete stages.[14]

Dualism. The first stage is a simple dualistic view. It is the characteristic state of college freshmen. These students

see the world as black or white, right or wrong,

perceive that right answers exist for everything and that some authority, usually a professor, knows that right answer, and

believe that if there is a diversity of opinion it is because someone is confused.

Multiplicity. Students at this stage

increasingly question the assumption that absolute answers exist,

are easily confused about different points of view, and

frequently base their decisions on personal bias or emotion rather than on supporting evidence or objective analysis.

Relativism. Students at this stage

no longer see knowledge as absolute,

combine both personal bias and emotion as well as objective evidence in their arguments, think analytically and can evaluate their own and others' ideas, and

consider the qualifications of experts in light of possible opinions and biases of the expert.

Commitment to relativism. The final stage is commitment to one's own position. Students at this level of development

define a role and purpose for themselves,

determine the style in which to carry out that purpose,

understand that as new evidence is presented their own points of view may need to change, and

tolerate other value systems.

What are the implications of this developmental schema on the library and on bibliographic instruction? It implies answers to the questions that librarians have about the efficacy of tool-based library instruction for freshmen in particular. If the entering student believes that truth exists in the professor's mind and that she or he must attempt to reproduce it, then library research is just a treasure hunt to find that truth and prevent it. Librarians become co-conspirators with the faculty in this hide and seek game. Barbara Fister says,

> The information they seek in the library—their "sources" or "evidence"— is perceived as hard and fast truth. They do not see their role in the research process except as hunters and gatherers. And many times the way they are taught to do research promotes the notion that knowledge is something on the shelves, to be pulled together into a paper, not something that the students construct for themselves with the collaboration of the sources they find to inform their thesis.[15]

Isn't this exactly the way Eadie has described library use? Suggesting that there exist clear-cut answers to be served up to students seems to imply that they also see the process of research in these simplistic terms. But there has also occurred a confusion between the concept of information and the concept of knowledge. Information is made up of those discrete bits of fact that can be presented at the ready reference area as virtually true. Knowledge, on the other hand, is the process of understanding the context in which these facts exist.

What most students must also learn, at first, is that information is not the same as knowledge and that facts are not understanding. Librarians who confuse the two do students, faculty, and their profession a great disservice. Bibliographic instruction often actually reinforces the belief that good thinking and good researching are the process of finding the answer that is closest to some predefined truth and thereby reinforce this lowest level of development. But even librarians who do not view research from this dualistic viewpoint often tend to confuse students because of their conflation of the terms information and knowledge. Perhaps the first step in bibliographic instruction should be to distinguish different stages of research: looking for the right answer (in an encyclopedia, as in grammar school), looking for an array of answers (as in a high school term paper, with a number of references as the goal), and the final step as creating new knowledge through research, entering the conversation through one's own discoveries, as the goal of college research.

What needs to be kept separate are the different ways of learning. For students in the dualistic stage,

> Morality and personal responsibility consist of simple obedience. Even "learning to be independent," as Authority asks one to, consists of learning self-controlled obedience. In the educational aspect of this world, morality consists of committing to memory, through hard work, an array of discrete items—correct responses, answers, and procedures, as assigned by Authority.[16]

In other words students can learn all the tasks and procedures that the librarian sets for them, collect all the information required without ever having a clue as to the reason or purpose for any of it.

It is most relevant for instruction librarians to understand how the students come to change from this level to the next. Perry clearly bases this change on exposure to a new world of ideas.

> The act of standing back is forced in a liberal arts college by the impact of pluralism of values and points of view. The shock may be intentional on the part of individual professors, as it is most frequently, though not always, in courses in General Education, or it may be simply the by-product of the clash of different professors, each one of whom is sure he teaches "the" truth. Only in the smallest and most carefully guarded facilities can this diversity be avoided.[17]

The conflict of ideas, values, and worldviews occurs in the social intercourse between peers inside and outside of the classroom. College is different from high school because it brings together students with a diversity of backgrounds who, perhaps for the first time, see that there is more than one way to view the world and that their assumptions about right and wrong, truth and beauty are not always commonly accepted and that they must either reject all they see around them or come to some understanding of this diversity. That understanding does not come in a flash of insight but must travel through levels also.

This is Perry's second-level multiplicity. It is exemplified by the student who comes to the reference desk seeking any two or three articles about a topic. That student no longer asks for the one answer, but thinks that any of the multiple perspectives, no matter how incoherent or unsystematic, are valid. The correlative of this is the justification of the truth of something by one's belief in it. "I believe this to be true and therefore it is true for me and no one can question it." The student has accepted the existence of multiplicity of thought but has yet to find any *systematic* explanation for the existence of that multiplicity. "How, in an educational institution where the student's every answer is evaluated, are answers judged? When even Authority doesn't know the answer yet, is not any answer as good as another?" [18]

Don't assignments in user education, with all good intention designed to teach the access tools, that ask the student to find a number of miscellaneous articles or books on a particular topic, just reinforce this stage? If the world is totally arbitrary then anything will suffice: all one needs to do is find lots of material.

Perry himself describes the development from the level of Multiplicity to the level of Relativism in the terms Thomas Kuhn uses to describe the revolution in scientific thought. He states that so many contradictions begin to occur in the students' world of multiplicity that his view of the world must be revolutionized into a whole new construct—one in which knowledge and truth are seen as belonging within contexts. The multiplicity becomes relational. Historical viewpoints, cultural diversity, and disciplinary perspectives start to become evident.

> We gather from what our students have told us that the educational impact of diversity can be at its best when it is deliberate. When a teacher asks his students to read conflicting authorities and then asks them to assess the nature and meaning of the conflict, he is in a strong position to assist them to go beyond simple diversity into the disciplines of relativity of thought through which specific instances of diversity can be productively exploited. He can teach the relation, the relativism, of one system of thought to another. In short, he can teach disciplined independence of mind. [19]

Critical thinking is one of the evident characteristics of this stage. This is the stage at which a student can argue and analyze any position. Neither side is seen as true, and so any consistent set of research can become the basis for any position—but the position still has no meaning within the student's life. It is still a game, but now a much more complex game, in which the rules are consistent but the sides don't matter. The multiplicity becomes systematic but as yet no commitment is made to any particular context. Library assignments that demand critical thinking skills and urge contrast and comparison of sources are appropriate to this level but they still often do not include that final stage in which evaluation takes place from a committed perspective. Either/or might well be true but there is no choice or decision by the student as to which is his or her perspective.

Perry calls Commitment to Relativism the stage of the mature student and the one for which all education aims. The student now has the ability to take the risk of stating a personal position. He or she has enough experience with the various possibilities and has come to some acceptance of personal limitations in coming to a problem, a research paper, a position paper in a chosen discipline and sorts the good from the bad, the relevant from the irrelevant, and those ideas that support his or her position from those that don't. Finally the library can teach the tools of research without the fear that these tools will be taken as the purpose of its existence.

It is this stage of development that Barbara Fister discovers in her interviews with students who have successfully completed research projects. She offers the kind of reality check that those of us doing bibliographic instruction need more often than we admit. For these college students, research and the writing are integrated into one process. "The students interviewed did not begin with choosing a topic, go on to seek information, and end up by composing a paper." [20] They did not depend upon a research model designed by those who are more familiar with library tools than with the learning process. For these students focusing a topic, finding and reading the literature, and clearly articulating a personal position are not distinct stages, as so often modeled, but a recursive and heuristic process of discovery.

Perry insists, and librarians must remember, no rule about human beings can ever be hard and fast. Students arrive at different levels at different ages. The levels often vary from discipline to discipline, so that a student who understands the diversity of opinion in one area may have a very dualistic concept in another. But even allowing for such variation, Perry's study gives the bibliographic instruction librarian just the kind of framework necessary for designing a program that will work with the developmental pattern of the undergraduate instead of, as we have so often done in the past, against it.

COLLABORATIVE CONVERSATIONS

Within the past few years collaborative learning has become recognized as a method of teaching that incorporates this social view of the nature of knowledge with modern learning theory. Working together in small groups or teams, students can cooperate on a research assignment, and bring together their results. And in this way, different points of view can be placed on the table and discussed, leading the students through the dualistic and multiplistic stages to a more sophisticated level than they could ever reach working alone.

Collaborative learning appears to be the "form of action" or teaching appropriate to the highest content level.

> Collaborative learning can be recognized by its methods and by its results: students work directly with each other and/or with faculty members in research, in teaching skills to their colleagues, in designing or revising courses of academic curricula. A common feature of the experience is that students share responsibility for shaping and teaching the subject at hand. Knowledge is not simply passed from teacher to student; instead students become aware of learning as a continuous process of creation through which they discover and extend the epistemology of their own learning. [21]

Even though scientists necessarily collaborate, students rarely are given assignments that allow them to work in this way. Patricia Bizzell and Bruce Herzberg explain how the word *research* can be defined differently: the scientist doing research means *discovery*, while students doing research means merely *recovery*; but in fact, research is a "social act":

What successful researchers possess that our students typically do not is knowledge, the shared body of knowledge that helps scholars define research projects and employ methods to pursue them. Invariably, researchers use the work of others in their field to develop such projects and consult others in the field to determine what projects will be of value. In short, all real research takes place and can only take place within a community of scholars. Research is a social act. Research is always collaborative, even if only one name appears on the final report. . . . This, then, is the third definition of research: a social collaborative act that draws on and contributes to the work of a community that cares about a given body of knowledge. . . . If the social act of research is successful, students have the opportunity to learn that knowledge is not just found, but created out of existing knowledge.[22]

Over and over scientists have demonstrated that working together, communicating frequently, asking for help and criticism lead to better, quicker, and more complete results and acceptance for those results than working alone. Support, encouragement, efficiency, and even natural (not imposed) competition of the group do more for learning than an individual could ever hope to do. The stereotype of the lone, mad scientist in a remote laboratory discovering the secret of life has long since died a deserved death.

Bibliographic instruction can continue to be a totally reactive enterprise. There is no doubt that most undergraduates will develop with or without library instruction. But can't instruction use this new view of the structure of knowledge and use Perry's study to design an instruction curriculum that facilitates and serves the ultimate goals of undergraduate education? Bruffee defines these: "the two most important things to learn if one sets out to become educated are how judgment is made within an assenting community, and how knowledge grows within an assenting community."[23]

In a later article, Bruffee finds the means to accomplish these goals when he observes students working collaboratively:

Students' work tended to improve when they got help from peers; peers offering help, furthermore, learned from the students they helped and from the activity of helping itself. Collaborative learning, it seemed, harnessed the powerful educative force of peer influence that had been—and largely still is—ignored and hence wasted by traditional forms of education.[24]

Teaching the tools and the vocational training aspects of user instruction must be set in this collaborative context. The main obstacle to doing this is forgetting that students need a framework in which to operate. Faculty and researchers have already identified and defined the structure of their fields. Graduate students are still learning the background and subtlety of that structure. Neither may remember that for undergraduates this framework and overview are not already in place.

Both teaching faculty and librarians often assume that the difficulties students have doing even the simplest research can be remedied by a course that teaches the use of the catalog, of indexes, of bibliographies and of all the myriad of tools available. What they don't seem to realize is that learning to drive an automobile has no meaning for anyone who has never been in a car, has never seen the places that it can take one, or understood the possibilities that it offers. And rather than teaching the joys of driving, many librarians are insisting that freshmen start by taking the engine apart.

The motivation offered to students in a BI session is often that if they pay attention they will be able to get an A on a library assignment or that if they learn the tools they will be able to get a good grade on a research paper. It encourages students to perceive the library's role in learning in the most simplistic and individualistic terms. Bruffee notes,

> We socially justify belief when we explain to others why one way of understanding how the world hangs together seems to us preferable to other ways of understanding it. We establish knowledge or justify belief collaboratively by challenging each other's biases and pre-suppositions; by negotiating collectively toward new paradigms of perception, thought, feeling, and expression; and by joining larger, more experienced communities of knowledgeable peers through assent-ing to those communities interests, values, language, and paradigms of perception and thought.[25]

Librarians cannot expect to encourage any sense of complexity and multiplicity by using library assignments that expect single right answers. Nor can they encourage critical thinking by expecting students to learn tools without a larger view of context and diversity. No one can expect undergraduates to understand that they are to learn to participate in the construction of understanding and knowledge unless we actually encourage the practice of construction.

What better way is there to teach how knowledge is constructed than by using the same collaborative method used to construct knowledge. As Barbara Fister says, "Group inquiry gives the students a working model of a scholarly community in the microcosm of the classroom."[26] Before a person is able to think, they must first experience direct social exchanges with others. In this view thought is dependent upon conversation. "The view that conversation and thought are causally related assumes not that thought is an essential attribute of the human mind, but that it is instead an artifact created by social interaction. We can think because we can talk, and we think in ways we have learned to talk."[27]

Collaborative learning requires the establishment of an environment in which the teacher does not have the answer. The questions asked must be so complex as to require analysis, debate, negotiation, and consensus before an answer can be suggested. "It is a setting where students are asked to do a lot, and are given the authority and the space to do it. . . . Research in this classroom requires sharing information, building on one another's ideas, and using written evidence as added voices in an extended conversation."[28]

Barbara Fister observes that in collaboration, students also learn the tools that are necessary to complete this research, but with a definite intellectual purpose in mind, not as ends in themselves. Much of how they learn the tools is through a process of discovery and a sharing among themselves of the fruits of their individual discoveries about the possibilities. For upper-division students working within the context of a discipline, it can extend the learning experience into the idiosyncrasies of the field that might include discussions of the importance of certain journals, subfields in the discipline, and new directions emerging.

Jean Sheridan details some of the changes that must take place in order for this method to work. The teacher must step out of the highly visible role of the lecturer and do much more in the way of preparation and communication. The clear objectives must be understood, techniques selected, and introductory material carefully prepared. Small groups must be configured, timetables set, readings and questions prepared. And perhaps most importantly the cooperative environment of trust and friendliness must be established in which this can work. Students previously led to expect a passive role must be motivated. Active listening to peers and tolerance for the styles and values of others are not always initially present.[29]

Elizabeth Simmons-O'Neill describes the procedure she uses while teaching a lower-division Medieval and Renaissance history class to introduce her students to the process of research in the library. She begins by having students read the introductions to works such as Huizinga's *Waning of the Middle Ages* and Marx's *Communist Manifesto* in order to establish the differences of approach and method that exist within the field. The students then attempt to place the author of their textbook within this context. They use the library to find as much information as they can about the textbook author to analyze what is said about him, what and how he writes in other articles and essays. By placing the writer of the textbook in a context they are able to extend the inquiry to see how other noted historians looked at the same events and people and to differentiate between the various possible interpretations of history and their presuppositions.[30]

Along the way the relationship between primary and secondary sources becomes evident. The students ultimately come to understand that the literature is an ongoing discussion, that the uncritical acceptance of any one side or source is mere redundancy, not very interesting and of little value, and that they are able to construct a new viewpoint using various sources and the contributions of their own insights, which in turn must be open to the criticism or consensus of the peer group.

> And it implies that collaborative learning as a classroom practice models more than how knowledge is established and maintained. The argument pursued here implies, in short, that in the long run collaborative learning models how knowledge is generated, how it changes and grows.[31]

CONCLUSION

The parallels between the changes that have occurred in the epistemology of science and the changes seen in the development of the undergraduate student are significant. Just as science has come to see that its understanding of the world is mediated, limited, and finally constructed by social consensus, so the undergraduate grows to understand the same thing in his life. And it seems that the collaborative model brings students' views into just such conflict that they can begin to understand how the context of the discussion determines the truth of a set of propositions or interpretation. Just as the Newtonian universe could no longer answer the questions posed by modern science, so also the dualism of the immature student cannot survive in the face of the multiplicity of viewpoints offered by peers and by teachers.

A recent software catalog offering a program that teaches collaborative writing says that roughly 75 percent of workplace writing is collaborative in nature. Scientists say that most of their work is done in close cooperation with their peers. Perry says that students develop because they must negotiate with themselves some meaning for the diversity that they encounter in their social and academic lives. The recognition that both knowledge and learning are social in origin must have wide-ranging effects on libraries that are intimately concerned with both. The paradigm of library as the conservator of culture, the well of wisdom, has become too static a metaphor in this time of radical change. Computer technology, online searching, full text databases, electronic journals are all pushing the meaning of what a library is to the limits of this old paradigm. Just as science has to throw over its outgrown vision of itself in order to progress—so libraries must do the same. These technologies seem to point toward the future dissolution of the book and printed text as we now know it and use it in libraries.

With this dissolution it is possible that the new paradigm, to be appropriate, must be one that goes back to before the origin of print and picks up on the social nature of man rather than his individual one. If this is true, then the metaphor of library as the locus for the conversation of humanity is most appropriate. And the implications of this paradigm in a democratic and diverse society lead to a sense of optimism not often present in libraries today. The human conversation in libraries will go on no matter what format the words take. A rich diversity of ideas will be available because of the ease of resource sharing and the digital image. And students will continue to outstrip the experts in their adaptation to these technological changes. The question appears to be whether librarians will choose to become leaders and innovators of this new vision, initiating collaboration with faculty and students in research activities. Will bibliographic instruction librarians come to see themselves as the hosts of this part in progress whose task is to send out the invitations to the newcomers?

NOTES

1. Michael Oakeshott, *Rationalism in Politics* (1962; reprint, New York: Methuen, 1974), 199.

2. Tom Eadie, "Immodest Proposals," *Library Journal* 115, no. 17 (1990): 42-49.

3. Hannelore B. Rader, "Library Orientation and Instruction—1989," *Reference Services Review* (winter 1989): 73-85; and "Library Orientation and Instruction—1989," *Reference Services Review* (winter 1990): 35-47.

4. David W. Lewis and C. Paul Vincent, "Reactions to the Think Tank Recommendations: An Initial Response," *Journal of Academic Librarianship* 9, no. 1 (1983): 5.

5. Lori Arp, "Information Literacy or Bibliographic Instruction: Semantics or Philosophy?" *RQ* 30 (1990): 49.

6. Eadie, "Immodest Proposals," 43.

7. Ibid., 45.

8. Susanne K. Langer, *Philosophy in a New Key* (New York: New American Library, 1948).

9. Jane Keefer, "The Hungry Rat Syndrome," *RQ* (spring 1993): 335.

10. Jacob Bronowski, *The Origins of Knowledge and Imagination* (New Haven, Conn.: Yale University Press, 1978), 54.

11. Thomas S. Kuhn, *The Structure of Scientific Revolution* (Chicago: University of Chicago Press, 1962), 2.

12. Gertrude Himmelfarb, "And of Terrible Truths," *New York Times Book Review* 24 (March 1991): 2. (Review of the revised edition of *The Crooked Timber of Humanity: Chapters in the History of Ideas*, by Isaiah Berlin.)

13. Joan M. Bechtel, "Conversation, a New Paradigm for Librarianship," *College and Research Libraries* (May 1986): 221.

14. See William G. Perry Jr., *Forms of Intellectual and Ethical Development in the College Years: A Scheme* (New York: Holt, 1968). There are three articles suggesting Perry's relevance to bibliographic instruction. See Constance A. Mellon, "Information Problem-Solving: A Developmental Approach to Library Instruction," in *Theories of Bibliographic Education: Designs for Teaching*, ed. Cerise Oberman and Katrina Strauch (New York: R. R. Bowker, 1982), 75-89; Mary Reichel, "Library Literacy," *RQ* 28 (fall 1988): 29-32; and Elizabeth J.

McNeer, "Learning Theories and Library Instruction," *The Journal of Academic Librarianship* 17 (1991): 294-97.

15.   Barbara Fister, "Teaching Research as a Social Act: Collaborative Learning and the Library," *RQ* (summer 1990): 506.

16.   William G. Perry Jr., *Forms of Intellectual and Ethical Development*, 59.

17.   Ibid., 35.

18.   Ibid., 89.

19.   Ibid., 35.

20.   Barbara Fister, "The Research Processes of Undergraduate Students," *Journal of Academic Librarianship* 18 (July 1992): 168.

21.   Jean Sheridan, "The Reflective Librarian: Some Observations on Bibliographic Instruction in the Academic Library," *Journal of Academic Librarianship* 16, no. 1 (1990): 23.

22.   Patricia Bizzell and Bruce Herzberg, "Research as a Social Act," *Clearinghouse* 60, no. 7 (1986-87): 304, 306.

23.   Kenneth A. Bruffee, "The Structure of Knowledge and the Future of Liberal Education," *Liberal Education* 67 (1981): 181.

24.   Kenneth A. Bruffee, "Collaborative Learning and the 'Conversation of Mankind,' " *College English* 46, no. 7 (1984): 638.

25.   Ibid., 646.

26.   Fister, "Teaching Research as a Social Act," 507.

27.   Bruffee, "Collaborative Learning," 640.

28.   Fister, "Teaching Research as a Social Act," 507.

29.   Sheridan, "The Reflective Librarian," 24.

30.   Elizabeth Simmons-O'Neill, "Evaluating Sources: Strategies for Faculty-Librarian-Student Collaboration" (paper presented at the Conference on College Composition and Communication, Chicago, Ill., March 22-24, 1990), 2-5. (ERIC Document Number ED321259.)

31.   Bruffee, "Collaborative Learning," 647.

13

Expanding the
Evaluation Role in the
Critical-Thinking Curriculum

Daniel Callison

Associate Professor and Director of School Media Education
School of Library and Information Science
Indiana University
Bloomington, Indiana

The role of the school library media specialist will continue to evolve during this decade. Definitions of potential change have been suggested in recent literature[1] and reinforced through principles outlined in the current national guidelines[2] for school library programs. A model will be outlined in this essay that rests on acceptance of much that has been proposed in terms of the teaching role,[3] but this model will give new depth to the collaborative and evaluative responsibilities of the school library media specialist.

This model may not be realistic when placed against the operation of most current school library media programs. If, however, the school library media specialist is to play a leading role in development of a truly critical thinking curriculum, the evaluative aspects of this model are essential. If evaluation is limited to materials selection and does not include evaluation of student information use, the school library media specialist cannot make a claim to being an educator on par with the classroom teacher.

Who will teach and test in the process of evaluating (determining the value of) information? Who will teach and test selection, use, and presentation of information? The individuals or groups who hold this powerful role can define the educational demands placed on both teachers and students. The greater the access to resource services in all forms (bibliographic and human), the greater the need for critical evaluation skills. The higher the critique level, the greater the need for education of teachers in methods aimed toward open discussion and analysis of information use. The educational mission is not only to develop an information-wise electorate, but to also increase the tolerance and patience required for frank debate of issues.

If we assume that the charge of schools (K-College) for the new age of education is to produce individuals who think, who know when they are thinking, and who think interactively with others, then curriculum design and support resources should include opportunities for practice of such skills. Above all else, students *and* teachers must be engaged in critical evaluation of the print and nonprint messages they encounter in both academic and nonacademic settings.

LITERACY REDEFINED

Literacy is not simply knowing how to read and write a particular script but applying this knowledge for specific purposes in specific contexts of use."[4] "An information literate person [is one who is] able to recognize when information is needed and [has] the ability to effectively locate, evaluate, and employ the needed information."[5] "Ultimately, information literate people are those who have learned how to learn. They know how to learn because they know how knowledge is organized, how to find information, and how to use information in such a way that others can learn from them.[6]

Literacy is a social phenomenon; its definition and its distribution shift constantly. Finding *who, what, when,* or *where* is descriptive and simply does not answer the questions inherent in a new definition of literacy.[7] *Why* becomes the demanding question, and the literate person does not stop with one answer nor with one conclusion, but seeks multiple options and determines where there is overlap and conflict. The literate person knows that information in any captured form is dated, inconclusive in and of itself, and usually presented in a biased manner. Ethical considerations must be part of the solution and the presentation of support data and these considerations are at the heart of judgment methods that must be taught to those responsible for increasing literacy in our society.

The principles associated with these higher demands on a literate information age generation must be taught at all grade levels. Methods and materials will vary, but the basic purpose should not change.

The definition of who shall be literate also shifts. Questioning, reflecting, discussing, and writing have always been a part of literacy for talented or privileged elites. But they have rarely been a part of what we consider important for students who were not gifted or clearly college-bound. A classroom where young women, learning-disabled students, poor and minority students, all read (not recite) and write about (not copy) Shakespeare or Steinbeck is an invention that is only as old as higher education for women, *Brown v. Board of Education,* and rulings on the rights of handicapped students. Our expectation of high levels of literacy for many is a radical, hopeful, and demanding departure.[8]

Resnick and Klopfer[9] write that "The Thinking Curriculum is not a course to be added to a crowded program when time permits. It is not a program that begins after 'basics' have been mastered." Skills in reasoning, problem-solving, making judgments, stating inferences need to spread from the top of Bloom's cognitive domain to all levels associated with learning. Each fact, each event, each concept presented should have a context and be questioned to the extent that relationships to the learner's personal abilities and individual needs are acknowledged.

This is not to say that learning is without steps, levels, or that there are no prerequisites. It is necessary, however, that students become aware of such increments themselves and that they construct their intellectual webbing based on as many informational items, thoughts, or conclusions as can be made relevant to their intellectual schema and relevant to their own current and possible future social contexts.

Resnick and Klopfer suggest that construction of any student's thinking curriculum should employ the following practices in what they term "cognitive apprenticeship."

Practice a real task. Writing an essay for an interested audience, not just the teacher who will give a grade; reading a text that takes some work (asking questions, discussion, comparisons) to understand; exploring a physical phenomenon that is inadequately explained by a current concept.

Contextualize the practice. Students would not do exercises on separating facts from opinions, but they would take on tasks of analyzing arguments (and statistics) on particular topics or participating in debates, both of which might engage them in a contextualized version of figuring out reliable information in a communication.

Observe models. Students need plenty of opportunity to observe others doing the kind of work they are expected to learn or to do. This observation (reinforced with the challenge to evaluate or critique) gives them standards of effective performance against which they can judge their own efforts.

The thinking curriculum is based on students practicing the process of raising questions, testing a variety of possible answers, and eventually voicing, writing, constructing, sculpting, drawing, and arguing the meaning of those answers. This inquiry process is founded on gathering information for the purpose of seeking various perspectives, not just a single conclusion. Most directly, it means that students must be engaged in a conversation and be shown how to enter, contribute to, and continue that conversation on their own and with others. The literature is rich with discussion as to how such conversations can be initiated.[10] The task remaining is to show how the school library media specialist can add value to the construction of critical conversations.

ESTABLISHED IMPLICATIONS

Craver[11] has given school library media specialists a superb summary of the implications from library and information science research related to new concepts in teaching critical thinking. Critical thinking was identified in four basic areas: reading, writing, group interaction, and speaking. These are four normal activities during which students may be engaged in the gathering and presentation of information, and, eventually, engaging in a conversation about the value of the information.

Successful methods in placing students in the critical thinking mode include the expectation that the student generate his or her own analysis of a given text or identify, organize, and raise questions concerning issues presented. Thoughtful discussion leaders and students reacting to peer opinions in groups tend to increase critical thinking. In a discussion situation, deliberate use of wait time conveys to students that they are expected to respond intelligently to posed questions. Open debate that results in capturing issues in written form followed by a cooling period in which students search for supportive or counter evidence may serve to raise the level of critical exchange.

Bowie[12] has listed very tangible activities that the school library media specialist and the classroom teacher can employ in order to challenge students in the reasoning process (her list has been paraphrased in interest of saving space):

- Ask a class to gather and sort opposing viewpoints on a social issue; use all possible sources; analyze merits of each opinion including the authority.

- Compile a file of popular advertisements (record television and radio spots as well) and lead students in a discussion of how information is manipulated (spoken and visual).

- Students should construct infinite bibliographies (or pathfinders) to show location of information through a variety of formats both in and _beyond_ the library, including human resources.

- Create activities that require comparison of maps, charts, census data over time and in relation to major events.

Bowie terms her activities _intervention strategies_. This term is important to note because intervention is a concept that must be broadened in the evaluation role of the school library media specialist and the teacher. The argument follows the rationale that information use instruction must be integrated with the curriculum in order to become effective and for teachers to understand its potential and relevance.

Intervention represents an opening created by the teacher/librarian in order to cue a point of instructional need. Intervention works best when collaboratively planned and classroom content grounded. Such intervention activities should serve as models to lead to actual change in the curriculum. The goal is to establish such critical thinking activities at the forefront of lesson planning to the extent that the adjective *intervention* can be dropped, and inquiry activities become the curriculum. Using varied resources, raising questions, presenting results of the information search become the standard, not the exception. Intervention by teachers and school library media specialists in inquiry activities becomes natural. Intervention becomes *the* strategy at a variety of evaluation points. Reflection on choices is found throughout the inquiry exercise not just at the culmination of the project.

Above all, the teaching methods that work best to provide an environment for critical thinking should be used by the school library media specialist in teaching information use skills. Instead of always lecturing and saturating students with "how-to" facts, actively involve them in learning, let them raise problems and suggest solutions. Use cooperative or collaborative learning whenever possible so peers can teach, learn from, and motivate each other. Supplement the library resources with access to human expertise found in other teachers, parents, or community contacts. To build activities within the limited confines of the school library is as undesirable as allowing a textbook to determine the parameters for learning. Bowie's recommendations of techniques for teaching critical thinking rest at the feet of the school library media specialist as well as the classroom teacher. Understanding how information can be used and presented in teaching students to think[13] leads to new initiatives in curriculum development.[14]

RESTRUCTURING MEDIA PROGRAMS

In order to teach, to lead, to model, to initiate critical thinking (not just support, supplement, or enhance), several changes must take place in how we manage school library media programs. Many of these changes have been suggested before,[15] but the emphasis here is within the context of the information skill activities described above, and with the understanding that the role of the school media specialist as curriculum developer will not become reality without such changes.[16] The role as evaluator of information, judge of student performance, and appraiser of the information/media/communication program becomes essential.[17]

Collection Development and information Access

In order to make inquiry units that are based on critical examination of information effective, students must have access to an extensive amount of materials. This means that a variety of resources should be available in terms of format, date, reading level, and points of view. There is nothing new in the idea that school library media center collections provide a variety of materials. What must be different in order to create an environment for critical examination of information is the depth of the school's library collection and the extent to which students truly have access to as many information sources as possible within and beyond the school.

First, collection development will need to take a sharp turn toward support of a few selected units. For these units, acquisition of materials should be as exhaustive as possible. Every relevant item should be acquired or access to such streamlined. More time will need to be given to discussing information needs and less time to specific (labor-intensive) classification and organization of materials. Information need, information understanding, leads taken, and leads unconsidered become the determining factors of the collection necessary for inquiry support.

Loertscher[18] has outlined such topic or unit targeting through the use of collection mapping, and has argued that special instructional units simply will not take place unless there are enough resources to support one or several classrooms of students. This is a shift from the approach that all areas of the curriculum along with leisure reading demands should be served. Resource support for units in which critical information analysis is expected will need to be even more extensive than Loertscher proposes for library-centered events. Dramatic changes in collection priorities will need to take place.

Units shaped around critical thinking activities will need support of files with special newspaper and magazine clippings, access to the local public and academic library collections, acquisition of materials that may not be reviewed or evaluated by the traditional selection tools. Emphasis may need to be placed on acquiring special index resources, which in turn lead to a greater use of interlibrary loan. The telephone and the fax machine may become the two very important reference tools. Online access to full-text information databases may need to be available in some classrooms as well as the library. Checking news services may need to take place each day or each hour in some events.

Use of fiction, historical or scientific, might be necessary for some units in order to provide a social context for the more factual items gathered. Historical fiction can give the student a greater appreciation for the social events being examined and science fiction can arouse the imagination in relation to what is actually known or theorized by scientists.[19] Oral tradition projects can result in a bonding with the community.[20]

In some cases, collections of unique resources may need to be gathered, boxed in special storage, added to over several years, and then controlled through a reserve system so that these difficult-to-obtain materials will be available to students when it comes time for the specific unit. As much as 20 percent of the annual budget might be invested over a three- to four-year period in order to create a rich, in-depth, multiperspective collection for one critical unit. We would no longer evaluate the collection by total volumes nor by the proportion of the curriculum it supports in some manner with books and magazines. Evaluations would include the extent to which choice areas of the curriculum are enriched, changed, and brought to the level of critical analysis. Are the depth of the collection and the extent of reference services great enough to meet the demands of forty or more students as each focuses on some aspect of a critical issue? Is it truly varied enough that all perspectives can be explored?

Second, the collection compiled in support of the critical information units should not be sanitized and should come, as much as possible, in its "real world" packaging. For secondary school-level students this means that tabloids and other "supermarket checkout line materials" take a place beside the respected news magazines and newspapers usually recommended to students. It means that extremes on both sides of an issue are easily available. The spectrum of arguments is full with right to left opinions. Access to factual data from government, private, and even personal records is pursued. Such massive gathering of materials would need to be relative to the information world encountered by the specific age group.

Students should have access to television programs and commentaries (previously taped and left unedited), and should view popular situational commentary found in television drama and comedy alongside the intellectual or investigative presentations. Examination of the messages delivered through the popular series should be made in context with real world events. What are the facts, emotions, and issues raised by the situations posed concerning sexual harassment in television's "Designing Women" compared to charges presented during the "Thomas Supreme Court Nomination Hearings"? What are local policies and opinions concerning the issues related to sexual harassment? Can students be educated and trained to ask such difficult questions of local audiences and can a forum be established to present their findings?

As much as possible, students should have access to government databases, statistical abstracts running back several decades, and yellow pages or specialized directories in order to contact possible experts either locally or via long distance. Yes, they need full access to the telephone or electronic mail, and should be taught how to approach human resources in order to gain the information desired or needed. Interviews should be preceded with student knowledge of the basic issues, practiced interview sessions, and a specific purpose established for the interview.

Third, the long march to move materials to a centralized location called the school library media center will need to take an about-face. The school library media center becomes a clearinghouse, a dissemination center, and an often-used experimental learning laboratory.[21] Classrooms will need to house and teachers will need to share informational materials as never before. In some cases, special collections of materials and artifacts for a given unit will need to be boxed and moved from one building to another as teachers select the area for the next class inquiry. Centralized district offices may serve to house such collections as well as provide centralized access to local electronic news services. Resources will flow in bulk in order to stimulate and establish the activity. Special services for seeking updated data will take students and teachers to a new insight each time the unit is processed.

Just as the new initiatives for literature-based language education depend on immediate access to and saturation with classroom sets of books, so too will units built on critical use of information demand access to resources in both the classroom and the library. When the unit is in full swing there should be little difference between the classroom and library resource environments other than greater contact with resources beyond the school will be provided through the community networks maintained by the school library media specialist.

Restructuring the Instructional Role

The instructional task becomes more complex in the process of teaching critical examination of information. School library media specialists would continue to recommend the "best" or most efficient sources and search processes. But added to this is the task of working with students to raise questions about the documentation they handle; why they selected what they did and why they excluded other information; what makes the information they have gleaned valuable to them and what do they need to do in order to communicate that information to others; how do they lead their audience to value what the student has to present?

Do students need to be educated in audience analysis? Should they be aware of the limitations and expectations of the audience destined to receive their report? The answer is yes if we include "the ability to present information in such a manner as to influence others with what you know" as a part of the definition of information literacy. The instructional role moves from location skills within a safe, sanitized, preselected environment to exposure to a massive amount of varied materials and opinions. It requires practice in selection of the most useful information to answer self-generated questions,[22] and to represent the findings convincingly to others.

Judgment calls, or information evaluation checks, will need to be negotiated at dozens of points, and the mediation role (teaching the meaning, the limitations, the potential of each source of information) becomes extremely important—so important that both the school librarian and the classroom teacher must be experts in teaching and modeling the use of information and the decision-making processes.[23] Students who display the ability to make such decisions will need to be recruited into roles as peer tutors or group leaders who in turn help other students practice analysis of information.

Liesener,[24] in response to the lack of attention to the library media field given in the government report *A Nation at Risk*, wrote, "The primary function performed by the school library media specialist or program can be viewed as a mediation function. From this perspective, the specialist plays the role of an intermediary between the incredibly complex and rapidly expanding information world and the client." The mediation task in relation to teaching critical information analysis skills is so demanding that the role must be taken by the teacher as well. In units designed to immerse the student in an information flood and to teach comparison and critical selection of information, the school library media specialist and the classroom teachers must be interchangeable parts.

The teacher, as well as the librarian, teaches the quality aspects of various information sources, how to conduct an efficient information search, when to seek information beyond the library, how to compare and contrast information gathered, and methods to present information effectively. The school library media specialist serves as one who also establishes the parameters of the assignments, defines the critical thinking skills to be demonstrated and measured, and evaluates the student through both process and product.

Division of responsibilities would take place on convenience for management of the activity, but the expertise relevant to selecting information, accessing information, using information, establishing assignments, and appraising student performance would be of equal merit in either camp. Such must be the shift from current roles divided between teacher and librarian if critical use of information is to move into the curriculum and become a dominant factor in molding curricular change.

The overriding goal for the curricular changes at as many ability levels and in as many disciplines as possible would be an increase in communication skills based on knowledgeable selection and use of information. Teachers and school library media specialists must have a command (not just respect) of each other's roles in order for such dramatic changes to take place.

Changes in Staffing

In larger schools, as the shift to the full teaching role of the school library media specialist evolves and selected teachers move toward information roles, the staffing expectations for operations of the school library facility may need to change. Coordination, policy setting, and planning aspects may actually begin to rest with a "Department of Educational Resources." The chair, similar to a chair of the reading department or the science department, will act as the director of the instructional components for this new department. The chair may come from either the teaching ranks or the library/media ranks, but the concentration of the chair's expertise should be in curriculum development and information management. Members of the educational resource department could be a mixture of those coming from either the library/media, educational technology, or various academic subject backgrounds.

The concentration of the cooperative efforts would be to model and demonstrate instructional methods best suited for the promotion of critical thinking skills. These include collaborative learning, free inquiry and discovery, and celebrations of student-teacher achievements within the community. The goal would be to create an environment in which teachers, students, and parents interact as a community of learners within a social curriculum.[25] Inquiry units that investigate local issues will generate the most visible community participation.[26]

Staffing for support of the resource center may include individuals who have training in the acquisition, processing, and organization of materials and who would serve the program on a paraprofessional level. The staffing cadre would include positions for clerical assistance and the usual student and parent volunteers. At least two district-level positions would become essential; one for networking of access and acquisition of resources and the other for coordination of critical thinking curricular efforts across all disciplines.

As the school media program has evolved over the past decades, new roles have been raised and "forced" on the school librarian without additional staffing support. Instructional television, multimedia production, instructional design, and development of integrated information skills programs have all faltered because of the lack of adequate professional staff. Development of the critical thinking curriculum is no different. Success will depend on a full staffing commitment.

NEW INTERVENTION
AND EVALUATION STRATEGIES

Although there are several useful approaches that have been recently published concerning the introduction of information search and use skills,[27] Kulthau's observation of the "typical" library research process by secondary school students gives the skeleton for new intervention strategies that must be practiced by both school library media specialist and classroom teacher in the critical thinking curriculum.[28]

Kuhlthau is refining her 1985 outline for the library research process,[29] but her basic structure is key to the approach for development of critical thinking assignments requiring a large resource support base. Most important to her strategy is the amount of time given to laying the groundwork. Emphasis is placed on brainstorming and preliminary discussion among students, with the teacher, and with the school library media specialist. Students explore the literature, raise questions, discuss the potential for topics before moving into the more extensive information search. Testing the information-base and determining the entry-level knowledge of students are critical. The "new" approach is that students learn to self-test for such limitations or richness themselves.

Several activities could be added or refined in this front-end portion of the Kuhlthau outline, for example, the need for priming the students through a common base of literature relevant to the general subject to be explored by the class. Textbook generalities and teacher-led discussion are not enough. Selection of important items (books, newspaper articles, films, guest lectures) should be shared by all involved in the unit in order to generate a context for the student project. From small-group discussions (led by teacher, library media specialist, and peer tutors) a common base can be identified as to "what we think we know," and "what we have before us to explore."

Modeling Critical Thinking

Too often the student is placed in the position of generating a product without preliminary knowledge about the issues, an understanding of the ideas or questions of his peers, or a challenge to move beyond the surface information provided in the popular media. Establishing an inquiry context includes knowledge of the foundation of common knowledge and concerns, student interest and ability levels, information parameters, and an understanding of where an individual's own inquiry may fit or not fit with others toward the end of the process. All of these front-end considerations help the novice visualize where they may eventually land at the end of the trip.

Students need access to models and examples. Not so much to tell them "this is the way it must be," but to help them visualize possibilities, critically examine products that have preceded their assignment, and challenge them in ways to achieve better results. Modeling should come in at least two forms: peer and mentor.

Peer products from similar assignments (not necessarily identical) should be examined. Presentations might even be made by students who completed a similar project the prior semester in order to discuss fertile contacts for information, dead ends and disappointments, and the need to (and how to) plan ahead. Students should challenge information presented and be placed in a position to consider how the process and products can be improved.

> Too often teachers do what they did today because that is what they did yesterday or because that is what they think others expect them to do. Just as potters cannot teach others to craft in clay without setting their own hand to work at the wheel, so teachers cannot fully teach others the excitement, the difficulty, the patience, and the satisfaction that accompany learning without themselves engaging in the messy, frustrating, and rewarding "clay" of learning. Inquiry for teachers can take place both in and out of the view of students, but to teacher and student alike there must be continuous evidence that it is occurring. For when teachers observe, examine, question, and reflect on their ideas and develop new practices that lead toward their ideals, students are alive. When teachers stop growing, so do their students. Unfortunately, schools are seen as places where children learn and adults teach.[30]

In most current curricula, mentors modeling information-use skills is almost unthinkable. In the critical thinking curriculum, it is essential.[31] Teachers *and* school library media specialists would immerse themselves in the inquiry process as well. Each would take a slice of the area to be explored and practice the same searching, interviewing, information gathering and presentation tasks as those demanded of the students. Enlightenment will be the result. Insight will generate new approaches and new inquiry units. Information location and use experienced by mentors will be the sparks leading to multiple discussion or intervention points throughout the process. As data and counter-data, opinion and counter-opinion are gathered, questions can be raised as to levels of relevance and authoritativeness. In the end, presentations and displays will be enhanced as mentors and students share their achievements. The conversation concerning human knowledge is initiated by all learners—students and teachers.[32]

During the information gathering process, Kuhlthau describes several intervention roles of the teacher and library media specialist. These roles are so important that, again, all should be played by either of the facilitators. These key interventions are at the decision points related to information gathering. Intervention is necessary in order to assist students in selection of information, use of charts and tables, understanding the context of a quotation, or tracing the roots of a given expert's true qualification. Data may need to be verified through other print sources or through contacting a primary source whenever feasible. Just as there is guidance in the focusing of the inquiry, so there must be practice and guidance in selection of information. Guidance is necessary at the initial point of selection, the point of deciding use, the point of editing, the point of revision, and the point of presentation. A given information item may change in value at each point.

Electronic databases provide open screen display that allows teacher and student (or students) to view the results of a given search together and to question at each citation or annotation (if necessary) the potential value of the source.[33] Discussing the potential value of each source leads to discussion as to the focus of the inquiry. It continues the process of raising additional questions to explore relative to the initial research questions identified from the front-end priming literature. It reinforces the practice of critical evaluation of information.

Electronic windowing environments will increase the potential for teachers and students to exchange opinions on sources. In some future databases, we may see a set of cues given that help the student select relevant sources. The credibility of a source used is one portion of the student's selection process that should be judged. Establishing credibility of a source may require intervention by the teacher or librarian in their role as information specialist. How one builds a case for credible, authoritative, relevant, clear, understandable evidence is a primary skill in the critical thinking curriculum.

Additional Aspects of Assessment and Appraisal

The final stage of the Kuhlthau outline currently centers on assessing the process. Self-assessment, process-assessment, and product-assessment are all needed in order to determine what worked and what can be improved.

The student, as Kuhlthau describes, should reflect on the experience and verbalize what would be done differently or similarly in the next experience. Sharing projects or end results is most important in the critical thinking curriculum. Students and teachers (including the school library media specialist) are placed in the position of presenting information to others, teaching what they have "discovered" and sharing the materials in as many ways as possible beyond the library and beyond the classroom. Parents, students in other schools, and local community groups are all potential audiences. Formats can include traditional video programs, pamphlets and posters, bulletin board displays, local newspaper articles, debates, editorials, term papers, and more.

Keys to making the products valued by others include any attempt that allows the product to be seen or heard by others and celebrated in some manner (an evening happening at the school at the end of the semester with an open house to display the products of the semester's inquiry units). Maintaining a collection of many of the projects for future students to examine and use as legitimate information sources and learning devices gives the products and the producers value.

The critical evaluation process of student performance is within the role of both teacher and school library media specialist. Such evaluation requires intervention in the process at specific check points with the intent to determine the progress of the student. It may be that there is a certain standard expected or the progress is measured relative to the unique entry level of each student, but the point to be established here is that judgments need to be made as to the quality of questions raised, sources pursued, evidence gathered, biases reconsidered, even ethical standards stemming from temptations to cloud or shade evidence through editing and lifting out of context. Use of electronic composition will open a new world for mentor intervention. Comments can be fed into electronic outlines and screen displays as they are constructed. Electronic mail will allow students to see critical comments at home as well as at school, and they can respond immediately.

Evaluation should be made concerning the ability of students to add value to their education experience. They are able to move from an entry point to some other level because of this experience. Knowledge gained through the experience should transfer to other areas of their learning environment. What does the student know at the end that they did not know at the beginning? What questions remain beyond the culmination of this project that they would like to explore? Evidence that the student took the initiative to continue the process, either on a new set of questions, or in another discipline, or another assignment, should be documented. We cannot measure lifelong learning, but we can measure changes within a student's academic life.

Process-assessment should include examination of the merits of resources identified and used, and considerations for seeking access to resources that seemed initially to be beyond reach. Did the student make the extra effort to obtain what was previously "off limits"? The critical thinking curriculum should allow for exposure to similar information channels encountered in "real life" as well as those that are hidden or even unknown at the beginning of the process. What tools best enable students and teachers to sort through information in order to construct their knowledge and eventually convey a message to others? Are these tools easily available for the next set of students?

Project-assessment should lead to development of other units as well as refinement of the one just completed. Questions should be raised concerning overlap or duplication of assignments, transfer of skills or building on skill levels, and how demanding the project was in terms of placing students in the position to make critical information judgments. This evaluation process should engage the opinions of several teachers and administrators. It should include those who are considering development of such units for the first time. The evaluation process thus becomes a learning and a teaching activity in itself. This process results in the bricks that construct the new units of the critical thinking curriculum.

The purpose of the interventions is to create an opportunity to engage the student concerning information choices and use. The goal is to nurture novice information specialists (librarian to teacher; teacher to student; student to student; and other cycles that allow learning within a social exchange).[34] A new cast of information access and use experts should evolve from the student population and their role as educators of other students should be recognized and rewarded.

Evaluation at each point can include a testing instrument. Tangible performances[35] can be identified and should be measured[36] along with a narrative record of teacher-librarian and student observations. Two points are necessary to remember, however. First, teachers as information specialists (including classroom teachers and the school library media specialist) should administer the evaluation and determine the merits of the experience. Second, evaluation should include the process and may even emphasize the process over the product.

New methods of evaluation should be explored as students may be judged on questioning techniques, search and location strategies, listening skills, organization skills, scripting and editing skills, and presentation methods. Just as a house is appraised and valued at several stages of construction, so too is the process by which students and teachers construct knowledge and intelligence from the information surrounding them. Foundation, framework, and finished product each have need for new appraisal instruments and new collaborative appraisers who have an inquiry method orientation.

NOTES

1. Philip M. Turner, *Helping Teachers Teach: The School Library Media Specialist's Role*, 2nd ed. (Englewood, Colo.: Libraries Unlimited, 1994); and Kathleen W. Craver, *The Changing Instructional Role of the High School Librarian* (Champaign: University of Illinois Graduate School of Library and Information Sciences, 1986).

2. American Association of School Librarians and Association for Educational Communications Technology, *Information Power* (Chicago: American Library Association, 1988).

3. Ken Haycock, *The School Library Program in the Curriculum* (Englewood, Colo.: Libraries Unlimited, 1990).

4. Sylvia Scribner and Michael Cole, *The Psychology of Literacy* (Cambridge: Harvard University Press, 1981).

5. Mary M. Huston, "Introduction: Toward Information Literacy—Innovative Perspectives for the 1990s," *Library Trends* 39, no. 3 (winter 1991): 187.

6. Patricia Senn Breivik, chair, *Final Report of the American Library Association Presidential Committee on Information Literacy* (Washington, D.C.: H. W. Wilson, 1989).

7. Lauren B. Resnick, *Education and Learning to Think* (Washington, D.C.: National Academy Press, 1987).

8. Dennie P. Wolf, *Reading Reconsidered: Literature and Literacy in High School* (New York: College Entrance Examination Board, 1988), 3.

9. Lauren B. Resnick and Leopold E. Klopfer, eds., *Toward the Thinking Curriculum: Current Cognitive Research* (Washington, D.C.: Association for Supervision and Curriculum Development, 1989).

10. George Hillocks, ed., *Research on Written Composition: New Directions for Teaching* (Washington, D.C.: National Institute of Education, 1986); Margaret A. Laughlin, H. Michael Hartroonian, and Norris M. Sanders, eds., *From Information to Decision Making: New Challenges for Effective Citizenship* (Washington, D.C.: National Council for Social Studies, 1989); Thomas C. Holt, *Thinking Historically: Narrative, Imagination, and Understanding* (New York:

College Entrance Examination Board, 1990); Dennie P. Wolf and Nancy Pistone, *Taking Full Measure: Rethinking Assessment Through the Arts* (New York: College Entrance Examination Board, 1991); Wolf, *Reading Reconsidered*; Edward A. Silver, Jeremy Kilpatrick, Beth Schlesinger, and Dennie P. Wolf, *Thinking Through Mathematics: Fostering Inquiry and Communication in Mathematics Classrooms* (New York: College Entrance Examination Board, 1990); and Diana Prentice and James Payne, *More Than Talking* (Caldwell, Idaho: Clark, 1983).

11. Kathleen W. Craver, "Critical Thinking: Implications for Library Research," in *The Research of School Library Media Centers*, ed. B. Woolls (Castle Rock, Colo.: Hi Willow, 1990), 121-34.

12. Melvin M. Bowie, "The Library Media Program and the Social Studies, Mathematics, and Science Curricula: Intervention Strategies for the Library Media Specialist," in *The Research of School Library Media Centers*, ed. B. Woolls (Castle Rock, Colo.: Hi Willow, 1990), 21-48.

13. Jacqueline C. Mancall, Shirley L. Aaron, and Scott Walker, "Educating Students to Think," *School Library Media Quarterly* 15, no. 1 (fall 1986): 18-27.

14. Michael B. Eisenberg and Robert E. Berkowitz, *Curriculum Initiative* (Norwood, N.J.: Ablex, 1989); Cindy Jeffrey Krimmelbein, *The Choice to Change: Establishing an Integrated School Library Media Program*, ed. Paula K. Montgomery (Englewood, Colo.: Libraries Unlimited, 1989); and Wisconsin Educational Media Association, *Online Information Retrieval: Teaching Electronic Access in the Curriculum* (Manitowoc, Wis.: WEMA, 1989).

15. Janet Stroud, "Library Media Center Taxonomy: Further Implications," *Wilson Library Bulletin* 56, no. 6 (February 1982): 428-33; Kay E. Vandergrift, *The Teaching Role of the School Library Media Specialist* (Chicago: American Library Association, 1989); and Kathleen W. Craver, "The Changing Instructional Role of the High School Library Media Specialist: 1950-84," *School Library Media Quarterly* 14, no. 4 (summer 1986): 183-92.

16. David V. Loertscher, *Taxonomies of the School Library Media Program* (Englewood, Colo.: Libraries Unlimited, 1988).

17. Daniel Callison, "Evaluator and Educator: The School Media Specialist," *TechTrends* 32, no. 5 (October 1987): 24-29.

18. David V. Loertscher, "Collection Mapping: An Evaluation Strategy for Collection Development," *Drexel Library Quarterly* 21, no. 2 (spring 1985): 9-21.

19. Millicent Lentz, *Nuclear Age Literature for Youth* (Chicago: American Library Association, 1990).

20. Eliot Wigginton, *Sometimes a Shining Moment: The Foxfire Experience* (Garden City, N.Y.: Anchor Press, 1986).

21. Daniel Callison, "School Library Media Programs and Free Inquiry Learning," *School Library Journal* 32, no. 6 (February 1986): 20-24.

22. Eleanor R. Kulleseid, "Extending the Research Base: Schema Theory, Cognitive Styles, and Types of Intelligence," *School Library Media Quarterly* 15, no. 1 (fall 1986): 41-48; and Diana Carr, "Living on One's Own Horizon: Cultural Institutions, School Libraries, and Lifelong Learning," *School Library Media Quarterly* 19, no. 1 (fall 1991): 217-22.

23. Carolyn Markuson, "Making It Happen: Taking Charge of the Information Curriculum," *School Library Media Quarterly* 15, no. 1 (fall 1986): 37-40; Lorraine Higgins, "Reading to Argue: Helping Students Transform Source Texts," in *Hearing Ourselves Think: Cognitive Research in the College Writing Classroom*, ed. Ann M. Penrose and Barbara M. Sitko (New York: Oxford University Press, 1993), 70-101; and Jennie Nelson, "The Library Revisited: Exploring Students' Research Processes," in *Hearing Ourselves Think: Cognitive Research in the College Writing Classroom*, ed. Ann M. Penrose and Barbara M. Sitko (New York: Oxford University Press, 1993), 102-22.

24. James Will Liesener, "Learning at Risk: School Library Media Programs in an Information World," *School Library Media Quarterly* 13 (fall 1985): 11-20.

25. Kathy Gnagey Short and Carolyn L. Burke, *Creating Curriculum* (Portsmouth, N.H.: Heinemann, 1991).

26. Karen Sheingold, "Keeping Children's Knowledge Alive Through Inquiry," *School Library Media Quarterly* 15, no. 2 (winter 1987): 80-85.

27. Carol-Ann Haycock, "Information Skills in the Curriculum," *Emergency Librarian* (September/October): 11-18; Hilda L. Jay, *Stimulating Student Search* (Hamden, Conn.: Library Professional Publications, 1983); M. Ellen Jay and Hilda L. Jay, *Designing Instruction for Diverse Abilities* (Hamden, Conn.: Library Professional Publications, 1990); Barbara K. Stripling and Judy M. Pitts, *Brainstorms and Blueprints* (Englewood, Colo.: Libraries Unlimited, 1988); and Michael B. Eisenberg and Robert E. Berkowitz, *Information Problem Solving* (Norwood, N.J.: Ablex, 1990).

28. Carol C. Kuhlthau, *Teaching the Library Research Process* (West Nyack, N.Y.: Center for Applied Research in Education, 1985).

29. Carol C. Kuhlthau, "An Emerging Theory of Library Instruction," *School Library Media Quarterly* 16, no. 1 (fall 1987): 23-28; and C. C. Kuhlthau, *Seeking Meaning: A Process Approach to Library and Information Services* (Norwood, N.J.: Ablex, 1993).

30. Roland S. Barth, *Improving Schools from Within* (San Francisco: Jossey-Bass, 1990), 49-50.

31. John Barell, *Teaching for Thoughtfulness* (New York: Longman, 1991).

32. *The Information Power Video* (videocassette, 19 minutes, color), comments in introduction from John Goodlad (Chicago: Encyclopaedia Britannica, 1988); and see chapter 2, "Enabling Critical Conversation," in Kathleen Dudden Andrasick, *Opening Texts* (Portsmouth, N.H.: Heinemann, 1990).

33. Daniel Callison and Ann Daniels, "Introducing End-User Software for Enhancing Student Online Searching," in *Online and CD-ROM Databases in School Libraries*, comp. Ann Lathrop (Englewood, Colo.: Libraries Unlimited, 1989), 128-46.

34. Jerome C. Harste, Kathy Gnagey Short, and Carolyn Burke, *Creating Classrooms for Authors* (Portmouth, N.H.: Heinemann, 1988); and Regie Routman, *Invitations: Changing as Teachers and Learners K-12* (Toronto: Irwin, 1991).

35. F. M. Newman, "Higher Order Thinking in Teaching Social Studies: A Rationale for the Assessment of Classroom Thoughtfulness," *Journal of Curriculum Studies* 22, no. 1 (1990): 41-56.

36. Stephen P. Norris and Robert H. Ennish, *Evaluating Critical Thinking* (Pacific Grove, Calif.: Midwest, 1989).

14

BI and the
Twenty-First Century:
An Opinion

Leigh A. Kilman

Bibliographic Instruction/Reference Librarian
Southwest Texas State University
San Marcos, Texas

As a relatively new bibliographic instruction (BI) librarian, I have many concerns about my field as it leaves the twentieth century and prepares for the twenty-first century. Thus, I find LIRT's invitation to answer the question Are the concepts of BI too narrow for functioning in the twenty-first century? far too tempting an opportunity to remain silent. There are several topics recently in debate that most assuredly will affect our professional transition into instructional services of the next century. In particular, I wish to address current debate topics such as: 1) BI librarian as a gatekeeper; 2) holistic librarians; 3) BI as an advocate of information literacy; and 4) "information empowerment specialists." Despite the following harangue, I find debate within our field invigorating. BI appears to have its share of protagonists and antagonists within and without our profession. However, I also fear that dissention within our professional ranks (as partly evidenced in this essay) is a greater potential threat than any technological advance the next century brings to information access.

GATEKEEPERS

The analogy describing librarians as gatekeepers or intermediaries in the flow of information is well known. Few people would argue this paradigm's imagery or accuracy. In BI, a newer generalization depicts librarians teaching patrons how to better utilize information resources so that these persons can gradually become more independent as information seekers and evaluators. The second example, of librarians as proponents, indeed educators, of information literacy skills apparently has its fair share of critics, especially as it affects our gatekeeping function (e.g., White 1992a). Why is it assumed that these two generalizations represent mutually exclusive concepts and practices? I certainly do not view them as concepts so different in nature that the two shall never meet. Indeed, as a BI and reference librarian I utilize both of these paradigms every day. Depending upon the topic and audience, I chop up digestible information modules from their larger simmering brew as my customers' regular diets. In other words, I deliberately regulate the amount and type of information access while simultaneously (and continuously) promoting the transference of this knowledge to potential information needs of today and tomorrow.

Unless the next century brings with it resources that are dramatically more user friendly, I think that the need to embrace both gatekeeping and instructional functions seems fairly prudent. Why should I help create co-dependent patrons, afraid to let me out of their sight, information needers too afraid to be seekers, afraid to touch a keyboard, too timid to turn a page, too unenlightened to criticize a piece of data? I find this vision horrific. And yes, I do believe that I make a difference on a daily basis. Thus I believe BI embracing the judicious responsibilities of gatekeeping and information literacy instruction is an essential and complementary component of our programs of today and tomorrow.

HOLISTIC LIBRARIAN

Lori Arp's carefully worded definition of bibliographic instruction (as offered at ALA's 1991 national convention) dramatizes the chameleon-like desire of BI librarians to be all things to all persons. In our rapidly changing environments of information sources and services, BI proponents despair at the thought of neglecting a patron in distress, someone in need of education. BI is altruistic to the core. I am not convinced that maintaining such professionally lofty and service-oriented underpinnings is necessary bad or "misguided" (White 1992b). However, the less eloquent phrase I coined before seeing Arp's more rigorous definition is the "holistic librarian."

Holism is concerned with wholes or complete systems. Arp's BI definition is "the contextual transmission of the conceptual foundation and organization of information sources and systems through a variety of communications methods" (White 1992a). I believe Arp's description is concerned with wholes or complete systems. If in BI we stretch to achieve Arp's holistic statement of being, then perhaps we are belittled by critics for dissecting information's concepts, organizations, sources, and systems into manageable chunks for teaching. After all, that practice doesn't outwardly appear to be holistic. We do seem to have very few converts from other disciplines singing our praises (Jacobson and Vallely 1992). Yet, what discipline doesn't educate their students through this method? If wholes or complete systems are analogous to fields of study, don't all schools, courses, and teachers parcel out disciplines into smaller, teachable units of inquiry?

The holistic BI librarian visualizes goals, end products, and how this all fits into the parenting institution's goals and end products. The librarian then establishes concrete objectives to achieve that educational vision that are appropriate to the particular learner and setting. Arp's definition is definitely broad enough to encompass all objectives as long as said objectives don't forget their raisons d'être.

INFORMATION LITERACY

There appears to be a trend in BI criticism insisting that many library customers don't wish to be "educated" only "informed" (i.e., "led to the answer" or "handed the answer") (White 1992a, 1991; Bessler 1990). Academic librarians are even chastised for their perceived unwillingness to complete patrons' research efforts for them as part of the library's informational mission (as opposed to the accepted educational mission) (White 1991).

My response begins with the thought of how such a patron will acclimate easily into the depeopled library of the far future, where a reference query might take place at a computer terminal without the assistance of another human being, especially not a librarian. The patron's functions in such a futuristic setting might be to: submit request, wait, and retrieve data. (Information retrieved in this future society will naturally be complete, accurate, and completely trustworthy.)

Returning to the present, certainly, I will "lead" a patron to an answer, if I know it. Nine times out of ten, I don't know *the* answer. Additionally, nine times out of ten, the reference query is not "simple." What I know instead is usually how to find these elusive pieces of data. The process of how to find and evaluate information is to me just as significant a mission at the reference desk as it is in a BI classroom. I believe that my customers are better served when I facilitate discovery (whether I am assisting a student, faculty, or community member). Data discovery (i.e., "research") is such a value-laden, personal learning experience that I simply cannot completely exclude the customer from the process (as much as the customer might like to be removed).

Reference and instruction are inherently interactive processes. On occasion, I have found that a patron's monologue simply doesn't work well in a reference interview: they describe the data needed; how they don't want to waste any time by actually researching; and that they only want to be handed the bottom-line information. Without a dialogue, a reference negotiation (as I currently know it) is essentially reduced to a directional question. Perhaps reference and BI staffs at other types of libraries can better justify the critics' need to *not* be educated in research, only "informed" (if that is possible anywhere). However, if I, as a university reference/instruction librarian, swallow such a line of rhetoric, then I am most assuredly in direct opposition to my university's educational mission statement. BI and reference are intertwined functions in my working environment.

I am such a BI enthusiast that I believe even the simplest of reference services can have an educational value. After all, life is an educational process. We learn in a library setting despite ourselves. I hope that such a professional and personal philosophy permeates the reference desk at my institution.

Critics argue that BI is also guilty of training people to help themselves through techniques (i.e., "tricks") that are likely to fail (White 1992a). Fail at what? Are librarians' objectives (or missions, etc.) being misinterpreted? I know that if in doubt, I teach the concept. When I teach concepts and a patron approaches me later at the reference desk asking, "what index should I use to find articles on this subject," I know that I and that patron have *succeeded*, not failed. I think that too often BI antagonists (including some reference librarians) and sometimes patrons themselves see the inability to regurgitate a list of exact titles or shelf locations as failure. I disagree. Even in BI classes, I hope to positively affect the question eventually asked at the reference desk, not to eliminate the need to ask further questions.

After all, system-specific skills are not an end unto themselves. Instead, specific skills are variables that in our technologically developing society will inevitably be changed. Yet, concepts regarding the nature and access of information potentially transcend library setting and should longer endure the test of time. I want my students to prioritize the internalization of concepts, before title lists, function keys, or shelf locations. Many help aids exist that perform memorization functions, such as catalogs, path finders, online tutorials, and so on. Granted, it is only after a patron's repeated exposure to information literacy concepts and enabling skills that these synthesize into a larger, somewhat holistic picture of information access. Yet, isn't this lengthy process true of any complex subject matter? System-specific skills (tricks or techniques) are only a means to a higher end, critical thinking or independent analysis. From my perspective, information literacy is better fostered through concept-oriented instruction.

If BI is ever reduced to the training of techniques, then I agree that we have certainly set narrowed goals doomed to fail today and tomorrow. I concur with the often stated premise that "change is the condition of libraries" and information access (e.g., Gorman 1991). Today's magic hat of training tricks most likely won't hold water a few decades from now. Thus I believe that BI must continue to embrace its commitment to information literacy instruction (Arp 1990) as we enter the next century. Otherwise, BI has written its own death certificate as a profession, supported the creation of the library as a service-poor information warehouse, as well as directly contributed to the creation of an information-poor subclass of American citizens.

INFORMATION EMPOWERMENT
SPECIALISTS

Another popular debate topic is the bashing of vocabulary used to describe bibliographic instruction as a profession, its courses and its philosophies. I have witnessed an enormous amount of debate both in print and via electronic mail (BI-L) about the true meanings of: training vs. instruction; BI vs. information literacy instruction; tour vs. instruction, and so on. Herbert White prefers the label "information empowerment specialists" to describe BI librarians and their mission (White 1992a). I like that professional label too. However, my young advice is that we are overanxious. You know those old sayings such as "The proof is in the pudding," or "What's in a name?" Let's call our instructional departments whatever we like. After all, if we don't prove useful, patrons won't come back. I find myself plenty busy enough, even with often using the misnomer "bibliographic instruction." (I also often use the label "Reference/ Instruction Librarian.") And yes, perhaps I too will eventually choose another department title. Frankly, I'm just too busy to worry about it. I prefer to change my BI and reference departments from the inside out. Changing department labels would be one of the last steps in remarketing services. If our professional and service images rest so heavily upon semantics, then I think we're passing on the wrong images to our patrons and parenting institutions.

CONCLUSION

Are BI concepts too narrow to allow librarians to be information instructors (facilitators or mediators, if you prefer) of today and tomorrow? I think not. Instead my estimation is that BI activists are overgenerous, overachievers.

Are BI concepts too broad? Well, not to instruction librarians. However, I perceive that our relatively new and enthusiastic efforts to embrace a wide variety of audiences may be confusing to some librarians and especially to professionals teaching in other well-entrenched disciplines. It seems to me that administrators, teachers, and librarians have not effectively communicated how their goals are mutually supportive.

Am I still fearful that dissenting opinions will adversely affect BI? I am somewhat afraid that dissenting and nonconstructive criticism within our ranks makes us appear less credible to other eavesdropping disciplines. However, I am comforted by the realization that all professions endure heated debate periodically in some sort of cathartic cleansing process.

Can BI effectively function in the next century? With careful proactive planning (along with the fostering of many other leadership and managerial talents), I believe instruction librarians can meet the complex demands of the future while supporting their parenting institution's goals. As a profession BI does not suffer from narrow vision nor narrow concepts, only from listening to narrow minds within and without our fields.

REFERENCES

Arp, Lori. 1990. "Information Literacy or Bibliographic Instruction: Semantics or Philosophy?" *RQ* 30, no. 1: 46-49.

Bessler, Joanne. 1990. "Do Library Patrons Know What's Good for Them?" *Journal of Academic Librarianship* 16, no. 2: 76-85.

Gorman, Michael. 1991. "The Academic Library in the Year 2001: Dream or Nightmare or Something in Between?" *Journal of Academic Librarianship* 17, no. 1: 4-9.

Jacobson, Trudi E., and John R. Vallely. 1992. "A Half-Built Bridge: The Unfinished Work of Bibliographic Instruction." *Journal of Academic Librarianship* 17, no. 6: 359-63.

White, Herbert S. 1992a. "Bibliographic Instruction, Information Literacy, and Information Empowerment." *Library Journal* 117 (January): 76-78.

———. 1992b. "The Perilous Allure of Moral Imperativism." *Library Journal* 117 (September 15): 44-45.

———. 1991. "The Variability of the Reference Process." *Library Journal* 116 (June 15): 54-55.

Bibliography

Compiled by the
Continuing Education Committee
Library Instruction Round Table

The following bibliography is organized around the following themes discussed at the 1992 Conference Program of the Library Instruction Round Table: technology, libraries, and the future; technology and information literacy; technology and remote users; and the human-machine interface (social and psychological factors).

TECHNOLOGY, LIBRARIES, AND THE FUTURE

Bush, Vannevar. "As We May Think." *The Atlantic Monthly* 176 (July 1945): 101-8.
Written at the end of World War II, this article anticipates the great post-World War II challenge: increasing access to information rather than just increasing the store of information. Bush presents the dream of the "memex," a proto-scholar's workstation emphasizing hypertext and associative linkages within knowledge domains.

Kurzweil, Raymond. "The Virtual Library." *Library Journal* 118 (March 1993): 54-55.
Predicts the demise of printed books by the end of the 1990s, with the advent of wireless technologies capable of transmitting full texts of books. These new technologies will allow libraries, to a large extent, to forego acquisition of traditional materials to concentrate on "just in time" delivery of electronic full texts, on demand, for patrons.

Malinconico, S. Michael. "Technology and the Academic Workplace." *Library Administration & Management* 5 (winter 1991): 25-28.
Discusses the workplace for librarians as an "electronic goldfish bowl," with libraries increasingly becoming agencies for information access rather than repositories of print sources. Adding value to information will figure more importantly in libraries of the future, as will teaching users to exploit a confusing array of information sources, both local and remote.

Roberts, Michael. "A Political Perspective on the Internet and NREN." *Computers in Libraries* 12 (May 1992): 58-61.

Summarizes briefly the history of NSFNET and ARPANET as precursors of the emerging NREN. Reviews the politics of setting priorities among all the players in the Internet community — the federal government, commercial services, and higher education. The author examines the implications of a National Information Infrastructure and poses questions concerning equality of opportunity vs. equality of access to information.

Roszak, Theodore. *The Cult of Information: The Folklore of Computers and the True Art of Thinking.* New York: Pantheon Books, 1986.

A humanist critique of the computer revolution and its impact on education and society. The author questions the information processing model of the mind and insists on the teaching of master ideas rather than "computer games."

Saunders, Laverna M. "The Virtual Library Today." *Library Administration & Management* 6 (spring 1992): 66-70.

Discusses recent developments in networking, full-text databases, and document delivery. Technical, administrative, and educational concerns are addressed in light of emerging NREN (National Research and Education Network).

Silverberg, Robert. *The Stochastic Man.* New York: Harper & Row, 1975.

A searching fictional examination of the possibility of order and certainty in the universe.

Wegner, Lucy Siefert. "The Research Library and Emerging Information Technology." In *New Directions for Teaching and Learning,* no. 51 (fall 1992). San Francisco: Jossey-Bass.

The author asserts that the "virtual library" of the future will define its service quality by access to, rather than by possession of, information. She also discusses the impact of international networks and the proposed NREN (National Research and Education Network) on academic libraries, and predicts a much more integrated role for libraries in higher education.

TECHNOLOGY AND INFORMATION LITERACY

Bechtel, Joan. "Developing and Using the Online Catalog to Teach Critical Thinking." *Information Technology and Libraries* 7 (March 1988): 30-40.

Describes an online catalog that forces students to make informed choices throughout the search process. Teaching the use of this catalog focuses on the critical thinking process necessary for formulating and researching a topic.

Breivik, Patricia Senn, and Dan L. Jones. "Information Literacy: Liberal Education for the Information Age." *Liberal Education* 79 (winter 1993): 24-29.

New developments in technology are explored along with a definition of a learning style that "fosters within the student the ability needed to be information-literate." The importance of information management skills and the need for standards for information literacy are emphasized, as well as the need for faculty and librarians to work collaboratively in developing information literacy programs.

Gratch, Bonnie G. "Rethinking Instructional Assumptions in an Age of Computerized Information Access." *Research Strategies* 6 (winter 1988): 4-7.
Reports on a study of the information-seeking behavior of users of several automated reference sources. A model for library user education that considers automated information retrieval is presented.

Lenox, Mary F., and Michael L. Walker. "Information Literacy in the Educational Process." *The Educational Forum* 57 (spring 1993): 312-24.
After defining information literacy, the authors look at its constituent parts, including the process of information access and development. They also emphasize that different ethnic groups have diverse learning information styles and that information literacy must develop different educational models and curricular strategies to address our society's diverse information needs.

Lowry, Anita Kay. "Beyond BI: Information Literacy in the Electronic Age." *Research Strategies* 8 (winter 1990): 22-27.
Describes a graduate information literacy course in the Humanities and History Division at Columbia University focusing on computerized information retrieval, scholarly communication, and textual analysis.

Marchionini, Gary, and Danuta A. Nitecki. "Managing Change: Supporting Users of Automated Systems." *College & Research Libraries* 48 (March 1987): 104-9.
In reviewing the training literature along with the results of three studies of patron interaction with an online catalog, the authors conclude that "[a]ttention to information-seeking strategies and judging relevancy should be the ultimate goals of most user training, not the mechanics of using a particular index or system" and that "instructional modules that address topics users need help with should be provided in short, intensive units and in a variety of media that allow self-directed study."

Oberman, Cerise. "Avoiding the Cereal Syndrome, or Critical Thinking in the Electronic Environment." *Library Trends* 39 (winter 1991): 189-202.
Discusses the instructional implications of the electronic information environment. The confusing complexity of the online environment requires the teaching of critical thinking skills that can be best taught through active learning models.

Saule, Mara R. "Teaching for Library Technologies." In *Teaching Technologies in Libraries: A Practical Guide.* Edited by Linda Brew MacDonald et al. Boston: G. K. Hall, 1990.

Discusses the challenges in teaching online information systems, including the problems of varying cognitive styles and backgrounds in end-users. Presents the costs as well as the benefits of teaching the basic concepts of computerized information retrieval, and describes a knowledge base that end-users should develop to become effective searchers.

Shill, Harold B. "Bibliographic Instruction: Planning for the Electronic Information Environment." *College & Research Libraries* 48 (September 1987): 433-53.

In an article intended "to convey the importance of strategic thinking and planning for developing bibliographic instruction programs . . . [and] to demonstrate to administrators the importance of including patron instruction programs in libraries' long-range planning activities," Shill takes a broad look at current BI practices and at the electronic information environment within and outside of libraries. In such planning, besides anticipating new technologies, ten other factors are identified that must be addressed.

TECHNOLOGY AND REMOTE USERS

Barbour, Bruce, and Robert Rubinyi. "Remote Access to CD-ROMs Using Generic Communications Software." *CD-ROM Professional* 5 (March 1992): 62-65.

Describes how to provide remote access to CD-ROMs simply using free shareware while maintaining security. A project involving remote access to several government CD-ROM products is outlined in detail.

Caren, Loretta. "New Bibliographic Instruction for New Technology: 'Library Connections' Seminar at the Rochester Institute of Technology." *Library Trends* 37 (winter 1989): 366-73.

Article describes a seminar presented to faculty at RIT, including instruction on remote dial-up access to library catalogs. Familiarizing faculty with new technology was the goal of the seminar, divided into a number of modules handled by different library staff and including "live" demonstrations of information technologies.

DiMattia, Ernest A., Jr. "Total Quality Management and Servicing Users Through Remote Access Technology." *Electronic Library* 11 (June 1993): 187-91.

DiMattia incorporates the concept of total quality management in serving information users through remote access technology. He emphasizes three key factors: personnel, user communication, and equipment support.

Kalin, Sally W. "Support Services for Remote Users of Online Public Access Catalogs." *RQ* 31 (winter 1991): 197-212.

Kalin discusses the needs of remote users of online public access catalogs (OPACs), including user expectations and problems encountered, as well as how these users' needs differ from traditional users. Support services are important considerations, such as instruction opportunities through printed guides, online help, or telephone assistance.

Kalin, Sally Wayman. "The Invisible Users of Online Catalogs: A Public Services Perspective." *Library Trends* 35 (spring 1987): 587-95.

Discusses user satisfaction with remote access to online catalogs, categorizes the types of assistance remote users require, and considers the library's responsibility to these invisible users. An outline of suggestions for improving service to remote users is provided. [CIJE abstract]

Lewontin, Amy. "Providing Online Services to End Users Outside the Library." *College and Research Libraries News* 52 (January 1991): 21-22.

Bentley College, a business school, provides undergraduates and faculty with a microcomputer for home or office use. Communications software used to upload and download from the college's minicomputer is ProComm, a versatile shareware program. Dial access to the library's online system and several databases is available twenty-four hours a day. The library offers what it now calls end-user counseling as well as providing handouts and specialized tutorials.

Millsap, Larry, and Terry Ellen Ferl. "Search Patterns of Remote Users: An Analysis of OPAC Transaction Logs." *Information Technology and Libraries* 12 (September 1993): 321-43.

OPACs are becoming increasingly sophisticated in search capabilities while transaction logs show users tend toward basic commands and single indexes. Authors suggest that BI librarians would benefit users more by concentrating on improving system design rather than instruction. Recommends how to deal with users' difficulty in reformulating unsuccessful searches.

Tiefel, Virginia. "The Gateway to Information: The Future of Information Access . . . Today." *Library Hi Tech* 11, no. 4 (1993): 57-66.

Ohio State University has developed a gateway to information that enables users to identify, locate, and evaluate the best information for their needs, regardless of the materials' format. Designed as a user-friendly tool for a wide range of patrons, the Gateway helps meet the demands of the information explosion in an innovative way.

THE HUMAN-MACHINE INTERFACE
(SOCIAL AND PSYCHOLOGICAL FACTORS)

Dalrymple, Prudence Ward. "Redesigning Access: What We Must Do to Help Information Seekers Succeed in the Electronic Environment." In *Information Literacy: Learning How to Learn.* Edited by Jane Varlejs. Jefferson, N.C.: McFarland, 1991.

Focuses on the problems untrained users have with electronic information systems, and discusses enhancements in these systems through artificial intelligence, natural language processing, and improved user interface design.

Hickey, Kate D., ed. "Technostress in Libraries and Media Centers: Case Studies and Coping Strategies." *Tech Trends for Leaders in Education & Training* 37, no. 2 (1992): 17-20.

Compiled by the ALA Community and Junior Colleges Library Section's Technology Committee, this article does an excellent job of briefly examining and presenting examples of the many reasons behind and some possible solutions to technostress in libraries.

King, David, and Betsy Baker. "Human Aspects of Library Technology." In *Bibliographic Instruction: The Second Generation*. Edited by Constance A. Mellon. Littleton, Colo.: Libraries Unlimited, 1987.

Examines the social and psychological dimensions of information seeking through library technologies. Emphasizes the development of clear mental models for understanding and using technologies rather than teaching narrow procedural skills.

Kirkland, Janice J., ed. "Human Response to Library Automation." *Library Trends* 37 (spring 1989): 385-542.

This issue explores, in formal and informal terms, the trend toward greater library automation and its effect on libraries, staff, users, and administrators. The introduction states that "if there is a consensus among the articles in this issue, it seems to be that people in libraries are adapting to automation but are feeling the stress of changes as they do so. . . ."

Marchionini, Gary. "Interfaces for End-User Information Seeking." *Journal of the American Society for Information Science* 43 (March 1992): 156-63.

In an issue of the journal focusing on "Perspectives on . . . Human-computer Interface," this article looks at the five components of information seeking (problem definition, source selection, problem articulation, examination of results, and information extraction); at how present systems address or fail to address those functions; and at recommended future research directions.

Smith, Kitty. "Toward the New Millennium: The Human Side of Library Automation (Revisited)." *Information Technology and Libraries* 12 (June 1993): 209-16.

Examines library automation in light of factors that can affect the successful introduction and adoption of automation; attitudes; management challenges; changes to organizational, social, and personal structures; the human impact; and the sociotechnical approach to leadership. Includes a good reference list on the topic.

Members of the Continuing Education Committee contributing to this bibliography:

Craig Gibson, compiler

Sally Lyon

John Spencer

Suzanne Holler

Trish Ridgeway

Tom Zogg

Bibliography updated by the following members of the LIRT Continuing Education Committee:

John Spencer, compiler

Craig Gibson

Suzanne Holler

Index

185